Hunter Davies was at the h...
Swinging Sixties, becoming ...
and especially Sir Paul McC...
bestselling books, as well as widely read columns for major
newspapers and magazines, for over fifty years. His most
recent books include *The Co-Op's Got Bananas*, *A Life in the
Day* and *Happy Old Me*. He lives in London and was married
to the author Margaret Forster.

Praise for Hunter Davies

'Affable, curious, unpretentious, never dull, Hunter is one of
the most agreeable egomaniacs I know.' **Michael Palin**

'Brilliantly funny.' *Daily Mail*

'Easy-going, humourous and a natural journalist, Hunter
Davies comes across as a thoroughly nice man.' *Sunday Times*

'Our own national treasure.' **Helena Kennedy**

C000245738

Also by Hunter Davies

The Co-Op's Got Bananas!

A Life in the Day

Happy Old Me

LONDON PARKS

A STROLL AROUND THE CAPITAL'S GREATEST GLORIES

HUNTER DAVIES

**SIMON &
SCHUSTER**

London · New York · Sydney · Toronto · New Delhi

First published in Great Britain by Simon & Schuster UK Ltd, 2021
This edition published in Great Britain by Simon & Schuster UK Ltd, 2022

Copyright © Hunter Davies, 2021
Illustrations © Jill Tytherleigh

This book is copyright under the Berne Convention.
No reproduction without permission.
All rights reserved.

The right of Hunter Davies to be identified as the author
of this work has been asserted in accordance with the
Copyright, Designs and Patents Act, 1988.

1 3 5 7 9 10 8 6 4 2

Simon & Schuster UK Ltd
1st Floor
222 Gray's Inn Road
London WC1X 8HB

www.simonandschuster.co.uk
www.simonandschuster.com.au
www.simonandschuster.co.in

Simon & Schuster Australia, Sydney
Simon & Schuster India, New Delhi

The author and publishers have made all reasonable efforts
to contact copyright-holders for permission, and apologise
for any omissions or errors in the form of credits given.
Corrections may be made to future printings.

A CIP catalogue record for this book
is available from the British Library

Paperback ISBN: 978-1-4711-9055-1
eBook ISBN: 978-1-4711-9054-4

Typeset in Bembo by M Rules
Printed and bound by CPI Group (UK) Ltd, Croydon, CR0 4YY

MIX
Paper from
responsible sources
FSC
www.fsc.org   FSC® C171272

For Claire,
who I hope will be walking with me for ever

Ex Libris:
Helen Powell

CONTENTS

Introduction   1

1 Hampstead Heath   11
2 Victoria Park   41
3 St James's Park   71
4 Queen Elizabeth Olympic Park   103
5 Hyde Park   131
6 The Royal Parks and their
   Chief Executive   159
7 Burgess Park   169
8 Greenwich Park   195
9 London Wetland Centre   225
10 Richmond Park   251
11 Battersea Park   279

   Appendix: Parks of London with
     Over Twenty Acres   309

INTRODUCTION

Are the London parks the capital's greatest glory? Let's think what the other contenders might be: the Thames? Good suggestion. The Thames has been there for ever and it flows through London and the heart of its history. In fact, the Thames is the main reason London exists at all. But other big cities, such as Paris, have pretty impressive rivers. And in the UK the Clyde is one of the prides of Glasgow and the Tyne is at the heart of Newcastle.

London's buildings? Yes, there are lots of stunning ones, but per square inch you would have to say that Venice beats London for architectural wonders.

The royal family? Unfair to drag them in. They are a national monument, not just a London one, though awfully well known throughout the world.

The theatre? London's West End does have more live theatres than any other city, with wonderful actors and great playwrights. There are currently 230 professional theatres in London, with seating for over 100,000. They attract a lot of tourists, and natives. Depending on your interests in life, where you live and what you do, you might well consider the theatres are London's best thing.

London's football clubs? This is not as daft as it sounds. London usually has five or six clubs in the top division and the Premier League, so the Premier League and Sky TV constantly tell us, is the envy of the world; the most watched, with the best players. Much though I love football, in another twenty years all the world's stars could well have left these shores and be kicking a ball around in China. So let's forget football.

My vote for our greatest glory goes to London parks. It's not new news. Critic and essayist John Ruskin once observed: 'The measure of any great civilization is in its cities, and the measure of a city's greatness is to be found in the quality of its public spaces, its parks and squares.' He had the honour of having a park in London's Denmark Hill named after him.

And the good news is that London parks are still growing, despite the temptation to build offices and homes for mighty profit in any spare square yard. Yet I can think of five major parks that were not here before the war, which together have added over 1,000 acres to London park life. Three I have included in this book – Burgess Park, Olympic Park and the Wetland Centre. Add to those Northala Fields and Beckenham Place Park. Amazing. Five new London parks, which I bet are unknown to most Londoners. London has recently announced itself as the world's first national park city, in recognition of all the wonderful parks and green spaces we are so fortunate to have acquired or created over the centuries.

We need our parks more than ever before, for our health and spirits, our bodies and souls, to keep us fit, to save us from pollution, to protect nature and wildlife. The parks are lungs. They do our breathing for us. Research says a leisurely walk in a park reduces your stress levels by 12 per cent.

During the lockdowns of 2020, caused by the coronavirus, what would we have done without our parks? The London parks, in fact all parks all over the nation, proved a vital escape, a tonic, giving health and spiritual uplift to everyone – and all for free.

I thought when I first started this book, back in 2018, that we would have no more new urban parks – but one of the effects of the virus is that the government is now promising to contribute towards new city centre parks in Manchester, Leeds and Sheffield.

Parks are being used more than ever before. Every park I visited just before the lockdown set in reported that visitor numbers have roughly doubled in the last twenty years. It's hard to estimate how many of us visit a park every year – they don't have turnstiles. But surveys show that the Royal Parks alone get 78 million annual visitors. Counting all London parks, big and small, royal and common, it must be at least 250 million a year.

There are eight Royal Parks in London, and I have included four. Their history is our history, the nation's story unfolded on their landscape. Visitors to Hyde Park can't believe that it exists, plonked right in the heart of the richest chunk of real estate in London, if not the world. Wow. How did that happen?

The Royal Parks have been with us for around 500 years and represent the first stage in the evolution of the London parks. The Royals originally grabbed some local land around palaces for hunting and fun, and then, over the centuries, they let in the great unwashed – or were forced to do so.

The second stage was in Victorian times. Enlightened persons and socially conscious local authorities decided that the toffs living near the Royal Parks should not have all the perks and parks. What about the poor and deprived in the East End? Surely they could do with some decent air? In fact, the notion that parks would benefit the wider public had been around since the start of the nineteenth century, voiced by luminaries including Scottish landscape designer John Claudius Loudon, who advocated for the installation of parks as 'breathing spaces' in the *Gardeners' Magazine* in 1829. Four years later a parliamentary select committee was formed to investigate how public walks might be a valuable addition to society. Its report observed, 'The provision of parks would lead to a better use of Sundays and the replacement of debasing pleasures.'

I'm sure not everyone was in agreement on that point, but during the Victoria era, around forty new public parks were created, a dozen of them in London. The best known in London is probably the aptly named Victoria Park.

The third stage, which even long-time residents of London might not really be aware of, is that since the war we have had some brand new parks, created from scratch, and not all for the same reason. Burgess Park, for example, in south London, was dreamt up in a wartime bomb shelter by some town planners who vowed that they would improve the lives of the people who lived nearby.

Northala Fields, near the thundering A40 in Ealing, has recently been created from rubbish tips and accumulated waste dumped over the decades to make way for Heathrow Airport, Wembley Stadium and other monster constructions. It is now a 68-acre public park with fishing lakes, sports fields and four hills to mask the traffic noise.

Beckenham Place Park in Lewisham, which opened as a public park only in 2019, used to be a golf course. Now, among other delights, it is a 237-acre public park with an enormous 285-metre-long swimming lake. It adds to the long-established open-air swimming places which other London parks have had for many years, such as Hampstead Heath and Hyde Park.

Open-air swimming, or wild swimming, to give it its new cool name, has become incredibly popular in the last ten years.

Today, 266,500 people in England swim in open water at least twice a month. In 2015, the number was only 93,500. One day in September 2019 the Serpentine in Hyde Park had 6,000 swimmers doing races up to two miles long. Global warming could make all-year-round wild swimmers of us all. Who will need to go abroad when we have the London parks and lidos to swim in?

It hasn't all been plain sailing for parks, which became notorious as hang-outs for gangs and criminals during the 1970s and '80s. Indeed, some parks are only now shaking off an image of being dangerous places after dark. Another problem has been money, or lack of it. Finances have been slashed down the decades, making it difficult for those in charge of parks to make ends meet. Yet they know what our ancestors knew, that parks are central to our well-being – and you cannot put a price on that.

So how many London parks are there? Oh God, I have struggled for over a year to answer that question. What is a park? That is the first question. It has to be public, it has to be mainly green, it has to have some facilities, such as a cafe. How big does it have to be to qualify as a park? Another hard question.

I decided to make a list of every park in London over 20 acres. What a mistake. It took me almost as long to compile as complete the book itself. In the old days, when the Greater London Council existed, which controlled almost all of the region's parks, you had some central focal point to contact for such information. Now the thirty-two different London boroughs individually own most of the green areas – and they all have different systems, different definitions, different departments, doing different things. Some hide their parks under Arts and Leisure, or Environment and Sport. Some have sublet all their parks to an outside body with a meaningless acronym. Often council workers don't in fact know how many parks and green spaces they have in their borough. Sometimes a large roadside verge is included as a green space, just because it has to be cut, which makes a total number of borough parks a bit of a fiddle and comparisons with other boroughs impossible.

I have listed my results in an appendix at the end and, by my reckoning, there are 370 parks of over 20 acres in the Greater London area. Twenty acres is roughly the area of fifteen football pitches, so quite spacious, but of course most of those listed over 20 acres are much bigger.

There are at least as many smaller parks, of under 20 acres, some of them with just as many delights. One of my daughters lives opposite Priory Park in Crouch End, which boasts a cafe, paddling pool, fountain, tennis courts and a history going back to the nineteenth century. It attracts 25,000 visitors a year. But it is only 16 acres, so did not make my cut. There are also a great number of smaller public green spaces, which are known and used by local people and I am sure most of them, when they go for a walk or take the dog out, refer to it as 'the park'. Overall, I should think there are around 1,000 parks in London, big and small, grand and modest, which locals love and use and view affectionately as their local park. As for the total number of green spaces, of all sorts and conditions and sizes, it must be 3,000.

How much of London is green? That is another good question – and equally hard to answer. It is usually estimated that 40 per cent of London is made up of public parks and open spaces. But if you add in nature reserves, cemeteries, churchyards, woods, along with private bits of greenery, such as residential squares and people's back gardens, then the total comes to 60 per cent. Beat that, you other major cities.

By the sound of it, Singapore might equal that one day. Their proportion of parks was 36 per cent, but they are still expanding. New York recently completed a target of planting one million new trees. All enlightened urban sprawls are trying to go greener. They know it makes sense. So far, though, London is the benchmark for public parks.

The object of this book is to give a hurrah for London parks. I decided to illustrate and illuminate their wonders by spending a year walking round ten different, carefully chosen, top London parks. It is not a guidebook, in the normal sense, though I hope it will be informative, as well as entertaining. It is my personal journey, what happened, what I thought, the people I met, my observations and reflections, the changes I observed, and the London memories I have accumulated, having lived in London these last sixty years.

I start on Hampstead Heath, beside which I have lived all my London life, and end up a year later in south London, in a famous park I am ashamed to say I had never visited before. This was the result of meeting a lady, a young woman of seventy, and wanting to get to know her more.

In every park, I made a point of interviewing the park superintendent, in his or her den, which is often hidden away. They don't want to be bothered all day long with walkers complaining about unruly dogs or mad cyclists. I wanted to hear their problems and pleasures, how they got the job, how they do it, what the future of parks looks like to them. I also knew they would reveal things, point out hidden delights, new attractions, which I would otherwise miss and which even regulars would not know about.

The book is also meant to be amusing. Parks, after all, are not just about greenery and nature or keeping fit or exercising the dog. Parks are meant to be fun.

Hunter Davies, NW5, October 2020

1

HAMPSTEAD HEATH

On Christmas morning, as I have done for over fifty years, I set off to watch the swimmers break the ice on the Men's Pond. Rarely in all these years has there been any actual ice to break. Christmas in London has always turned out mild, middling, damp, compared with the Christmases I used to spend at home in Carlisle where it was always freezing. Put your bare feet on the lino when you got out of bed and you could be stuck there till Easter. For most people, having no central heating at the time, all houses, no matter how grand, were freezing all winter long.

When I first came to London in 1959, I used to tell the folks back up north that here there was no sign of winter till late January. In fact, in London it was often hard to tell what season it was.

All the same, I would not fancy swimming in an open-air pond on Christmas Day – or any day until mid-summer. That's when I do regularly go swimming in the Men's Pond, or the Mixed, or the Lido. We are so lucky, we folks who live near Hampstead Heath, having all these places to swim. I just have to go out of the back door from my garden, along a hidden mews, across Highgate Road, and bingo, I am straight onto the Heath. Or onto the Fields, which is what most locals used to call this side of the Heath – after Parliament Hill Fields.

I do like to see young people, and not so young people, men and women, being brave and hardy on Christmas morning, before tucking onto their turkeys.

During sixty years of living near the Heath, the numbers of Christmas Day swimmers have grown considerably. This time there were at least thirty people throwing themselves in, men and women, doing a quick dash, then back just as quickly, while their friends and supporters and passers-by cheered and clapped. You have to get into the Men's Pond compound early, and squeeze your way towards the lifeguard's hut and the diving board, in order to get a good view of the action, as several hundred people now turn up to watch, turning it into a jolly social occasion. They come from all over north London, and most of them I don't know. I suspect they are merely Christmas Day visitors. We regular Heath walkers, who go there every day, like to think we know or at least recognise everyone.

There has been a huge increase in what they now call wild swimming, which we just used to call open-air swimming, meaning more lifeguards are needed, to be on the safe side. Wild swimming makes it sound awfully adventurous. My daughter Caitlin, the only one of our three children who has turned out to be a writer, has written two books about wild swimming – one about the history of swimming on the Heath and one about swimming in the Thames.

There used to be a trumpeter, whom I got to know, who played Christmas carols before the Christmas swim began. The sound of his bugle could be heard miles away, as if calling the faithful to play. He was called Dave and he was also a professional bagpiper, playing at Burns suppers and weddings. Haven't seen him this year. Perhaps I missed him – I was a bit late. Living on my own these days, I don't rush out of the house as I used to when my wife was alive. I would leave her to start the magic of Christmas Day while I sloped off to watch the swimming.

One of the big attractions these days is the hot mulled wine and mince pies – yum yum. They are presumably meant to reward the swimmers, but it's the friends and supporters who scoff them. As usual, I pushed myself to the front of the queue and had two. I don't know who pays for them – presumably the Highgate Lifebuoys Club, the club for men swimmers based on the Men's Pond.

I remember a few years ago, when the City of London took over ownership of the Heath, there was a move to have hot showers in the changing room. I was all for it, as the changing area is open and concrete and horrible and the showers freezing. But the regulars vetoed it. They wanted a cold shower, as they always had done. Hot showers would just attract the wrong sort of swimmer.

I spoke to two of the parkies – to use a term that many of us knew in childhood, covering anyone who worked inside park gates – who are both called Paul. Paul Jeal, whom I have known since he was a little boy, as he went to school with my son Jake, is now the senior swimming facilities supervisor, based at the Lido. Paul Maskell is in charge of all the events at this end of the Heath, such as the live shows on the bandstand and the cross-country races.

All regulars at parks, in London and elsewhere, like to think they know some of the parkies by name. They become snobbish, showing off about which ones they know, and are thrilled when they in turn are addressed by their first name. Proves we exist, part of the community. Do you know how long I have lived here?

I also spoke to Dan Fawkes, who works at the Lido and ponds, whom I have also known for decades, being great friends of his parents. I do like to think Hampstead Heath is my Heath. I rather resent these offcomers who turn up once a year for the free mulled wine. Yes, I will have another glass, Paul, how kind.

The Men's Pond is the second pond you come to when you enter the Heath from the Highgate Road end. The first pond is officially on the maps as the Highgate Number One Pond, but I have always known it as the duck pond. Now it has become the dog pond. Every time I go past it there are dog owners throwing sticks in for their overexcited dogs. Some are also throwing bread for the ducks, swans and pigeons, which of course they should not. The dogs churn up the water and mud and reeds, making this end of the dog pond dirty and unattractive. So I walk on quickly.

The Men's Pool in the summer goes equally murky and very green with all the algae. I know strangers who shudder at the sight of it and can't believe it is safe for swimming. It can look horrible at times, but in all these years I have never picked up any lurgy or heard of anyone being ill. Recently, the body of a man in his fifties was found drowned in the Men's Pond. He lived nearby and was a good swimmer. But he suffered from undiagnosed coronary heart disease and, after having a heart attack, his body sank from view. In the middle, the pond goes down to a depth of 20 feet. It was an unusual event. I can't think of any other deaths in the Men's Pond in recent decades, though there was one in the Ladies' Pond in 2013.

After the Men's Pond you come to the Boating Pond, meaning model boats, not rowing boats, as, unlike lots of other London parks, the Heath does not have any rowing. Alas, the model boat enthusiasts seem to have disappeared. Back in the 1960s, there were races at weekends among the model-boat owners, which was very entertaining, and attracted quite large crowds. Perhaps the recent massive work on the ponds put them off and they have not yet returned.

For about two years, this end of the Heath was turned into a vast building yard as over £20 million was spent on constructing spillways and aquatic planting schemes. The string of ponds on this side of the Heath was the original source of the River Fleet, one of the many rivers which flowed into the Thames, long built over when London started expanding. The name lingers on locally in Fleet Road, and Fleet Primary School, and of course in Fleet Street, where the River Fleet went into the Thames. Fleet Street, when I came to London, was the home of the nation's newspapers. Now all the papers have dispersed, or closed, their homes often purely in the clouds these days, not on the ground. Fleet Street though remains as a generic term for our national press.

The next pond along is the bird pond, which is a nature reserve with no public access. Then comes the Ladies' Pond, which is the prettiest of all the swimming ponds, beautifully secluded and sylvan. I have not had the pleasure of swimming there, but I often think, on a really hot day, when the Men's Pond is so crowded and noisy, if only I could just enter and dive in. Surely in this day and age there is no discrimination allowed against men? Since last year, they are now at least more inclusive, allowing in those who identify as women.

There was nobody in the Ladies' Pond, as all the excitement on Christmas morning is of course at the Men's Pond. I walked on, as I was there on a pilgrimage, not just to see the Christmas Day swimming races, but to visit a memorial connected to my late wife.

In 1985 we celebrated our silver wedding anniversary. What should we do, we thought, to commemorate this remarkable achievement – at least in *our* lives? We had a silver wedding party. Two parties, in fact – one at the Groucho Club, which had just opened in Soho, and one at home for our local friends. We also wanted to do something that would be more permanent and somehow connected with the Heath – but what?

We had married on 11 June 1960, the day after my wife sat her last exam as a student at Oxford. We moved into a flat in the Vale of Health, a little oasis, which even many locals don't know is there, tucked into the middle of the Heath on the Hampstead side, off East Heath Road. Shelley sailed paper boats on the Vale of Health Pond and Keats lived nearby. Although by 1911 it was described as 'vulgarised' by the presences of the pub, tea gardens, merry-go-rounds and slot machines, plenty of famous folk made their home there, such as writers D. H. Lawrence, Leigh Hunt, Compton McKenzie, Edgar Wallace, artists Stanley Spencer and Sir Muirhead Bone and newspaper proprietors Alfred and Harold Harmsworth.

The name Vale of Health is supposed to come from the fact that this little enclave was one of the places to escape the Great Plague of 1665.There is no historical proof of this, but traditionally it has always been considered a pretty healthy place.

It did not quite work out that way for me. The Vale has its own pond, which our bedroom window overlooked. In the winter the misty, moisty air crept into our bedroom and caused me to have the most awful asthma attacks. I had asthma as a boy and until that moment thought I had outgrown it.

We only stayed there two years, saving like mad to put down a deposit on a house. Margaret was working as a supply teacher in Barnsbury, going on the Overground from Hampstead Heath station, and I was a reporter on the *Sunday Times*. I was just twenty-four and she was twenty-two when we got married, with no money and no help from our families, yet in two years we had saved £1,500 – enough for a deposit on a house. A modern couple, on similar wages, at a similar position in life, would probably today have to save for fifty years before they could raise one-third of the price of an average London house.

We could not afford to stay in Hampstead itself, as a house in Flask Walk cost £7,500, so we bought a house on what was considered the wrong side of the Heath, the Kentish Town side, off Highgate Road. It cost £5,000 – which I tell every new person who moves into our street, just to see them being sick on the pavement. It did have a tenant on the top floor, but by 1985, when we celebrated our silver wedding, she had gone.

After twenty-five happy years living on or beside the Heath, we decided to mark our silver wedding by having some sort of memorial to ourselves, possibly somewhere on the Heath itself.

I enquired at the Greater London Council, then the owners of Hampstead Heath, about having a bench on the Heath engraved with our names. There was a long waiting list and, traditionally, memorial benches are for someone who is dead. It took time and some faffing to get them to agree. I think, from memory, we paid £200.

We were given a choice of location, and picked one which we thought was secluded and attractive, and also, by chance, a bit of a visual joke. So that was what I was off to see, on that Christmas morning, hoping no one was sitting on it, or had vandalised it.

Our seat is situated to the left of the entrance gate to

Kenwood House, a Georgian stately home, up a sandy, windy track, which these days, aged eighty-three, I find a bit steep for my dodgy knees. It overlooks a section called the South Meadow, which has a sort of valley at the bottom, and lots of trees, an area which never attracts many people. Most folks are heading straight on, through the gates to Kenwood.

Our seat, which faces towards London and the City, sits under a silver birch tree. In fact it is now a little clump of birch trees. It seems to have spread over the decades. As we all have.

The inscription on the back of the bench, carved into the wood, is very simple.

TO HUNTER AND MARGARET ON THEIR
SILVER WEDDING, JUNE 11, 1985

I wonder how many people, who have chanced upon it these last thirty-five years and rested their legs, have been aware of the visual pun? Celebrating a silver wedding – in front of a silver birch tree. Good joke, huh?

And I wonder how many Heath walkers have realised that it was the only memorial seat on the Heath in memory of a living person? And at the last count, at least, one of us is still living.

I sat for a long time, thinking of course about Margaret. She died in February 2016, four years ago now, after fifty-five years of marriage. I have lived alone ever since, though I now have a lady friend who often visits. In turn I go on the wonderful Overground railway from the station on the Heath at Gospel Oak to visit her. She lives elsewhere in London, but she does have her own local and very well-known park, which I plan to visit for this book, a book which will be about my year walking London parks – if, of course, in a year's time, we are still chums. Otherwise I will finish on another park. There are loads to choose from.

Margaret loved the Heath, walked on it every day, almost to the end of her life. She was always a better walker than me, and stronger. I used to get her to carry our rucksack when we were hostelling in the Lake District as students – until we passed through a village, when I carried it so as not to look a total wimp.

I spent a long time on our seat, just looking at the view, thinking, as always, about how lucky all Londoners are to have so much greenery within walking distance, wherever they live.

Hampstead Heath is probably the most remarkable park of all, in that it is so near the centre of London – just four miles from Charing Cross – yet so extensive and so varied, with its hills and lakes, that you can feel you are in the countryside. Not quite the Lake District. But at certain spots, on a quiet day, in a quiet place, by narrowing your eyes, looking down on the ponds, you can pretend you are on Ullswater.

For sixty years, I have boasted about the Heath to all relations and friends visiting from the north. They often say how can you live here in the Smoke? I tell them how you can walk for three hours, doing the whole circuit of the Heath, taking in Kenwood, Sandy Heath, the Heath Extension and Golders Hill Park – and yet only have to cross one road. There are endless facilities, a stately home with old masters, cafes and restaurants, and every sort of sport available.

Perhaps over the year, as I plan to visit several parks I have never been to before, I might decide there are other London parks just as wonderful – possibly even more so. We shall see.

It was of course not a matter of luck and chance, or even God's goodness, that Hampstead Heath today is 800 wonderful acres, free and open to all. A lot of battles had to be fought, and still have to be fought, to make it as it is today.

The name Hampstead comes from the Saxon Hampstede, meaning home stead, which in those days usually meant a farm, and until well into the Middle Ages, farming was the main activity, especially pig farming. By the sixteenth century, it had become more like a village, with its own specialised activity − washing. It was full of laundresses, using all that free-flowing local water and natural springs, who washed the dirty linen for the high and mighty down the hill from the Hampstead heights. The London aristocracy and even the royal family sent their dirty linen up to Hampstead. On a dry day, it was said that Hampstead was turned into a snow-capped mountain, with all the lines of flapping linen.

In the early eighteenth century, Hampstead became a popular watering place as people flocked to the spas on Well Walk which were supposed to have medicinal qualities. Fine houses were built in and around Church Row and the High Street, and Hampstead became a fashionable place to live and for visitors to enjoy themselves, attracted by a racecourse on the Heath and other associated pleasures.

By the nineteenth century, Hampstead was becoming still more refined, where successful chaps who worked in Bloomsbury or the City settled down with their families in what they liked to imagine was rural, sylvan bliss. As the village grew, so the Heath began to shrink.

It had been wild scrubland, full of gorse; hence it had always been described as a heath, not a park. Various enclosures and housing developments had gobbled up surrounding open land, such as Highgate Common. The Heath itself in 1818 covered only 250 acres. The lord of the manor, Sir Thomas Maryon Wilson, maintained he had rights over all the Heath, including the rights to enclose even more of it.

In 1829, when extensive building work was going on all over London, he tried to cash in his inheritance by announcing he was going to develop it all – which resulted in local uproar. He might have got away with it when the main local residents were washerwomen, but all the affluent, professional classes knew their rights. They insisted it had always been common land, took legal advice, mounted protests, and for the next forty-two years there was open warfare. They put up legal objections when he tried to get enclosure bills through Parliament, a route taken by numerous landowners to get legal control of land previously used by others. He replied by charging the washerwomen for drying their clothes on his Heath and builders who took away his sand. As a final warning, he built a road across the Heath from East Heath Road and erected a large viaduct over a pond, the first stage in a grandiose housing development he had planned.

This viaduct is still there, and its road, and the pond below. When we first moved nearby into the Vale of Health in 1960, it seemed so weird, this huge bridge, in the middle of nowhere, going nowhere. I was not interested in local history at the time, or any sort of history, even though I did read history at Durham.

There was a plan to buy the Heath from him when the price was said to be £400,000, but the locals could not raise the money. Ten years later, in 1856, he had put the price up to

£2.5 million, which of course was just trying it on, to frighten off all his enemies. It was his death in 1869 which finally solved the problem and in 1871 the Hampstead Heath Act was passed. His brother, who inherited the Heath, agreed to hand over his manorial rights to the Heath for £45,000. It was bought by the Metropolitan Board of Works, later the London County Council and, later still, when we moved in, it was owned by the GLC.

Over the next few decades after the Hampstead Heath Act, there were further campaigns and battles – this time to extend the Heath. In 1886, Parliament Hill and its surrounding fields were taken over for £302,000. In 1899, Golders Hill was purchased for £38,000. The most spectacular acquisition was the purchase of the Kenwood estate in the 1920s.

Since then, there have been other, smaller bits acquired, which has resulted in Hampstead Heath today covering 800 acres, compared with just 200 acres in 1871 when the Act was passed and it first went into public hands. A stirring, uplifting, moral story to please the hearts of all campaigners and environmentalists everywhere.

I have been a member of the Heath & Hampstead Society since 1960, when we first moved into the Vale, and over the years I have got to know much more about the history of the Heath. When friends living elsewhere in London moan about encroachment or development on their local if rather pathetic patch of greenery, I tell them that if Hampstead can do it, so can they. They roll their eyes and reply with a cynical shrug. All right for you; if we had the great and good living locally, all those lords and ladies, judges and famous actors they have in Hampstead, we could probably move mountains, if not pull a few influential strings . . .

During all these years, these decades, of boasting, and thinking I know everything about the Heath, even at one time leading conducted tours, you would think I'd be best friends with the Hampstead Heath superintendent. At least I would know what he looked like, doff my cap to him, say good morning, squire. I would know where his office was, where he lived.

But blow me, once I started thinking about it, knowing I would have to go and interview him, I realised I didn't even know the name of the Heath's current big boss, despite being on first-name terms with so many of the Heath's managers and parkies.

Back in the 1980s, when Dave King was the superintendent, I knew which house on the Heath he lived in, said hello to him most mornings on my walk. I had assumed, because I had not come across him locally, that the present superintendent was perhaps based at the Kenwood yard and lived in one of the rather handsome Georgian cottages over there, on what we always consider the posh side of the Heath.

There have of course been huge changes in the ownership and running of the Heath in recent years, especially after the demise of the GLC in 1986. I was bound to be a bit out of date.

I remember at the time there were lots of local worries about what would happen. Would we want Camden Borough Council to be in charge, which might subject us to political pressures and whims? We were all quite relieved when the City of London Corporation emerged as the new owners, whoever they were, whatever they owned. They at least would appear to be above party politics, an ancient and affluent left-over organisation from the great days of the City of London.

It did seem a bit strange at the time, as the Heath is not in the City of London. But, on the other hand, a remote body might not be as tempted to interfere.

Would today's superintendent even still be called superintendent? I didn't even know that. I do like that traditional terminology for a chief parky. So many public bodies these days prefer to use the term general manager or chief executive.

Superintendent did turn out indeed to be his official title – hurrah – but I was surprised and rather disappointed to find out where he works from. Not from some secluded little Georgian gem hidden away behind Kenwood House, or even a little wooden camp in a bosky glade. He turned out to have his office in an anonymous modern brick building on the horrendously noisy Archway Road. Poor feller, I thought, having that traffic thundering outside.

Then there was another surprise. When I happened to say he must be disappointed not to live at Kenwood, he revealed that as superintendent of Hampstead Heath, he is no longer responsible for Kenwood House or its grounds. Oh goodness – tough luck – should we get up a petition?

I had assumed, like most locals who walk the Heath, and all visitors carrying the map of the Heath, that it is all one entity. When you walk past the ponds, past the path to my seat, and go straight into Kenwood, there are no gates, no barriers and no demarcation lines. It must clearly all be Hampstead Heath.

I had forgotten, or more likely never took it in, that when the GLC packed up in 1986, Kenwood and its 74 acres of grounds did not pass over to the City of London. It went to English Heritage.

I suppose it does make sense. Looking after a famous stately home, with all those famous paintings, is a job for arty sorts and well-bred architects, not rough-hewn parkies.

Today's superintendent is called Bob Warnock, aged fifty-two. No relation to football manager Neil or philosopher Mary. He was born in Kingston, Surrey, where his dad was an architect. He got a diploma in nature conservation and worked his way up from being a ranger to being a park manager, from Dartmoor to Surrey. In 1991 he joined the City of London Corporation and was working on a large nature reserve in Surrey, at Ashtead, which had been taken over by the City of London. Seems a long way from the City?

'That's what we first thought, but the City of London has a long tradition in acquiring green spaces within twenty-five miles of London – in order to protect them – which was how it came to take over the Heath.'

The City of London Corporation currently owns a huge swathe of London greenery. Sorry, its old-school aldermen and councillors don't like the word 'own'. They prefer to be termed custodians. Their empire, sorry, domain, includes Epping Forest, Burnham Beaches, Highgate Wood, Queen's Park in Brent, and Hampstead Heath, plus about 80 acres of small parcels of greenery in the City of London itself. Altogether, they are custodians of over 11,000 acres. They spend over £19 million a year on their green spaces, which comes from the City's long-standing funds, plus grants and donations.

Bob became superintendent of the Heath in 2014, never having worked in London before. He was immediately struck by how busy it all was. He was amazed by all the people, all the activities, going on all the time, every day, all day.

He had to move house and his wife had to give up her job as a teacher. One of his two daughters had to commute for a year back to Surrey, as she was still doing her A levels at her old school. Now, both his daughters have just graduated – one from St Andrews and one from Exeter.

So where does he live now? Surely not in some modern block on the Archway Road? Phew. He does have a very attractive tied house at Golders Hill. It is inside the park boundary, so he gets locked in at night, Golders Hill Park being the only patch of the Heath that gets locked up.

Altogether, thirteen of the Heath staff have tied accommodation – five living on the Heath itself and the rest with flats in their Archway Road premises. Getting staff, on humble wages, is otherwise hard in London, as people cannot afford the accommodation.

Did he feel a provincial, coming to work in London after all these years out in the sticks? That's how I felt, back in 1960, moving in with the quality in the Vale of Health.

He says he didn't. Nor did he feel intimidated by all the poshos, the famous judges and actors who live beside the Heath in Hampstead, many of whom he has to deal with as they all tend to be passionate about the Heath.

'Yes, there are some very famous and clever people here, but we do have our experts – ecologists and arboriculture consultants who are very good at their job. We all get along well.'

His job is much bigger than I had expected. Though on paper the Heath itself is smaller, with the loss of Kenwood, his empire is bigger, for he also looks after Highgate Wood, which is just behind his Archway Road office. In addition he looks after Queen's Park in Brent and Keats House in Hampstead.

The Heath's gardening team – which cares for the gardens at Golders Hill Park – also looks after the Keats House garden, with excellent support from the Heath Hands volunteers.

Altogether, he controls a staff of 130, which is more than any one of the Royal Parks has. All are employed directly by the City of London. Everywhere else in London, the majority of parkies you see working away in London parks are contract staff.

He has six management staff in his office with him. Most of the rest are based in yards on the Heath itself, such as at Parliament Hill. Twelve rangers patrol and care for the Heath. There are sixteen involved with sports and recreation, a dozen who look after the Lido and the ponds, an education team, an ecology team and other teams whose names I never got. There is also a constabulary – two sergeants and ten constables, with two patrol vehicles – to deal with incidents ranging from medical emergencies to indecent exposure. The constabulary is based at Kenwood beside the nursery. The nursery, which also has a splendid garden, open to all, is part of the Heath but is managed by English Heritage.

Bob arrived at a fraught time in 2014, for him and for all Heath lovers. It was right at the beginning of the £20 million Dams Project – which became a term of abuse, dreaded by all locals, criticised by the local press. I even signed a petition wanting it not to happen.

The City had told us that, with the threat of major flooding coming with global warming, the ponds would rise and overflow and the roads and houses in Highgate Road and Gospel Oak would be filled with water. It was implied that hundreds of locals could drown in their beds – which would have included me. So something had to be done. Massive dams and barriers and underground pipes had to be installed to regulate these potential floods.

It seemed to me, and many others, that the risk was a minor one, and far away in the future. The City was being alarmist. Why ruin the Heath for two years with massive digging and landscaping, when it might never happen? There was clearly too much money washing about and the Corporation just want to spend it. So some of us believed.

Bob arrived when legal arguments and complaints were still going on and a judicial review was under way. He found himself, as a newcomer to the Heath and the area, having to attend endless meetings and answer countless questions.

'Flooding was a serious threat. Work really had to be done whenever there was a storm warning, we had to use a telemetry – which is a way of measuring water level electronically. We were eventually able to download it on our mobile phones – then rush out and inspect where it was happening. We couldn't actually do much about it – just prepare storm flood alerts and warn local residents of the danger and what they must do. The storm warnings had been getting more frequent. So we knew something had to be done.'

One of the things he had to do was liaise with all the so-called Heath stakeholders who were entitled and keen to have their say. He counted twenty-six in all, ranging from the long-established powerful ones, such as the Heath & Hampstead Society and the Highgate Society, to smaller pressure groups representing various niche activities, such as fishing, tree-spotting and birdwatching.

The work went ahead with all the mess and chaos that it

entailed. It really was appalling, so I thought, making myself sound like Prince Charles. The ponds, on both sides of the Heath, Hampstead as well as Highgate, became one huge horrible building site. It was like an army encampment. You had to trudge for miles to get round the cordoned-off building sites. For two years, I gave up trying to get to our memorial bench. The detour took too long. I feared it would never end.

It was amusing, though, when they totally drained the Boating Pond as they found something rather strange at the bottom – an ancient 1960s Ford Cortina. It was rusty and mud-caked, but still relatively intact, in that its number plate was clear. How it had got there? There is no direct road access to the Boating Pond. So who had driven it into the water, and how?

One theory, according to the *Camden New Journal*, was that it was the wife of a fisherman. She had become suspicious when night after night her husband said he was on the Heath doing night fishing, but in fact was off with another woman. She took his car, drove it through a barrier, across the grass, to the spot beside the pond where she knew he said he had gone fishing. She got to the edge, took off the hand brake, and let the car slide into the water. A plausible story, but no one has yet come forward to admit it.

Today, now that the enormous upheaval is long over, I have to confess, through gritted teeth, that all the chaos and mess was worth it. The ponds on either side of the Heath are better landscaped than they were before. You can't now see any of the scars left by all the building work. There are new trees and, best of all, the Boating Pond, which was a fairly boring, rectangular shape, now has dinky curves and a very pretty island, which is a bird sanctuary. So hurrah for the City of London Corporation.

It is now a pleasure again to walk round the ponds every day. They do appear even more natural than before. And it is reassuring, I suppose, to know I now won't be drowned in my bed.

Bob was a bit defensive when I suggested that the City of London is a moneybags corporation, able to spend almost what and when they like. And with the number of swimmers doubling in a decade, money becomes a greater issue.

In 2005 a voluntary charge was brought in for the Men's, Ladies' and Mixed ponds – which I have to confess I don't always pay. The Lido has always had an entrance fee. In 2019 the combined income from the three swimming ponds came to £67,000. However, £747,000 was spent on the three ponds and the Lido during those twelve months. On a busy day, the Lido alone has twelve lifeguards and, with the numbers of swimmers increasing, more are needed.

With that in mind, an Act of Parliament was passed in 2018 giving the City of London powers to license commercial activities on the Heath.

Commercial dog walking on the Heath is one of the more recent growth industries. Agencies in Hampstead which specialise in dog walking have their own offices and designated vans. Dog walkers go out with up to seven dogs at a time. A lot of employees are not of course full time, but out-of-work actors or the retired or unemployed, on minimum hourly rates.

Many of them, from my observations, spend a lot of their dog-walking time sitting smoking and chatting to other dog walkers, in various cafes, especially the summer cafe near the bandstand. Meanwhile, their dogs rush around, chasing each other and being shouted at. Professional dog walkers are constantly getting into arguments with ordinary walkers – and most of all with runners, who trip over the leads, or get attacked by unruly dogs. Yes, I am not a dog lover, though my children are, as is my girlfriend. Until she met me, she had told herself that when she got to her next – seventieth – birthday, she was going to get her own dog. So far she has not got one. Phew.

At the moment, as I write, there is no limit to how many dogs a dog walker can walk. The only rule is that they must all be properly controlled. But there is an ongoing discussion about imposing a Code of Conduct for Dog Walkers, which is obviously going to happen. That will ensure all dog walkers are insured and will limit the numbers of dogs they can walk at any one time.

The other huge increase in recent years, and a clear sign of the times in which we live, is in fitness coaches. One group is called the British Military Boot Camp. I see them most weekends, about twenty-five sweltering men and women in matching tops, being shouted at, ordered around, made to run up and down Parly (Parliament Hill), or do endless mad press-ups. The properly organised, professional fitness schools now pay a fee for permission to use the Heath for their activities, unlike dog walkers.

But there are also now dozens of one to one freelance fitness trainers who arrive with a skipping rope and a mat and a client they have just hooked on the internet. Bob thinks they will be hard to control. When apprehended by a parky, they always say they are not professional, just helping a friend to keep fit.

I asked about the schools that use the Heath. On the Hampstead side, where there are forty different schools in a one-mile radius, most of them private, you often get whole classes of prep school kids in their immaculate uniform using the Heath as a classroom, spending whole afternoons playing games on the Heath, taking advantage of the facilities – without paying.

Yet parents are paying the schools to look after their children. Is that not commercial activity?

Bob sighed. He would be wary of charging any schools, state or private. One of the fantastic opportunities the Heath provides is outdoor learning and play for children of all ages, all types.

Schools do of course pay a modest fee to use the race track and changing rooms for their sports days. Almost every day in the summer term you see a school sports day taking place. I love watching them and think: happy days. I am thinking not just of my own children, who all went to local schools, but of my own appearance in a father's race. This was when my children were at Brookfield Primary. I beat one of the teachers who had just appeared in the Olympics. True. Except I always forget to add that he was a wrestler, not a runner.

There are many, much bigger events held every year, which bring in more people. The biggest is the National Cross Country Championships, which can attract up to 10,000 runners – and twice as many spectators. Then there is the Southern Counties championship, which usually has 4,000 entrants. The Night of the 10,000 Metres, where well-known runners try to improve their PB, lasts all day and most of the evening, in the dark, with the floodlights on. It is part of the qualifying process for the UK's Olympic and Commonwealth 10,000-metre team.

There must be tens of thousands of people from all over Great Britain, who have memories of trailing to Hampstead Heath to compete in some sort of race, coming in a special coach, setting up their club marquees, and then whizzing off again, without ever realising what Hampstead Heath is, what it contains, what its other attractions are. They must go away thinking it is a just a big muddy racecourse.

The Affordable Art Fair is a newer annual attraction, which gets set up on the fairground site beside East Heath Row – a massive construction, which takes a week to erect. The parkies don't have to do any work putting it up – they just collect a rent for the site.

All London parks, and all parks everywhere, are constantly trying to think of money-making activities that won't of course detract from their normal attractions. Few can have as many as Hampstead Heath, but then it has been attracting crowds for a long time. Its most famous annual event is the Hampstead Heath Fair, which has been going since the 1800s – and is the origin of the expression 'Appy 'Ampstead. It takes place on the three main Bank Holidays. It used to be on two sites, but in the last few years it has been restricted to one site, at East Heath Road.

When I lived in the Vale of Health in the early 1960s, the Fair had an equally large site centred there. We had to leave home when it was at its height as the noise and crowds were unbearable. In those days there was still a large old Victorian pub in the Vale of Health, backing onto the pond. It is now a rather boring modern block of flats.

Until recently, the Heath itself licensed each side show and fairground attraction, which meant hundreds of forms had to be issued and filled in. Now they have handed over the job to the Showmen's Guild of Great Britain, who do the licensing themselves. In September each year there is also a big circus.

Recently there have been sheepdog trials on the Heath, part of the BBC TV *Countryfile* series. I went that particular day, not knowing it was taking place – and what a glorious and wonderful sight, real sheep being rounded up on the slopes of Parliament Hill. So rural, so agricultural, I imagined for a moment I was back in the Lake District. Then I raised my eyes and could see all the skyscrapers and famous buildings just a few miles away, down in the City.

Each year now there is another rural sight – haymaking. They do it on the slopes of Parly and near Kenwood. I did a little video last year on my mobile phone, of the haymaking machine and the bales of hay, and sent it to my friends in Loweswater, asking them to guess where I was. No one guessed I was on the Heath, just four miles from Big Ben.

Another annual delight is the shire horses. They appear and do a day's work after one of the mass cross-country races has turned the Heath into a quagmire. Motorised tractors can't cope, so the shire horses pull chain harrows, raking over and smoothing out the boggy bits. It is always remarkable how in just a few weeks the Heath turns from a mud bath back into sylvan green. The shire horses are just on loan for a couple of days from Richmond Park. Parkies do like to help each other.

In August 2019, Bob managed to bring back sheep onto the Heath for a trial period. In my collection of more than 200 vintage postcards of the Heath, there are wartime photos showing sheep grazing on the slopes on the Highgate side of Parly, with the sheep looking down towards the Men's Pond. During the war, sheep grazed the Heath to increase our meat supply. The purpose of the 2019 trial was to have the sheep grazing rough grass which can't be controlled by mechanical means. And of course sheep cause less noise and pollution than diesel-driven tractors.

There were just five sheep, all rare breeds, either Oxford Down or Norfolk Horn. They were in a little fenced-off area beside a copse at the top of a mound near Parliament Hill. The mound is known locally as Boudicca's Mound and, according to legend, was her last resting place.

Hampstead Heath, like all good parks, likes to think it has a social and educational purpose, not just sporting and recreational. All the extra attractions have of course attracted more people than ever, which is their aim. Living in London, people want and need to go somewhere to breathe clean air. The downside is all the litter. Humans can be so untidy.

'We are now trying to think of ways of encouraging people to take their own waste home, and recycle it themselves,' said Bob 'We do already recycle all the green waste, but plastic, paper and food are the problems.'

Despite the size of the Heath, and the fact that most of it is open twenty-four hours a day (except Golders Hill Park and the Pergola, which close at dusk), there isn't a huge problem with rough sleepers. The rangers and constables see to that.

'One worry this year has been knife crime, which has increased all over London. We have had awful incidents nearby in Camden. Our constabulary have upped their patrols around Parliament Hill.'

They bring around twenty prosecutions a year, mainly against people with unruly dogs, or cyclists cycling where they should not. 'We warn a lot more than we ever take to court. We do have to protect the rights of the public to enjoy the Heath safely.'

I told Bob about my memorial seat, and how I always tell people we were the only living people to have one. He thought this was probably still true, but would have to check.

I told Bob that I had recently seen notices appearing on lots of the memorial seats, asking anyone who had been involved in installing them to contact them. What was the point of that? Wanting more money?

He explained that there are now 800 memorial benches on the Heath, far more than I had imagined, with a waiting list of 120. They don't really want to introduce any new ones, so you have to wait till one falls to pieces and needs to be replaced.

Back in the 1980s, when we had ours erected, as far as I remember, your seat was there for life, or longer. My £200 fee covered upkeep, which usually meant an annual coat of varnish.

In recent decades, the system has changed. You now 'sponsor' your seat for ten years. After that, if you want it to remain, you have to pay another fee to have it repaired or renewed. So they have been trying to contact families of older memorial seats which have fallen into disrepair.

'We give them a year to contact us, and if they don't, we replace it, offering the dedication to someone on the waiting list.'

The fee is now £2,000, just for ten years. Wow, quite an increase. But the cost of the wood, engraving it and an annual oiling has greatly increased as well. The well-chosen words for the seat have to be agreed. No politics or religion. They encourage people in the wording to mention how the beloved person loved the Heath. This of course is good PR for the Heath, making passers-by reflect on how much they too love the Heath. As we all do.

Will I love other London parks just as much? The ones unknown to me, which I have never visited before but will do this coming year? And when I get to the park where my girlfriend lives, will I still love her as well?

Best Things About Hampstead Heath

1. The view from Parliament Hill of London and the City. Study the plaque, trying to work out all the landmarks, till you go dizzy.

2. The three open-air swimming ponds – one for men, one for women, and one mixed, plus the Lido. Has any park anywhere got as many places to swim?

3. Kenwood House – a real stately home but open to all, with paintings by Rembrandt, Van Dyck, Gainsborough, Reynolds, plus landscaped gardens. Spot the fake wooden bridge over the pond. But don't try to walk over it.

4. The enormous variety of landscapes, with hills and lakes, woods and meadows. Yet so near central London. You can walk for three hours, see no one, and only have one road to cross.

5. My memorial seat, near the entrance to Kenwood as you come from the Highgate ponds. Erected in 1985 to celebrate our silver wedding.

2

VICTORIA PARK

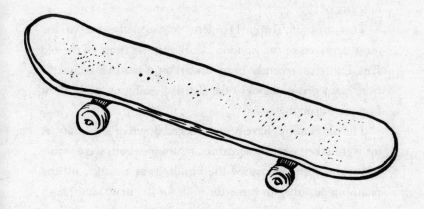

I came out of Hackney Wick Overground station and was immediately confronted by the most awful concrete dual carriageway, the hell known as the A12. The roar of the traffic was deafening, the speed of so many mad drivers frightening. The filth and fumes made me choke. How could any human live and breathe anywhere near such a nightmare?

There appeared no way to walk over the road, but then I noticed a concrete footbridge and raced across it as quickly as I could, my hands over my ears.

I looked back and saw a large hand-painted sign on a derelict building announcing to the world, SHIT HOUSE TO PENTHOUSE.

This area of Tower Hamlets, traditionally one of the most deprived of the London boroughs, the heart of the old East End, has recently been undergoing massive regeneration, with private blocks of smart flats going up, as in most London boroughs.

The old factories have been knocked down or left empty. A lot were taken over by squatters, many of whom were artists of various sorts, who used the buildings as a canvas till the planning permissions came through for the new, brash, flash developments, and they were all chucked out. Hence this cry of pain about their Shit House being turned into yet another penthouse. A squeal of protest, or an appeal to the powers that be, somewhere up in the heavens.

So far, it had been entirely unlike my dear Hampstead Heath, with its ever so tasteful surrounding streets and, of course, its ever so tasteful locals and regulars, such as, well, my own dear self. But so many young Londoners, young professional IT types of people, a lot with beards, who have recently moved into newly fashionable Hackney, had been telling me about the wonders of Victoria Park, its fascinating history, and how a park like Victoria Park was absolutely vital in the East End of London – more than Hampstead Heath is to its community. They could not believe that during all these years living in London, I had never been. I wasn't even sure where it was, hence all the blinking and staring, confusion and deep intake of breath at some of the modern horrors of urban life as I came out of the station and tried to find the park.

But once over the road bridge and just a few hundred yards further on, peace prevailed. I could not believe the change in the atmosphere, as if nature had been turned on. And there was Victoria Park – not that I could see much of it at this stage. I entered through the Cadogan Gate and after a few hundred yards it all felt green and attractive.

I was so delighted to have escaped the traffic that it didn't strike me at first that at this end of the park, where I had entered, despite the greenery, it was in fact pretty boring, with flat stretches of grass, filled with football pitches, and without much character. It reminded me of a pathetic park I had once traipsed miles to visit one day in Manchester, when I had first arrived, not knowing my way around. Municipal parks everywhere, in London and our other big cities, have tended to conform to a pattern, especially if all they have is a flat stretch of empty grass. They were tended by decades of municipal park keepers and council gardeners who grew the same plants, cut the same hedges, chased the same kids off the floral clock.

I walked down an avenue of trees and noticed that some of the fruits had fallen and were lying on the ground. I thought at first they were cherry trees till I picked some up and bit them and realised they were little crab apples. Very sour. So I spat them out. Eventually, when they get soggy and start fermenting, the wasps will probably eat them, get themselves drunk and go around stinging the locals, especially those with beards.

As I slowly progressed, the park began to reveal its true self, opening up and displaying its treasures and delights. I then began to understand why Victoria Park is considered one of the wonders of east London, the jewel in Tower Hamlets' crown, with Victorian monuments seen nowhere else, and why it has been regularly voted the most loved park in the UK. Beat that, Hampstead Heath.

It is a man-made park, first opened to the public in 1845 in a deliberate attempt to bring greenery to the East End and to provide a park for the people – as opposed to the local quality, which was who the Royal Parks in the middle of London had mainly catered to when they were first created.

It was the Crown Estate that purchased the 218 acres needed to create Victoria Park, land which had been spoiled by the extraction of gravel and clay. A bishop's palace was also pulled down to make way for the park. The intention was to reproduce a Royal Park only for the poor of the East End. It would be reminiscent of Regent's Park, as it was laid out by the notable architect and planner Sir James Pennethorne, who had been a pupil of John Nash, who had of course helped to create St James's Park (see p. 71)

It is bordered on two sides by canals – the Regent's Canal and what was once the Hertford Union Canal, which opened in 1830 as a mile-long link to the River Lee Navigation, when it was often called Duckett's Cut, after investor Sir George Duckett. When it failed to turn a profit, it was incorporated first into the company that ran the Regent's Canal and, in 1927, the Grand Union Canal.

The canals are still used by narrowboats and there are moorings in the park, popular with those who have beautiful boats. Who wouldn't want to wake up in a park such as this?

In addition to canals, there are three lakes, for fishing and swimming and racing model steam boats. One is over-looked by a pagoda. In 1936, a splendid Lido was added, enjoyed by generations of East End children, their first and often only chance of free open-air swimming, although this hasn't endured.

From the beginning, Victoria Park was known as the People's Park and it became a centre for political meetings, rallies and public events, often with a left-wing, revolutionary feel. In 1848, just three years after the park opened and when the rest of Europe was engulfed in revolution, noisy Chartists gathered here for a demonstration. Their aim was to win the vote for working men. (At the time, democracy was largely the preserve of the wealthy and landed.)

The police response was immediate and overwhelming. An extraordinary 1,600 constables, 100 mounted policemen and 500 police pensioners turned out to confront the demonstra-tors. The stage was set for an almighty showdown. However, after a summer thunderstorm erupted, everyone retreated and the skirmish was averted.

This tradition continued, however, with regular soapbox orators attracting huge crowds, whether arguing for socialism, Calvinism, Darwinism, Salvationism or anarchy. Over the decades, star speakers included William Morris, who was not only a famous textile designer but also a revolutionary social-ist, trades unionist Annie Besant and women's rights champion Christabel Pankhurst.

The park attracted wealthy upper-class patrons and bene-factors such as Baroness Angela Burnett-Coutts, who funded a magnificent pink marble and granite drinking fountain, erected in 1862 at a cost of £6,000, which is equivalent to about half a mill in today's terms. Coutts was fabulously wealthy, having inherited a fortune from her grandfather Thomas, who had founded the family bank. Upon his death in 1837, she inherited £1.8 million, equivalent to £160 million today. A friend of both the Duke of Wellington and writer Charles Dickens, she invested much of her money in assisting the poor by financing schools. She also loathed animal cruelty and made it her business to provide dog fountains for thirsty canines. When the mighty canopied fountain that she paid for in Victoria Park was opened, 14,000 people came to mark the occasion. On it there are cherubs and urns and inspiring advice for life: 'Temperance is a bridle of gold'.

The point of the lavish fountain was to provide clean, fresh drinking water for the poor of the East End as those were the days when fresh water was not universally available. She was one of the first women ever to be made a peer in her own right. Unsurprisingly, she was courted by many chancers, hoping to get their hands on her wealth, and she did not marry till she was sixty-seven – to a twenty-nine-year-old American who had been her secretary. He then took her surname. When she died in 1903, she was buried in Westminster Abbey. There was national mourning for the woman known as the Queen of the Poor.

For several generations the park figured largely in their childhoods, as they drank from the fountain, bathed in its pools or raced boats on the water. Some were drawn to more formal games and by 1900 there were thirty-two cricket pitches and thirty-seven free tennis courts. British champion Fred Perry, who dominated at Wimbledon between 1936 and 1939, practised there.

Inevitably, many of the children who played here were Jewish, after about 100,000 families fled persecution in Russia, Poland and other parts of Eastern Europe during the closing years of the nineteenth century. That's why there's a Yiddish song, dating from about 1890, that mentions Victoria Park, which Tower Hamlets has put online for people to hear. The poverty that affected most people who lived in the neighbourhood began to ease in the twentieth century.

But with the Second World War everything changed. London's East End suffered heavy German bombing, with most of the bombers heading for the London docks. The park was turned over to allotments and a pig farm while iron railings were pulled up as part of the war effort. Ditches were dug around the park to provide air-raid shelters, the biggest capable of holding 1,386 people, and there were barrage balloons drifting above, in the hope of deterring bombers. But as politician Stanley Baldwin predicted in 1932, 'the bomber will always get through', and when the park was struck during enemy action on 15 October 1940, fifteen people in that mighty air-raid shelter perished. Worse was to come for residents as some of the park was given over to anti-aircraft guns. The colossal noise of the Z Battery firing its three-inch missiles is thought to have been responsible for one of the biggest tragedies of the war.

The Bethnal Green Tube disaster in 1943 claimed the lives of 173 people who were crushed as they rushed for the safety of the Underground. There had been tension in the air, as people knew Berlin had suffered mammoth bombing raids during previous nights. Punishing retaliation by Hitler seemed likely. So when the siren sounded there was panic, and hundreds of people pushed into the Tube station at the same time. The tragedy unfolded as some of the early arrivals tripped and fell near the bottom of the stairs. Bodies piled up, with one suffocating the next. Everyone thought they had heard German bombers above, but some eyewitnesses later reported that the noise was caused by the new anti-aircraft guns based at Victoria Park. It was the biggest single loss of civilians during the whole of the Second World War, but the government tried to keep the whole tragedy quiet, not wanting to affect national moral.

Soon a prisoner of war camp was set up along the north-east side of the park, housing German and Italian POWs. One of the most poignant reminders of the war is the St Augustine's Church stone, standing near the gate of the same name. It's where a square-towered church built in 1867 stood until the end of the war, when it was deemed too wrecked to repair. The stone marks the spot where the altar once stood and trees were planted to reveal its outline.

Victoria Park, like Hampstead Heath, was owned by the Greater London Council until 1986, when it was handed over to the boroughs of Tower Hamlets and Hackney. Since 1994, Tower Hamlets Borough has looked after it.

The park is in two parts: East and West Park, with a road between the two. I had come by chance into the larger section of park, the East Park, which is the one nearest the less affluent area.

I was heading for the so-called Hub, where the park manager is based, not knowing what it was. It turned out to be a rather modern, attractive building, which contains the park cafe – closed that day, as it was a Monday – and also a display area on the history of the park and a couple of community rooms.

I couldn't find where the parkies were hidden, so I wandered round the back, banging on windows as I could not see a door. I suspected they must be inside, crouching. I did have an appointment, but I was in fact early, so I should not blame them for not having a welcome committee waiting for me.

I eventually got inside and into a small open-plan office where I found the manager of the park and his staff not crouching, but working away on their computers and their walkie-talkies.

Parkies traditionally don't like being spied upon or accosted in their lairs. They like to hide away, get on with their parky life, without people banging on their windows or barging in with moans and complaints. Lucky is the Hampstead Heath superintendent, safely cut off on the Archway Road, well away from nosy blighters or bossy boots.

Dave Hime, the manager, introduced me to several of his assistant managers and they all seemed to have rather fancy titles, the sort BBC officials and civil servants all love these days and get mocked for in satirical programmes. I didn't take them all in but there were two park development officers, one community officer, one infrastructure officer, an education liaison officer and a nature operative. I think that is roughly right. In the old days, all parkies were just parkies, apart from the superintendent. Now they all have titles, special duties and skills, and most with college degrees to prove it.

Dave the park manager was tall and burly with a shaven head and looked very fit and strong. He had done eighty lengths that day in a local swimming pool before coming to work. He and his staff looked more like policemen or security services. Most, even sitting at their desks, were wearing yellow hi-vis jackets with very serious-looking walkie-talkies hanging from their belts, burbling away.

Dave is fifty-seven and was born locally – on the Isle of Dogs – though he now lives in Essex. As a boy he remembers coming to the Lido in Victoria Park – and how cold it always was. He joined the council forty years ago from school as an apprentice gardener in the Bethnal Green Gardens. When he joined, there were eight gardeners in that one little park. Now it has no full-time gardeners assigned to it at all. It gets done by outside contractors, when it gets done.

He has been at Victoria Park for ten years, most of that time as monitoring officer, whatever that means. I did not quite understand it, but it had something to do with contracts. He took over as park manager in July 2017 when the previous manager, Ron Cain, died after a short illness.

Dave had not thought of applying for the job till he realised how well qualified he was, having sat beside Ron in their office for so many years, observing what the work entailed.

There are four on the management team, including Dave.

They look after events and liaise between the community and the environment. Then there are six park rangers who wear blue uniforms and do a lot of cycling round, keeping an eye on things and enforcing the bylaws, when necessary. The rangers work shifts, and do more in summer than winter, when the opening hours are longer.

Then there is the 'Green Gang', numbering eight, not to be confused with the gardeners, of which there is a head gardener and two others, plus three apprentices.

Altogether then, under Dave's command, there are normally twenty-three full-time staff members looking after the 200 acres of Victoria Park. Pre-war, there were at least fifty full-time workers.

Clearing up the rubbish, as in all parks, is a mammoth, never-ending task. At Victoria Park, the work is contracted out, in this case to Veolia, who appear these days to do most of the dustbin and rubbish work in the London boroughs.

The whole of Victoria Park is enclosed, with a railing or fence all the way round, and gets locked at night. There used to be twenty-six gates, almost all of which in the old days had a handy pub right beside it. Most of these pubs have gone but one of the older ones, in the West Park, has recently changed its name. It is now calling itself the People's Park Tavern. Very Hackney.

There is a new gate, making the total twenty-seven, created in 2010 for the Queen's Jubilee. When the public was asked what it should be called, suggestions included the Justin Bieber Gate, the Michael Jackson Gate and the Dogs Gate. The winner was the most obvious one – the Jubilee Gate.

The gates open every day, all year round – even on

Christmas Day – and close at dusk. In the summer this can be pretty late, which is why the rangers work shifts. It is their job to close and open the twenty-seven gates.

There are special security locks on all the gates, opened by what are known as FB keys, short for Fire Brigade keys. Police and firemen have copies of these so they can get in quickly in case of emergency.

Alas, in this modern age, some clever but wicked people have been selling repro keys on Amazon for only two pounds. They have had to change the locks several times, which recently led to some confusion. Some burglars, being chased, managed to climb over one of the gates, followed not far behind by the police, who then got stuck behind the closed gate as their security key did not work.

Dave's routine problems are less dramatic, though – mainly to do with minor grumbles. People always seem to have something to upset them, whether noise or disputes between dog owners and cyclists, each of whom think they own the park and that it is all organised for their benefit. And of course litter is a constant bugbear.

'So many people just stand up when they have had a picnic – and walk away. They think if they don't chuck it about it doesn't count as littering.'

He recently had occasion to admonish a woman whose dog had fouled a path. She had just walked on, not clearing it up with a little bag as she should have.

'I'm not clearing it up,' she replied. 'It's a bit runny.'

'All the more reason to do so,' said Dave. 'Children might walk through it.'

She suddenly started shouting and swearing at him, calling

him all sorts of names. 'Did you not get it from your wife last night,' she yelled. 'Is that why you have the hump with me?'

Dave decided to take a photo of the dog shit as evidence. While he was doing so, the woman lunged at him, striking him in the face.

'I reported the incident to the police and they did put out an arrest warrant for assault, but nothing ever happened. They either couldn't find her or gave up. I did happen to see her a few months ago. She carefully avoided me, moving away sharpish.'

He always advises staff to avoid confrontation at all costs. When they come across someone committing a misdemeanour, he instructs them to talk into their walkie-talkies, saying they have been called to the scene 'because there has been something seen on CCTV'. This is to frighten the miscreants who now know that their behaviour has been caught by the cameras. This generally avoids any likelihood of a personal slanging match.

There are lots of CCTV cameras all over the park. In his office I could see a bank of sixteen screens, each showing a different view. I thought later that they must have seen me, entering by the Cadogan Gate, picking crab apples, then snooping round the hub, banging on the windows. It's a wonder I was not arrested for acting suspiciously.

Several of their cameras in the busiest areas, such as the skate park, have an audio element. So a parky sitting in a video room can see trouble and then speak directly to the culprits from the camera – which always startles them.

In fact there isn't a lot of antisocial behaviour. The park is locked up every night, so the rowdies and gangs can't get in.

And unlike many public parks, they have had no serious drugs problem, judging by the fact that discarded needles or drugs paraphernalia are rarely found.

A lot of Dave's work each year is concerned with raising money, particularly from public events held in the park. The political rallies have all gone, as present-day councils don't like to be seen encouraging extremists and agitators, or even evangelicals. In place of politics they have pop music. Victoria Park has become one of the leading venues in London for open-air pop concerts, attracting audiences of 40,000. Madness have performed there, and so have The Clash. Many films, TV dramas and TV commercials, such as the John Lewis Christmas one featuring Monty the Penguin, have been set in the park, which has earned them good money.

The big pop concerts are organised by an outside agency, but the park itself organises Family Fun Days, which can attract 8,000 people of all ages. Each year they have a Great Day Out, when they bring the seaside to the East End with donkey rides, Punch and Judy shows and a pop-up sandy beach.

All these events, about the most held in any London park, including Hyde Park, bring in almost £250,000 a year. They have to keep finding new money every year in order to fund all the improvements and new services they want to provide.

Even without these one-off events, there's still plenty going on. With nine football pitches, a changing room, three cricket fields, three lakes, a bowling green, three play areas, two cafes, tennis courts and so many regular events, activities take up twenty pages of the park's programme. They include Family Fun Days, history walks, bird walks, chess for children, fishing, canoeing picnics, first-aid training, outdoor nature classroom, teddy bears' picnics, tea dancing for the pensioners and a farmers' market every Sunday.

And everything is free. There is no admission charge for any of these events, hence a continual need to find a source of income in order to keep offering so many attractions.

There is a charge for the football pitches, though, as you do get changing premises and hot showers, plus nets and goal posts provided. The fee is £32 per game for twenty-two players.

The average number of visits each year is now nine million, which is a lot, for what is a fairly small park, compared with Hampstead Heath. It also explains why it is regularly voted the best-loved park in all Britain.

I didn't know there were such awards, so Dave took me proudly to see where their framed certificates are hanging. The most important accolade in the parks world is a Green Flag, which is awarded by the Keep Britain Tidy campaign. Victoria Park won the main award five years running, then the rules were changed and there was no outright winner any more. Instead, the top ten most popular parks were announced, in no order. And, oh horrors, in 2018 Victoria Park was not one of them, nor was any other London borough park. Could it have been anti-London prejudice? But in 2019 Victoria Park did make the top ten in the UK again, the only London Park to do so. Phew.

Dave agreed to start me on my walk round the park, taking me first to the nearby skateboard park. I had noticed this bru-tally modernistic creation, all double slopes and curves and hollows. There was a boy, in all the skateboard gear, with helmet, going across at such fantastic speed I was sure he was going to crash into the end wall, but then he flew up in the air, turned and came back down again.

Dave pointed to what he called the cradle, a concrete cave, in which the experts can turn 360 degrees in the air. It is apparently one of only two full cradles in the whole country. On a busy day there are up to 500 skateboarders, who come from as far away as Brighton.

'Skateboarders are all well behaved. They queue patiently and wait for their turns. And if any leaves get blown in, or any rubbish appears, they will come and politely ask to borrow a broom and brush it all up. So it is self-sustaining.'

The site occupied by the playground and skatepark was at one time the Victorian bathing pool, but it fell into disrepair and was eventually closed. One day Dave would like to see the Lido rebuilt, but doubts if it will get funding.

In 2010, the park did manage to do some massive improve-ments which cost £12 million, £4.5 million of which came from a National Lottery grant. The Hub was one of the new things that got built, and there were repairs to some of the Victorian bridges, buildings and playgrounds.

Another source of income these days comes from a so-called Section 106. When Tower Hamlets Council grants planning permission for certain commercial properties, an extra payment has to be paid which goes towards local amen-ities. So when yet another new luxury apartment block goes up, the community as a whole gains something.

'We also charge volunteers to come and work in the park,' said Dave.

You what? I thought I had misheard. They pay you?

Yes, said Dave. Corporate volunteers pay £35 each time

they come and do a day's work in the park. They tend to be from corporate companies, big City firms, who once a year allow their staff a day off to come and volunteer to do work in the park – and pay for the privilege.

Twenty volunteers, all employees of Société Général, were coming the next day. Dave was going to get them to move a large mountain of gravel, which had just arrived, and lay it out in a playground, under the direction of one of the rangers.

He then took me to the Old English Garden, which seemed a bit wild to me, full of grasses and a bit overgrown. There used to be some very high hedges round the garden, but these had been taken down for security reasons.

In 2003, not long after Dave joined the park, the body of a woman jogger was found. She had been stabbed in the neck, though not sexually assaulted. Her assailant had jumped out from behind a hedge. The murderer was never found, though there was a long investigation. CCTV cameras were few in those days. The woman was an American who lived locally, and was a talented artist.

Dave took me over to a large fig tree where a clay model of a face had been fixed to the trunk, about six feet up. The face was not of the murdered woman but of a piece of pottery she had been working on, given to the park by her family in her memory.

I would have missed it if I had not been with Dave. Even if I had spotted it, I could not possibly have known its significance. There is no plaque or explanation. But the sight of it is poignant and provoking.

All the sporting facilities are well used – except for one. The poor old bowling club, which has a handsome, well-cared-for lawn and an attractive clubhouse, is struggling to get new members. It has tried open days for young people and introduced barefooted bowling, which made it into the local newspapers, but after initial interest, the numbers fell away again. I suggested nude bowling. When global warming makes our summers tropical every year, that would surely be attractive. That would at least get them some national publicity.

Perhaps the single most interesting old building in the whole park is the Burdett Coutts Fountain. A lot of the £12 million regeneration money was spent restoring it. I had read about it but did not expect it to be so large and impressive, like a slightly smaller version of the Albert Memorial, with a cupola on top, elaborate inscriptions and engravings all the way round. Beside the cleaned-up, gleaming fountain is a very well-written plaque, giving the history of the fountain. I do hate it in parks when clearly fascinating monuments or buildings are not properly explained.

A lot of money was also spent on another splendid Victorian edifice: the Pagoda. The original dated from 1842 and was originally in Hyde Park, part of a Chinese exhibition which is said to have inspired Gilbert and Sullivan to write *The Mikado*. It was moved to Victoria Park when the park was opened, but a century later it had fallen into disrepair. Now it has been completely rebuilt, with crimson pillars supporting a roof with upturned corners, along with the bridge that leads to it.

The nearby lake has also been cleaned up, a new water bore drilled and two islands made. On one of the islands you can see two other original Victorian creations – the Dogs of Alcibiades. They were a gift from another Victorian philanthropic woman, Lady Regnart. Originally they guarded one of the entrance gates to the park but jokers continually took various liberties with the dogs, sticking silly things in their mouths. They are now safely situated on the island, which is not accessible.

The ones sitting on top of the gates today are repro versions. They are based on dogs which appeared on classical statues dating back to the fifth century. Dave was very surprised recently, when on holiday in Rome with his wife, he came across statues of the dogs near the Vatican. 'Hmm,' he thought, 'exactly the same as the ones in our park.'

The smaller West Park contains most of the ancient Victorian monuments, not the East Park where I had come in, and where all the football pitches are, so it was a delightful surprise to keep coming across them.

The West Park has a smarter, more upmarket feel. The iron work benches are fancier, the bridges more ornate. This is the up and coming end. There are now million-pound houses along Grove Road, bordering the park. Victoria Park is now Grade II listed, which, entering at the other end, I had found hard to believe. But now I could see why. The local estate agents, always alive to any social changes and rising prices, have rechristened this bit Victoria Park Village.

Dave is fortunate that he has only one local community organisation to deal with, the Victoria Park Friends. With some parks, you can have several groups, often competing, with different objectives. And of course most such groups, being volunteers, often fall out among themselves.

The chair of the Victoria Park Friends is Richard Desmond. I met him in the park for a coffee. He lives right beside it – not in one of the posh houses, but in a tower block. He is an electrician working in the West End theatres and sports some fine tattoos on his arms. He was born and brought up locally and when he was aged three, he drank a bottle of Fairy washing-up liquid. He was rushed to the Mile End hospital where his stomach was pumped. Out of it came a mass of bubbles. His parents from then on called him Bubbles, a nickname which he has now managed to discard, though he has retained a tattoo of some ink bubbles.

The Friends are awfully egalitarian and socially conscientious. There is no membership fee, anyone can join, and all their activities are free. On their Facebook site they have 5,000 regular members. As members and locals, at both ends of the Park, are on the whole very pleased and approve of the park, they don't get many arguments or splits among themselves. 'If people are happy, they don't complain,' said Richard.

'Councils do not have a statutory duty to provide parks and green spaces for residents. And lots of course do and put a lot of effort and money in. But it is not compulsory, the way they have to provide schools and hospitals. This means people who love parks and use them have to do their bit, to look after them for future generations.'

The Friends keep an eye on the noise levels in the park and try to limit the number of pop concerts that can be held each year. Local residents get very upset and start complaining if they can't sleep. There is now an agreement with the park and the borough council that there will be only six days of big pop concerts in any one year. Tea dances and brass bands in the bandstand don't count.

Dave, the superintendent, recently lost a battle over the children's playground area. A lot of money was being spent on improving it and he did not want to put a fence round it, feeling it spoiled all his new landscaping. But certain mothers in the Friends protested, saying that keeping it unfenced posed a danger to their children playing: they could easily wander off and into the lake.

'They said to me, who is going to stop them doing that? And I said they will, as their mothers. You go to the seaside and there is no fence to stop children going into the sea. But they were not convinced. They then had a public demonstration, the mothers lining arms all the way round the playground to symbolise a fence. It made the local papers. The council gave in. So I lost that one. I had to put up a fence.

'But if you look carefully, you can see we have now added bamboos. When they are established, they will cover up the fence.'

Dave seemed to be amused rather than upset by their protests, saying it is in fact very rare that there is a difference of opinion with any of the local residents. Generally, they all work together.

He suddenly stopped as we were talking and rushed off into the bushes. He had spotted a small tent deep in the undergrowth. I don't how he had seen it.

No one is allowed to stay in the park overnight, hence the ring fence and the secure gates, or of course to sleep in it, though courting couples have been known to stay pretty late, before climbing out.

I followed Dave into the undergrowth and could see him bending down, looking at a small orange tent, quite new-looking; the sort pop fans buy for Glastonbury, then discard when it is all over.

'Are you okay?' Dave was shouting through the canvas.

The tent was quite small, but might have contained one or two persons. Personally, I would not have got so close to the opening in case someone came out and hit me.

'I'm leaving at two o'clock,' a low voice eventually could be heard, in what might have been an East European accent.

'That's okay then,' said Dave. 'Just make sure you do. If you are needing somewhere to sleep tonight, we can put you in touch with some homeless organisations. Okay?'

The voice gave a grunt.

On his walkie-talkie, Dave then rang the head ranger, Marcello, a Bolivian who has been in this country sixteen years, and told him what he had spotted. He said that one of his rangers should check the site later in the day.

We later came across another encampment, a homemade shelter, with old blankets and a tarpaulin draped over a tree, right beside the boundary fence. Whoever had been using it had clearly long departed.

It was in a small wood and the gardeners had spent a lot of time and money edging the paths with logs. Last winter, the logs had started disappearing, which baffled the park staff. Who would steal old logs, and why? Then one night, someone from one of the boats on the canal was spotted creeping into the wood in the dark, followed by several others. They were taking the logs to burn in their stoves on the boat.

I later told Richard, the chair of the Friends, about Dave finding someone sleeping in a tent, and he nodded, not noticeably shocked. 'This is the nature of London today. There is such a huge disparity between the rich and poor today and it's getting worse. You have so many homeless with nowhere to go'.

If you need a sit-down you might choose one of the stone alcoves that once stood on Old London Bridge – that's the one before the one before this one. Fourteen alcoves were added to the busy bridge in 1762 to provide shelter for pedestrians. After this bridge was replaced in 1831, two of the alcoves found their way to Victoria Park.

As I wandered round Victoria Park, I examined all the park benches, thinking of course of my own memorial bench on the Heath.

'In loving memory of Reg Hutchinson and all of the wonderful times spent in the park.' Not quite as literary as some of those on the Heath, but simple and moving. There seemed to be more of them at the Western end than the Eastern, presumably because it is prettier, and the ironwork on the benches better. It costs just £1,000 – half the price of a bench on the Heath – if you want a brand new one, from scratch. And even less if you get a reconditioned one.

People are now also being encouraged to consider planting a memorial tree. You don't get your name on it, but you do get a warm glow knowing you have paid for it. About ninety memorial trees a year are being planted. You can also place cremation ashes under the tree. However, scattering human ashes on the flower beds isn't permitted. 'There is something in human ashes which can burn some of the young plants,' explained Dave.

On one seat I met an elderly couple having a rest. He was wearing a Hawaiian shirt which I admired. 'It's to match the flowers,' he said, 'give them some competition.'

The couple come into the park every day of the year. He goes off to the East Park to pop into the bowling club, see if any of his friends are there. She always goes to the West Park to the flower garden to admire whatever is out. Then they meet up on this same bench.

They were now on their way to the Community Centre, right beside the park. She was going to have a massage. He was having his feet done. 'It's our life. Our life is in the park. We live our life here.'

The garden with all the flowers is known as the Sunken Garden and is filled with annuals, so it's always more colourful than the more verdant Old English Garden. It has featured in loads of wedding photographs and videos. Happy couples can drive along the little road nearby, which crosses the park, and pose in front of the flower garden. No one admiring their wedding photos later is to know that they had not hired Blenheim Palace for their special day but are in fact standing on a road in front of railings in a public park in the East End of London.

I had lunch in the Pavilion Cafe. Ten years ago, so I was told, it was a greasy spoon cafe. Now it is chic and cool and trendy, not things I associate with the heart of the East End. This of course is a silly, snobbish, Hampstead-type thing to say. Hackney has been the home of hipsters for at least the last ten years. The building is modern, with a glass domed roof, so there is loads of light, with finely scrubbed bare wooden tables, inside and out.

Owner Rob Green, a healthy country-looking man in his fifties, was originally from Yorkshire. At one time he used to be a social worker in Sri Lanka. While living there he became fascinated by tea, so when he came back to live in London he started importing tea, which he sold in Borough Market. Then he started a bakery.

'Ten years ago I heard that this cafe was up for grabs. It had been derelict for a while. I applied for the lease and got it. I sold my house to pay for it, even though I was getting divorced at the time. A lot of work needed to be done to it.'

A year ago he turned it into a vegetarian restaurant – quite a brave thing to do, as their meat dishes were very popular. The week before I met him he had done something even more daring, if not foolhardy: he had decided to go alcohol-free.

As everyone knows, the mark-up on bottles of wine in restaurants is outrageous. He stands to lose a lot of his profit, but he thinks it will be worth it. It will be good for the environment, good for humanity.

His next project is to go totally waste-free. By which he means that the cafe will re-process all its food waste and dispense with all plastic and other non-degradable materials. I had already noticed that all the straws on the counter were black, something I had never seen before. I asked one of the girls who worked there and she said they were made of paper, not plastic.

One challenge is going to be disposal cups. The day before, a Sunday, they had sold 1,800 coffees – all in plastic cups. If the cafe changes to glass or china cups, how can it cope with all those customers? The dishwasher would have to be the size of the pagoda.

He and his staff are now working on possible solutions, as they are determined to go waste-free. One idea is to sell proper cups to customers at £5 each. You would get a free coffee when you first buy the cup, then 20 per cent off every time you brought your cup in for a coffee. It would be your cup, which you washed at home. Or you could bring your own, and use that each time.

Decisions, decisions. They had not worked it all out yet. It was just the first week of their announcement about going waste-free, or at least telling themselves they were going waste-free. I said I would try to come back in a year to find out how they had solved the problem.

It is of course a problem which faces the whole globe. We all have to be environmentally aware. We don't want our beaches and oceans bunged up with even more plastic.

I stood for a long time admiring the menu. I even took a snap of it on my mobile. It was a little work of art in itself, written by hand in beautiful script in black pen on a white board. I was torn between the pancake with crème fraîche, fried eggs, harissa and greens on sourdough toast, avocado poached eggs with coconut sambal on sourdough toast, wild mushrooms with poached eggs on sourdough toast, or kippers with potato cakes and poached eggs on rye toast. Phew.

I didn't know what some of the items were. The chef apparently is from Sri Lanka so was including some of his native dishes. I plumped for something I did recognise – good old kippers. And they were excellent.

I had never expected to walk into an East End park I had never been to before and feel in touch with so many of our modern-life trends and present-day concerns, and meet right-thinking people trying to come to grips with them.

And it is not just humans in Victoria Park who are being encouraged to eat healthily and well and help save the planet. The birds and the ducks are also being targeted.

The lake in the West Park, which is very attractive and nicely landscaped, with rowing boats and an arty fountain in the middle, has always been popular with a lot of elderly people and children. Alas, many unthinking people have been feeding the ducks and birds with stale bread, which they bring with them for that purpose, as families have done in parks all over the land for generations. I used to do it with my own children when they were young, without thinking.

'People don't properly realise it is like feeding them junk food,' said Dave. 'It is so bad for them. So we had to think of a way of discouraging people from giving them stale bread, without banning it.'

Eventually they came up with a smart solution – to sell the public packets of corn and birdseed, available from the boat-house at the lake at the very low price of 50p a packet, making it clear how much better it was for their beloved feathered friends than stale white bread.

'But we ran out of the packets yesterday. I had an old lady complaining to me. She said she had brought her grandson specially to feed the birds. I said I was sorry, the previous day there had been so many people in the park that we ran out.

'I wanted to add that there was no reason why she could not buy her own birdseed and bring it with her, but of course I didn't. We always try to avoid confrontation.'

During my walk in Victoria Park I also learned the truth concerning a well-known story about our dear prime minister, Boris Johnson, when he got stuck on a zip wire.

It occurred in August 2012, at the time of the Olympic Games. I remembered the story, but had never realised it had taken place in Victoria Park. Boris sets off to sail through the air on a harness, trussed up a like a big fat turkey. He is holding two Union Jack flags, beaming and waving them, and generally showing off. You can hear him shouting how splendid it all is, how it is working effectively, how well organised it all is. Then, suddenly, Boris comes to a standstill: the wire has stopped and Boris is marooned mid-air.

You can still watch it on You Tube, which 408,639 people have already done, according to the number of recorded views on the day I viewed it. It is very funny. You can see his surprise and then slowly his fury and panic. He begins shouting at someone down below to get a rope and pull him down. At the same time, he realises it must appear very funny to everyone watching below, him getting stuck on the wire, and people must be enjoying his humiliation at his stunt collapsing. So he is also trying to be appear not bothered – which he clearly is, growing angrier and more worried. When he is eventually pulled manually to safety, and is back on solid ground, he then tries to laugh it all off. He tries some jokes, blaming it all on someone having left a brake on.

What never came out at the time, so Richard Desmond, chair of the Victoria Park Friends, explained to me, was that it was Boris's own fault.

'The wire worked because there is a counterweight at the end, heavier than the person being pulled, which goes down and pulls the person all the way across. But Boris had not provided his correct weight, so I was told. The weight was not heavy enough to pull him right across. So it suddenly stopped halfway, leaving him suspended in mid-air.'

It couldn't have happened in a more appropriate park, one traditionally known as the People's Park, beloved by all good socialists in the olden days and now by all right-thinking environmentalists. It is, after all, a park of the people, for the people, not just for our elite.

The Victoria Park audience that day enjoyed enormously the plight of a right-wing Tory politician and Old Etonian, the sort who often give the impression that they are above ordinary people. Which, of course, Boris was for a while that day . . .

Best Things About Victoria Park

1. That it exists, in the once deprived East End. It was created by the Victorians in 1845 as a People's Park, to give the poor the same quality of park as the toffs had in the Royal Parks.

2. The smaller West Park is prettier and lusher, with lakes and Victorian monuments. The East Park is flatter, with all the football pitches.

3. The Burdett-Coutts Fountain – a monument to admire and wonder at, rather than just have a drink of water.

4. The Pavilion Cafe – so cool, so chic, and even though it is veggie and does not serve alcohol, the food is excellent.

5. Skateboard park – looks concrete and brutal, but wow, watch them go. One of only two full cradles in the UK.

3

St James's Park

St James's Park is bounded by the Mall to the north and Birdcage Walk to the south. To the west there is the Queen Victoria Memorial, while Horse Guards Road makes up its eastern border. At one end is Buckingham Palace. All these are A-list London landmarks. So how lovely and handy and neat and refreshing to have a little oasis of green, bang in the middle.

St James's is the oldest of all the Royal Parks. It was once a boggy marshland attached to St James's Hospital for young women suffering from leprosy, a scarring infectious disease that romped around Europe in the twelfth and thirteenth centuries. The women were shunned by society and lived in seclusion and fed their hogs on this damp, scrubby land.

In 1531, Henry VIII snapped up the site and built St James's Palace. He had the land drained, using most of it for hunting deer and hiving off a bit as a garden. For the next hundred years it was a high-class adventure playground for the royal family, where they could enjoy cockfighting, bowling, drinking, playing games, watching military reviews – the sort of ordinary, mundane pastimes which for the most part our royals still enjoy. Almost from the beginning it contained a menagerie that included camels, crocodiles and an elephant, as well as exotic birds. There are records in 1626 of a keeper being paid to look after 'the beasts and fowls'.

Today, the park is still best known for exotica in the shape of its six pelicans, gigantic creatures with the second-largest wingspan of all living birds; at about 10 feet it is smaller only than that of the great albatross. These remarkable creatures live nonchalantly alongside mallards and moorhens, without any apparent regard to how enormously gawky and out of place they seem to passers-by.

And there are many of those. St James's Park is the most visited Royal Park, despite being remarkably titchy, covering just 58 acres (93 acres if you include The Green Park). It's probably the most visited park in all England – nay, the universe – as every year over 17 million people pass through it. Tourists trundle along its paths as they pass between Buckingham Palace and Horse Guards Parade, or having visited exhibitions at the Institute of Contemporary Arts en route to the Guards Museum. Civil servants who work at government buildings nearby lunch there.

St James's Park is a showcase – a ceremonial park, surrounded by famous buildings and public monuments, government offices and royal residencies. No wonder visitor numbers are so high. But few stop for long in St James's Park and realise that what they are walking through is British history.

On 30 January 1649, which was a Tuesday, King Charles I took his final stroll through St James's Park. He walked from St James's Palace, where he had been confined for the three days since his death sentence on charges of treason and tyranny, with a phalanx of guards and his pet dog. At the Palace of Whitehall, a special scaffold, draped in black fabric, had been erected and he was executed at 2 p.m. by an anonymous axeman paid £100 for the grisly task. It was a bitterly cold morning, so the king had asked if he could wear two shirts, as he feared that any shivering would be misconstrued among the crowd as fear. Witnesses said a mighty groan rippled through the crowd as the sharpened blade fell. While Charles I was a curious combination of acutely shy and breathtakingly arrogant, and had made a poor fist of ruling, there was little public appetite for his death. Certainly, the subsequent years dominated by over-arching joyless puritanism rapidly diminished any favour Oliver Cromwell had among the people, and eleven years after Charles I died, his son, also Charles, was on the throne.

Charles II was very fond of a new type of bowling game he had picked up in France, known as *paille maille*. It was something like billiards, played on the ground using a mallet and iron rings, and was the precursor of croquet. He laid out a special surface for it to be played on, and eventually it came to be known as Pall Mall.

One of his mistresses, Nell Gwynne, who was both kind and canny, acquired one of the new smart houses nearby – very handy for visiting the king. 'Pretty, witty Nell' was a former theatre orange-seller, popular among the people, not only for being a protestant but also for her racy humour, which felt like a breath of fresh air after the cloying Cromwell years. The diarist John Evelyn was shocked when he overheard some rather ribald chat between the king and Mrs Nelly, as she was also known, called out over her garden wall as he was passing.

Today, famous and eminent folk still walk through St James's Park most days: Whitehall mandarins going to work, the chancellor having a stroll before revealing his budget, ministers on the way to have a quiet word with the monarch.

John Nash, George IV's favourite architect, turned the canal that cut through the park into a more natural-looking lake, which now makes up 20 per cent of the park's area. He also re-established Duck Island, which had been taken out as a health hazard. Nash was an accomplished architect, respon-sible for Luscombe Castle in Devon, Ravensworth Castle in

Tyne and Wear and his own East Cowes Castle on the Isle of Wight, among others. In Brighton he helped formulate the oriental style of the Pavilion, while in London he left his mark on Regent Street, Regent's Park and Marylebone. It was while working on Buckingham Palace, extending and tarting it up, that Nash became somewhat unstuck, after costs rose to much more than double his original estimate. With the death of George IV in 1830, Nash lost his royal protection and died in 1835, before the royal palace was finally finished.

Soon after the park's makeover, the Ornithological Society of London presented some birds to the park and built a home for a birdkeeper, which looks for all the world like a small Swiss chalet. Both Duck Island Cottage and the post created back then remain today.

Everyone who goes through the park will be aware of the pelicans. Waddling pelicans have been part and parcel of the park experience since 1664 when the Russian ambassador presented them to Charles II. At the time, his opposite number was Tsar Alexander II, a prominent reformer – not that it did him any good, as he was assassinated in 1881. Since then more than forty pelicans have called St James's Park home.

Today there are Isla, Tiffany and Gargi, the latter arriving after a family woke up to find a pelican in their back garden in Southend, Essex. He liked it so much he stayed and was named Gargi by the family. But the expense of keeping a pelican on a fish-rich diet is no joke and the bird was duly donated to St James's Park. His wings are not clipped, though, so after the daily feeding time there he's likely to fly across to London Zoo in Regent's Park for another meal.

Then there are Sun, Moon and Star, recent arrivals which

were hand-reared at Prague Zoo. Although they are used to human contact, there's a great effort made among park staff to keep them semi-wild. Not too hard when their favourite hangout is Pelican Rock, at the centre of the lake. Of course, it's tempting to try to make friends with the pelicans when they walk along the paths or squat on the seats. But, unless you have a fresh roach in your pocket, they won't really want to know you.

Pelicans are beloved for the stretchy pouch that hangs from the lower half of their bill, which they use to scoop up prey. Normally dinner is waterborne, but not exclusively so. And the victims are not chewed but swallowed whole – eventually.

These unorthodox eating habits helped the pelicans become an internet sensation in 2006 when one was photographed eating a pigeon. While anxious wildlife experts insisted it was an extraordinary occurrence, visitors weighed in with their own accounts, which seemed to point to the pelicans being quite the pigeon scoffers. One man saw two pelicans eating pigeons at the same time. 'There was a bit of struggling and the pelicans filled their bills with water to drown or wash the pigeon down.'

Don't worry – there are plenty of pigeons left and they themselves have all learned to target first-timers in the park who are brave enough to bring lunch. Perhaps the pelicans are trying to eliminate the opposition so they can have the sandwiches all to themselves?

Pelicans can live to a ripe old age: the oldest known in St James's Park was Peter, an Eastern White, still remembered, who died in 1951 aged fifty-four.

They put one in mind of a limerick by Dixon Lanier

Merritt, loved by most for using made-up words that are so wrong, they are right.

A wonderful bird is the pelican
His bill can hold more than his belican
He can take in his beak
Food enough for a week
But I'm damned if I see how the helican

The pelicans get fed on fresh fish every day at 2.30 p.m., near Duck Island. But all day long you can spot other waterbirds from all over the world – black swans from Australia, mandarin ducks from China, Bahama pintails from the West Indies, as well British species such as coots, shelducks and wigeons.

The luckiest of visitors might see the balletic mating rituals of the great crested grebes to brighten up a grey February day. The first indication it's about to happen is that the chestnut ruffs around the necks of the performing pair fan out. There's some shallow diving and a spell of neck arching followed by head shaking, with one bird expertly mimicking its mate. Then both will dive down to pick a bouquet of pond weed to present to the other, rushing towards each other at speed when they surface, with feet paddling on the top of the water.

Great crested grebes have faced down a conservation crisis and come out the winners. Disaster loomed after their plumage became a favourite fashion accessory after the Great Exhibition of 1851 and the resulting trade reduced their population to an estimated thirty-two breeding pairs. However, protection measures saved the birds, which can now be found all over the United Kingdom.

Inevitably there are Canada geese, and it was here that these bold, honking hoodlums were first introduced to the UK. Today, population numbers across the UK top 62,000 breeding pairs.

The abundance of wildlife does lead to problems – as it does at Victoria Park and elsewhere. Visitors insist on feeding wildlife sandwiches made with white bread and filled with cooked or processed food. There are notices and leaflets telling them not to, but this seems to make little difference.

St James's Park is also noted for its London plane trees, extensively planted in the Victorian age after the hybrid was discovered, almost certainly the product of an oriental plane and an American sycamore. It became popular for its resistance to pollution, in an era when smoke from steam trains made London a lot smoggier than it is now. Still, its popularity continues. In 1996, Nelson Mandela, on his official visit to London, walked from Buckingham Palace in the early morning to plant a plane tree in St James's Park. The Mandela Tree – strong, dependable, long-lived – is still there, complete with a discreet plaque, but I failed to find it. Apparently it is on the side of the park towards the Mall.

Mark Wasilewski is the manager of St James's Park. He has a house that goes with the job, a three-bedroom bungalow, hidden away in the staff yard, which itself is obscured by some trees, at the rear of the large military monument, the Guards Memorial, at the main entrance to St James's Park from Horse Guards Parade.

The nearest permanent resident to where he lives is the Chancellor of the Exchequer. As the crow flies, Number 11 Downing Street is his closest neighbour.

'If I suddenly wanted to borrow a cup of sugar, I suppose I would probably have to go there.'

Prince Charles, the Prince of Wales, is about the next nearest, at Clarence House across the Mall. Going for sugar from the queen at Buckingham Palace would be a bit of a trek – probably take him about nine minutes to get there.

Downing Street is the nearest street with anyone living in it full time, just a couple of minutes' quick walk away, across Horse Guards Parade. In the middle of the night, Mark is often visited by Larry, the 10 Downing Street cat, on his nocturnal prowls. Mark has a cat flap so Larry is always able to pop in and deposit anything he has managed to capture – very thoughtful.

Most of the Royal Parks, and grander London parks, have quite a few staff lodges, but St James's has just the one, where Mark lives. But I bet no more than a handful have ever spotted Mark's house, or been aware that he lives there full time, on his own, the only permanent resident of St James's.

Don't you get scared at night, all on your own, in the middle of an empty park, in the very middle of London?

'No,' he said. 'Even the hubbub of the central London location has been eliminated now, thanks to the miracle of double glazing.'

Mark first arrived at St James's Park almost thirty years ago. Being a country boy from Somerset, he was wandering round, getting his bearings, when he overheard people looking at their London maps and saying to each other, 'Oh, I wonder if this park has got a name?' One of the many tasks he set himself was decent signage with proper signposts, indicating exactly which way and how far to Buckingham

Palace and the rest. Over the years he has added a lot more than just mileage. If you keep your eyes open, look up from your maps, or your sandwiches, you will be able to read some excellent information boards. They inform you of the history of all the monuments, the wildlife and the story behind the park itself.

'So many people don't seem to know the wonderful history of this park. And I have to admit I didn't know it myself until I started work here.'

Mark Wasilewski's father was Polish, serving in the Polish air force before joining the RAF during the war. He rose to the rank of squadron leader, working for a while with SOE on Special Duties, winning a Distinguished Flying Cross medal and bar.

Mark's mother was Scottish. During the war she was working on an RAF base in the east of England. She and her friend Barbara were moaning about the lack of eligible young men on their base, as of course they were all away at war. One day, they heard that some Polish airmen were arriving.

'According to my mother, she and Babs decided to bag one each – which they did.'

The family moved around a lot due to air-force life, and Mark was sent to board at Douai Abbey School, at one time a well-known Catholic public school in Berkshire. It closed in 1999, following various misdeeds committed by one of the monks.

'I don't remember that monk in question. But I remember the school governors getting worried that applications would drop and they would lose money and have to close. Which is what happened sometime after I had left.'

Mark went to Liverpool University to read geography, with no idea what he eventually might do. He was drawn to the idea of keeping the family tradition alive and becoming a pilot, but lacked the requisite qualifications.

His dad, on his retirement, had bought a house with a big garden in the West Country. Mark became fascinated by the garden and decided to go into horticulture. He got a job as a gardener at a local psychiatric hospital with grounds of 112 acres, including sports pitches, kitchen gardens and landscape gardens. He stayed there for eleven years, advancing to management level.

'It then became clear that these huge Victorian institutions, many of them former asylums, had had their day. People with mental health issues were now being cared for in smaller units. The enormous old Victorian buildings were being sold off.'

He moved to the Royal Parks in 1989, working at Greenwich Park in their nursery. He first arrived at St James's Park as park supervisor, which at that stage was number two in the St James's Park hierarchy.

'I had never been to St James's Park before, and I didn't know London that well. When I first walked round the park, and saw how small it was, I thought this will be a doddle.'

In 2002 he became park manager, responsible for the whole of St James's Park and The Green Park, which is the adjoining stretch of greenery. The Royal Parks' hierarchy insists on the definite article always being attached to The Green Park. They are therefore not pleased that the local Tube station is simply called Green Park. Appalling – did they not go to school?

Apart from St James's and Green Park – oh God, sorry, The Green Park – Mark is also responsible for Horse Guards

Parade, the Mall, the Queen Victoria Memorial Gardens in front of Buckingham Palace and two of the grander monuments in front of the palace.

The superintendent of St James's also used to be responsible for Admiralty Arch, but now that has been sold to a private developer and is currently being turned into a luxury hotel.

'But I still have the ancient key to the gates of Admiralty Arch,' Mark beamed, and went off to open a drawer and pull out a massive if rather rusty iron key, promising to hand it over when the hotel opened so it could be displayed in a glass case.

Admiralty Arch was the work of Sir Aston Webb, one of the architects who helped change the face of London. He was responsible for Romanesque-, classical- and Gothic-style designs including the Victoria and Albert Museum, the Victoria Memorial and the main façade of Buckingham Palace, which was remodelled in 1913.

'People don't realise that the road leading from Buckingham Palace to the Admiralty Arch was built especially as a processional route,' explained Mark.

Webb – who was also responsible for the Royal Naval College at Dartmouth – introduced naval references where he could. With the British Empire proud of the might of its Royal Navy, the lamp posts on the Mall have little galleons as part of their decorations.

Goodness. All these decades I've been going down the Mall for various reasons and events, I had never noticed that.

The Mall is still a triumphal route, used for national and royal events – royal weddings and state visits. In 2019, Mr Trump, US president at the time, went down the Mall, but not in the traditional horse-drawn open gold carriage. He was in a bullet-proof giant limo.

Every time there is a big national event involving Buckingham Palace or the Mall, Mark and his merry band have to work hard to make sure that St James's Park and The Green Park look absolutely stunning. And afterwards, oh heck, there is the nightmare of clearing up all the mountains of litter.

Mark has a staff of five Royal Park people, plus twenty-two contract staff, but they are all billeted together in the staff compound hidden behind the main gate, where Mark has his office and his own house.

As a national focal point and a royal institution, they try hard to keep St James's Park classy. Not for them any money-grabbing events like vulgar pop concerts, which now of course happen, alas, in some other Royal Parks, which shall not be named. Not yet, anyway.

In St James's and The Green Park there are never any com-mercial events. Nor are there any sponsored fairs, corporate events, or even discreet hospitality tents, which must be a relief to Mark and his staff. Imagine having in your park a Winter Wonderland which attracts hundreds of thousands and goes on for weeks. The noise, my dears, and the people – how could Mark ever sleep?

But they do allow sporting events, at least down the Mall and Horse Guards Parade, which of course are also his concern.

'The Marathon now finishes in the Mall, which is a bit of a headache. Over at Greenwich, where the Marathon begins, Graham the superintendent has to get up incredibly early, but by lunchtime, his day is done. During the London Marathon, I usually don't get to bed till three in the morning.'

During the 2012 Olympics, the women's beach volleyball was held in Horse Guards Parade, which created endless worries for his staff, but also a lot of fun and excitement and entertainment for the global TV audience.

'The stadium was put up especially for the event and housed 15,000. During the fourteen days of the competition, over 380,000 came and watched it, plus millions on TV. In the stadium itself, there was one day when 17,600 pints of Heineken were drunk.'

He enjoyed the volleyball, even though it often went on till midnight. It was all happening just 240 feet from his bedroom, so he could hear every cheer, every shout, every yahoo.

Another sporting activity is making inroads into the park these days, the Cycle Super Highway. Once, cycling was not permitted in the park itself, just on the Mall and surrounding roads. But cycling is now being officially encouraged as it is environmentally friendly and routes are being opened all over the place.

Trooping the Colour is one of the biggest annual events, held in June, and each year a special grandstand holding 6,000 has to be erected in Horse Guards Parade, where the prime minister and VIPs have the best views at the front.

Mark and his staff always get up at four in the morning to rake the parade ground – which is covered in golden gravel. In 2018, thanks to the heatwave, they had to water it as well.

An event like a state visit will bring several thousand into the Mall. A royal wedding can attract 100,000. Normally there have been two state visits a year, but as the queen has aged, these have been cut down.

About the biggest event in Mark's career so far was the

queen's Diamond Jubilee celebrations in 2012, which ended with a monster pop concert outside the gates of Buckingham Palace. Grandstands were specially built to accommodate guests. Almost 140,000 were in the park that night.

'Afterwards, when it was all over, we had 200 extra litter pickers, apart from our own staff, report for duty. They were in their uniform and when walking through the park at night in long lines they looked like storm troopers. They worked all night till six in the morning.

'I just had two hours of sleep. It was so quiet when I eventually got to bed I shed a little tear.

'Early the next morning, after the procession, I walked the Mall with a police chief superintendent. They were still clearing up the horse manure. The superintendent said to me, "I never thought the pinnacle of my career would be checking on horse muck."

'I replied to him, "This *is* my career."'

The horse manure these days is picked up off the roads by mechanical sweepers and dumped. But in the park, they do recycle all their own leaves, trees and dead flowers.

As a lot of MPs and top civil servants walk through the park each day, not all of them famous faces, Mark always warns his staff to be wary.

'I always tell the staff to be careful what they say, to anyone. You never know who they might turn out to be, perhaps a new cabinet minister or someone newly ennobled on the way to speak at the House of Lords.'

David Cameron, when prime minister, took a regular morning jog round St James's, then changed his jog to The Green Park. He realised there were fewer people there.

'He told me one day that at the far end of The Green Park he had often smelled pot. I wanted to ask him how he recognised the smell . . .'

The foreign secretary, whoever he or she is, is often seen in the park, walking between their office and official residence of 1 Carlton Terrace.

Boris, on becoming PM, did for a while take his morning jog in the park, or at least a speeded up shambling shuffle, till he got abused by some boorish members of the public and retreated to a more private place – the grounds of Buckingham Palace.

There have been several occasions when ministers have been walking through the park carrying important documents, thinking no one was watching, and then got photographed, with the words on the documents clear. 'One politician was photographed getting rid of his papers in one of our litter bins early in the morning on his way to Whitehall.'

There was once a complaint on behalf of Prince Charles. Someone rang from Clarence House to ask if the street sweepers on the Mall could start a bit later. The prince apparently sleeps with his window open and the noise was keeping him awake.

There are a lot of rough sleepers in the park, far more than in most London parks, partly because of its central position – and there is an ample supply of solid benches to sleep on. The park officially only opens from five in the morning till midnight, but as there is no perimeter fence, you can get in any time.

'When St James's Park cafe was renovated a few years ago, outside electric sockets were installed and all-weather cushions were also left outside. This could not have been handier for rough sleepers. They could charge their mobile phones and get a comfortable sleep. Oh yes, so many have mobile phones. I like to think we do get a better class of rough sleeper in St James's.'

This of course is probably partly true. There are so many clubs nearby, and smart hotels, so when a gentleman has had too much to drink, he might as well kip down for a few hours.

'You can always tell from the rubbish what sort of people use the park. In Richmond Park, the biggest single type of rubbish collected is dog poo. In St James's, it is wine bottles.'

But, of course, the majority of rough sleepers are the real homeless. Up to thirty of them have been found sleeping overnight in the park. There is no park patrol or park police on duty at night-time. It is left to the Metropolitan Police to sort things out.

'Our policy these days anyway is to be humane. We don't automatically move them on, as we used to do. We try to help, referring people to homeless charities or health workers.' Gaining the trust of someone who is struggling to grasp even the bottom rung of life's ladder can be a time-consuming job. If this is one of the sadder sides of the job, there are many quirky ones.

One morning, Mark was alerted to a strange object which had appeared in the lake overnight. 'A flashing light had been spotted in the middle of the lake. When I went to look, I could see a notice beside it saying DANGER: RADIATION. Very strange; we had not put it there, and it had not been there the night before.

'I was rung by someone from the Atomic Energy Authority and asked about it, but I said I didn't know anything about any leak. The caller said that I didn't seem to be taking it seriously.

Anyway, later that day we took the light out of the lake and dumped it.

'About two years later, I happened to read a book about Banksy, the artist, and it described how he had put a Radiation Warning in a Royal Park lake. I rushed to the dump to find the light, but it had gone. I fear we might well have destroyed a valuable piece of artwork.'

The biggest change Mark has noticed in his thirty years in the park is not just the huge increase in the number of visitors but the fact that they come all year round. There is no off season for foreign visitors.

'They tend to come in coaches, with a leader. It means that you can have a party of sixty walking along one of our paths – who then meet another party of sixty going the other way. Our paths are not very wide, so half of them have to step aside on the grass. It means our verges are getting more worn and need constantly repair.'

St James's Park, like most glamorous or well-known London parks, receives constant requests from film companies. One of them was for *Mary Poppins Returns*.

'We agreed to permit night-time filming in the park, and also night-time filming on Horse Guards Parade. That involved a lot of smoke being generated. I was phoned by Downing Street the following morning who complained that in the night it had set their fire alarms off.'

Over the years, Mark has had many telephone enquiries from people contacting the wrong St James's Park.

'I can't tell you how many phone calls we get asking what time kick off is.'

This is often from Geordie fans. The ground of Newcastle

United is of course called St James's Park. Exeter City also plays at a ground called St James Park and that has led to similar confusions.

'When I was working on business once in London for the RHS [Royal Horticultural Society], I couldn't understand why they had bought me a return rail ticket to Exeter.'

St James's used to be one of the only London parks without its own Friends – community groups who take an interest in their local park, support it, or keep it up to the mark. St James's Park does not have locals in the normal sense – ordinary residents who live beside the park and walk on it every day.

The nearest community-minded group was the Thorney Island Society, which mainly concerns itself with planning applications around Parliament Square, keeping an eye on proposed changes to the local buildings or streets.

A former Royals Parks chief executive decided that the park should have a group of Friends like all other parks. He approached members of the Thorney Island Society and asked them to adopt St James's Park, along with all their other planning concerns. And they agreed.

The name Thorney Island comes from a small island, covered with brambles, which was located in the Thames in medieval times, roughly opposite the Houses of Parliament, now long gone. There is a legend that it was there that King Canute thought he could control the tides. Formed in 1985 after successfully campaigning to save London's first public library in Great Smith Street from demolition, the society protects and promotes the heritage of Westminster generally, which mainly means buildings and monuments. But now they also concern themselves with the green grass and wildlife of St James's Park.

'They are very helpful,' said Mark. 'They don't raise money nor do they raise problems – but they support and help us.'

Their remit is to protect the park, as far as they are able, so that Nash himself would still recognise it. Some things have changed, of course. Marble Arch, once in front of Buckingham Palace, has since been moved to a site of splendid isolation at the junction of Oxford Street, Park Lane and Edgware Road.

The area outside Buckingham Palace was altered at the beginning of the twentieth century to accommodate the Victoria Memorial, an imperial masterpiece that's run through with naval imagery, as well as images in white marble of the old queen alongside representatives of courage, constancy, victory, charity, truth and motherhood. In 1911 it was unveiled by Victoria's grandson, by now George V. Nearby stand grand gates, once again evoking the glory of Empire, dedicated in turn to Canada, Australia, and South and West Africa. Once again, it's the work of Aston Webb, with others. The memorial gardens nearby were part of the scheme to honour the queen. In the summer there are 22,500 plants in situ, including scarlet geraniums to match the tunics of the Queen's Guard at Buckingham Palace. In winter there are some 50,000 yellow wallflowers and red tulips. Planting for each takes about two weeks and needs some ten staff to complete.

Meanwhile, the suspension bridge that crosses the lake is not the elegant original but a stout concrete version that can better cope with the extreme usage.

I talked to Mark for far longer than I had planned, his stories being so good, his descriptions so colourful, but eventually I started my own walk proper around and inside St James's Park.

I began, as most new visitors approach the park, by walking down Whitehall from the Houses of Parliament.

I had a gape into Downing Street, thinking as ever that it is such a shame that ordinary members of the public cannot walk down it any more, which they used to do when I was young. So many ordinary families on outings to London took snaps of themselves in front of Number 10 – including Harold Wilson as a boy.

In 1989 they put up steel barriers and erected a security entrance. The murder of Lord Mountbatten in 1979 and the Brighton bomb five years later convinced Mrs Thatcher she needed to be properly protected.

Over the years, in the line of work as a journalist, I have been into Number 10 several times. I interviewed Harold Macmillan towards the end of his reign. He was worried about how he would use a telephone when he returned to civilian life. During his years in Downing Street, all his calls had been made for him and he had forgotten how they worked.

I got into the PM's private quarters once when I interviewed Sir Alec Douglas-Home's wife, Elizabeth. She was charming, but totally scatty.

When I went to interview Harold Wilson, George Brown was hanging around outside his office, rather the worse for drink. Marcia Williams, Wilson's private secretary, was going 'tut, tut', trying to shoo Brown away.

I got invited to one of Tony Blair's so-called Cool Britannia parties when he became prime minister in 1997. My wife and I were at our Lake District home in Loweswater at the time, where we spent every summer for thirty years. I came in from a walk to the lake and could hear my wife on the phone, talking to someone, saying no, sorry, we can't. Then she put down the phone.

I came in and asked her who it was. She said someone from Downing Street, inviting us to a reception. I said what? You turned it down?

Yes, she said. We have always agreed not to go to London while we are up here. You know that.

On your bike, I said, I would have broken our rules for that.

I managed to get a number for Number 10 and rang to say, 'Er, if you have another party in the autumn, we could come to that. Please.' An invitation duly arrived.

At the reception, we were both introduced to Cherie Blair. It turned out she was a great fan of my wife's novels. That was probably the reason we had got invited, not my amazing career as a journalist and writer.

I then walked past Admiralty Arch, remembering how I once went there to meet John Prescott. He was deputy prime minister and had a flat in the building. He had asked me to ghost his memoirs, which I did.

When they first moved into Admiralty Arch, Pauline, his dear wife, went downstairs to inspect the impressive front entrance. She came back upstairs rather perturbed. 'John,' she said, 'I can't find anywhere to leave our milk bottles.'

I walked across Horse Guards Parade, having forgotten just how enormous it is – big enough anyway for 1,400 officers and men to Troop the Colour to mark the queen's birthday. I checked the surface. Mark had mentioned how it is covered with golden gravel which needs to be raked. Who knew? Not me.

I noticed there was the Household Cavalry Museum, opened since I was last there. At the front entrance of this living museum was a video on a loop showing the guards going about their duties. It also contained various questions visitors might ask, such as 'Who guards the queen?' Another question, over a shot of a guardsman doing a rather stiff and formal march, was, 'Why is he walking like this?' I wondered how many visitors, British ones, anyway, think of their own rude explanation.

I then entered the main gate of St James's Park, past where I now know Mark and his staff have their office, and headed to the park's restaurant. It is swish, with good home-cooked food, and was very busy, even though it was late in the afternoon. It does have a very clever upstairs bit, a turf roof, where you can sit and have a drink, which was designed by an old friend and neighbour of mine, Michael Hopkins. Alas, it was closed. So I had coffee downstairs and then set off round the lake.

I tried to remember when I last actually walked through St James's Park. When I first lived in London in the 1960s, like any provincial from the north, I made a point of visiting all the major London sites, to gape at names I had only ever seen on the Monopoly board. In due course, when our relations from Carlisle came to visit us, I drove them round places like Buckingham Palace, showing off my knowledge. You wouldn't drive any visitor around central London these days by car. Anyway, I no longer have a car.

I think I probably last walked St James's Park in the 1980s. Goodness, what have I been doing all these decades? Walking on the Heath is the answer.

The first change to strike me was the noise of helicopters overhead. I don't remember hearing any back in the 1980s. The threat of all sorts of terrorism is now constantly with us.

These days there always seems to be a big march or demonstration taking place somewhere around Westminster – protesting about Brexit, climate change, Donald Trump, save the whale, free TV licences for oldies. The police like to have their helicopters hovering overhead, keeping an eye on proceedings and any oldies getting too stroppy.

The army regularly has flights into Wellington Barracks for senior army personnel (three-star generals and above) ever since Chelsea Barracks was closed down. There are also air ambulances, rushing to accidents. The sky over Westminster these days is almost as chocker and noisy as the M1.

Then, of course, whenever there is a big news story around Whitehall, a terrorist bomb or a joyous occasion like a royal wedding, the media companies feel they must use a helicopter. I remember watching on TV as David Cameron drove to Buckingham Palace to tender his resignation to the queen. There were two TV helicopters following him all the way. The coverage went on for ages, showing damn all.

I stood on the bridge crossing the middle of the lake, which affords some of the best views in all London. It's called the Blue Bridge, a new, simple concrete bridge, built only in 1957, the third over the lake. An earlier one was built by John Nash. When I first stood on the bridge back in the 1960s, I was stunned by the richness and depths of the views, back to Horse Guards Parade, or the other way, towards Buckingham Palace.

The skyline towards Horse Guards Parade had probably the best views, with so many unexpected towers and minarets and domes, which you are hardly aware of at street level. I remember taking a snap of it and asking my wife if she thought it could be Istanbul or St Petersburg.

I was looking forward to enjoying that view again, but I had forgotten a newcomer on the horizon – the London Eye. I had not realised how near it is to the park, and how it dominates the view.

Mark had said that when it was first erected in 2000, there had been some concerns. 'I don't think the previous chief executive made a formal complaint, but I know he was worried it would ruin the view from the bridge. However, we were given free tickets for rides on the Eye . . .'

As I walked along the lake, I looked out for any famous MPs or lords having their lunchtime stroll. They must have been hiding. I did see a lot of Civil Service types though, striding purposely through the park in their pinstripe suits, dark overcoats and highly polished black shoes. They were such a contrast to the majority of walkers in the park, mostly young tourists in tatty trainers, worn anoraks, awful hats and rucksacks, stuffing their faces with fast food in plastic trays. I should not criticise, of course. My walking clothes are worse.

I then crossed the Mall and went into Green Park. I don't think I am going to add the definite article any more – it looks so pedantic.

Green Park, unlike St James's, is empty. It is simply a stretch of open grass. No flower beds, no lake, no facilities. More like a field than a public park. But I did notice a difference since I was last there – some sort of new building made out of brown marble. When I got nearer, I realised it was the sun gleaming. It was not a building, as such, but a war memorial, in honour of the Canadians who died in the last war.

I then headed towards Buckingham Palace, stopping on the way at the massive golden Canada Gates. They must be the biggest, grandest gates in London. They are normally kept closed, which makes them excellent for photo opportunities. They were created in 1911, along with the Queen Victoria Memorial nearby, as part of the grand processional route between Trafalgar Square and Buckingham Palace.

I stared for a long time at the front windows of the palace, wondering if the queen was looking out from any of them, staring at me, staring at her, which is pretty silly. I have been to the palace several times and know that her quarters are hidden at the back, well away from the hordes and the traffic.

I first went to the palace thirty years ago when my brother-in-law, Roger, was awarded an OBE. He took with him his wife Annabelle – my sister – and children Ross and Lindsey, and me as his chauffeur.

Roger was suffering from MS, confined to a wheelchair, though still struggling to do his job as a senior civil servant in Whitehall, commuting each day in the guard's van of the train from Leighton Buzzard.

When the invite came, a parking permit was also included for his chauffeur and I volunteered. It detailed where his driver should park and where he should wait during the ceremony.

I had a black Ford Granada Ghia at the time, a model that many government ministers were driven around in. I was also still collecting railway memorabilia. So I put on a railway inspector's black hat, the sort chauffeurs used to wear, and a dark suit, and drove them through the gates of Buckingham Palace, flashing my pass. I dropped off my passengers in the inner courtyard, and then went as instructed to park the car and wait.

It was by a little coach house where there were some proper chauffeurs sitting waiting, drinking tea from flasks. Most of them were rubbishing their bosses, the people they worked for. I praised my boss, Roger – a pleasure to work with, I said, not revealing our relationship.

My next visit to Buck House, as we regulars call it, was as a proper guest, along with my wife, to a garden party in 1981. They never tell you why you are invited. My wife did not want to go, but I talked her into it. I had not realised how many other people had been invited; thousands of them, a bigger crowd than at Brunton Park to watch Carlisle United.

The queen was there, and about half a dozen other royals, each of whom stood in their own little roped-off circle on the lawn. You could pick which you would like to meet. You gave your name, queued up politely, and after a long wait you were allowed a handshake.

My wife went off walking round the grounds, hoping to see the corgis. She had no interest in meeting the queen, or any of them, though her knowledge of the royal family was always amazing. She was able to recite the names and dates of birth of even the most minor royal.

I could see that the queue for the queen was enormous, then I spotted that Lady Diana Spencer had arrived. She had recently got engaged to Prince Charles. I think this was probably about her first public outing.

There was an immediate rush in her direction, which I followed, pushing my way in. Eventually, oh joy, I got introduced to her.

She even addressed a few words to me, personally, privately, which no one else could hear. Protocol has it that you should not repeat what any royals say to you, but as she is long dead, I don't think any harm can be caused now.

'Over there,' she said, bending down towards me, 'I think you will find some very good choccy cake.'

My next Buckingham Palace visit was in 1985 when I went there on a job. I was presenting a weekly BBC Radio books programme called *Bookshelf*. The invitation to be a radio presenter had come out of the blue and surprised me. I did not have a lot of radio experience and, anyway, I was always being told I mumbled too much and was always interrupting. Also I had a northern accent.

But I enjoyed it, and even thought for a while I might go on to become a full-time broadcaster. But after three years, I decided I much preferred working on my own, doing books and columns.

I was at the palace to interview Prince Philip for *Bookshelf*, about a book of his collected speeches. It so happened that both his publisher, Christopher Sinclair-Stevenson, and his literary agent, Giles Gordon, were also my publisher and agent. It was they who had fixed with Prince Philip's office for me to interview him at the palace.

What a bollocking I got from the BBC hierarchy. I was not aware there was a special BBC official whose job it was to co-ordinate all requests to the palace. I should have gone through him first.

Anyway, the interview was allowed to go ahead when the head of *Bookshelf* decided she would come along with me, and be my producer for the day.

We got shown into a library, in the prince's private quarters. I was going along the rows of books, desperate to find either a book by my wife or by me, when suddenly part of the row of shelves I was looking at opened wide. It was in fact a secret door. I think I must have touched a button by mistake. Through it I caught a glimpse of the prince sitting in a little room in front of an old-fashioned one-bar electric fire. It seemed somehow pathetic, in this massive palace, that he should have to crouch to keep warm.

The secret panel closed just as suddenly, and then a few moments later a flunkey appeared, through a proper door, and led me into a formal sitting room where we did the interview with the prince. It went well; he was amusing and self-deprecating. I can't remember now what exactly he said. All I remember was that glimpse of him in front of his sad little fire.

In 2012 I myself was awarded an OBE (drum roll, please) – for services to literature no less, which amused my wife and children. She of course refused to come to the palace. She said she would have divorced me if I had been awarded a knight-hood, thereby making her a lady.

When receiving an honour, you are allowed a trio of guests, so I was able to invite my three children, not thinking they would want to come. But they all jumped at it and we had a lovely day. It was surprisingly intimate and personal, very efficient and well organised, with only around 100 others receiving awards.

You don't know till the day you arrive which member of the royal family will be on duty. We all had our fingers crossed it would not be Prince Andrew. But hurrah, we got the actual queen.

I had a chat with her, and made her laugh. Everyone afterwards, watching from the audience, asked me what I had said to her. They said it was the only time she had laughed during the whole ceremony. I had reminded her about a recent visit she had made to the British Library, for the opening ceremony. Although invited, I was not actually there, as we were in Loweswater that day, but I was told later that she had spent a lot of time in the Manuscripts Room, examining some original lyrics handwritten by the Beatles. She only spent a few seconds in front of Magna Carta, her medieval Latin not being very strong. But she had carefully studied a copy of 'Yesterday' in Paul's handwriting, as of course she can read English, and knows the words, as we all do.

I repeated all this to her, and asked if it was true. She said yes! And then she started laughing.

(The Beatles lyrics, by the way, were donated by me to the British Library. Only saying . . .)

When you have lived in London for over sixty years, and been a journalist who specialised at one time in interviewing well-known people, writing books about well-known people and places, and going through life accepting almost every invitation, one of the joys of old age is all the accumulated memories. It happens to every oldie, of course, if they have lived long enough. We constantly find ourselves coming out with these memories to our dear ones, sparked off by some connection, even though these days the reaction is very often, 'Spare us, Grandpa, you've told us that loads of times.'

On my own, I find myself wandering around central London, in the Royal Parks and the famous streets, looking up at so many buildings, and in my mind I can see and hear long-gone images, conversations, sights and sounds and smells of people long dead whom I once met.

I had not actually anticipated that, when I began this walk

through the London parks, just walking idly through them would spark off so many memories. Sorry about that.

Right, that's enough self-indulgence. Now on to the next park . . .

Best Things About St James's Park

1. All that history back to 1530, all those royals, all those national events. Make sure you do some research beforehand or at least read all the excellent plaques.

2. The setting – just off Horse Guards Parade and Whitehall, jolly handy for the Mall and Buckingham Palace. No park is surrounded by more famous streets and buildings and monuments than St James's.

3. The lake and all those lovely birds, and the pelicans. Ah, but please don't feed them.

4. Spotting the famous politicians, lords and top-drawer civil servants having a stroll. But please don't feed them.

5. The views from the Blue Bridge over the lake – looking one way towards Horse Guards Parade or other way to Buck House. Each is stunning.

4

Queen Elizabeth Olympic Park

Until recently, I was rather confused by the notion of an Olympic park. I have been reading references to it since the 2012 Olympics and worked out, being clever, that it must have something to do with the Olympic Stadium. But how can a stadium become a park? How big is it? Must be titchy. What does it contain and where is it, anyway?

I have just been. And it turns out to be enormous, the biggest new park in Europe for the last 150 years, and the most surprising park I have ever walked around.

It is not a park as we normally know them – a nice bit of greenery, a few paths, some pretty flowers all in row. It does have some of that. But it is more of a revolution in open spaces, turning the whole concept of parks on its head.

The first revolution in parks came in the eighteenth century when our royals first started enclosing and laying out chunks of choice land for their own amusement. In the nineteenth century, enlightened Victorians decided major cities should have their own public parks.

With the new Queen Elizabeth Olympic Park, we now have an urban park. It could be the way forward for parks in the future. If, of course, we can ever find the space, and the money. Which seems unlikely, after the virus.

I had read that the Olympic Park was in Stratford, but I always get confused by Stratford and how to get there. There is Stratford International railway station, that new brutal concrete station that you whizz through on the high-speed train from St Pancras, on the way to France or to Broadstairs. I always think ugh, horrible, glad I don't live here. There is the old Stratford Tube station, which I have looked upon in my mind as Stratford East. Then,

Stratford High Street DLR station, plus there is Stratford Overground station.

Stratford has always been a railway hub, with trains operating there from 1839. What began life as an engine shed in 1840 expanded to become a mighty manufacturing site. In 1891 there was pride and lusty cheering among the workers after they built a six-wheel coupled engine and tender in ten hours, an industry record. It was the pinnacle, and little did they know that in not much more than a century the workshop would have shut. All evidence of this history was erased with the construction of Stratford International station.

Living in north London for sixty years, south of the river is a foreign country to which you rarely venture, while the East End is deprived and scary. This is all snobbism and prejudice and silly, of course. But where is the East End, anyway? Where does it begin and end? And is it not all part of Essex?

I did go once to Stratford East, back in 1967, to the Theatre Royal in Stratford, to see Joan Littlewood's signature production of *Oh What a Lovely War*. It was brilliant; so energetic and entertaining. It's a shame about the drag of getting there. No satnav in those days. But I did take my passport.

My car, the first I ever bought, a 1947 2.4 Riley, broke down on the way there, as it often did. I opened up the bonnet, gave it a few kicks and drove off again. It was only the next day I realised that when bending down I had lost my 1967 diary. It must have fallen out of my jacket pocket. I did wear a jacket in those days. I was distraught. I had kept a daily diary from the moment I had started work in 1958, partly to help when doing my expenses so I could remember where I had been, what I had spent, which I would then double. Yes, disgusting. But we did that sort of thing in Fleet Street. You had an agreed but unofficial weekly expense which you had to reach, regardless of what you actually spent.

I have all my diaries back to 1958, right to this very day, on my shelf, in chronological order, but my 1967 diary is blank for the first three months of that year. I had to buy a new one, but could only fill it in from April onwards. I always blamed Stratford.

I had not realised, till starting my tour of London parks, how great an impact the London Olympics of 2012 had on not just London life, but on London parks, as we have already seen at Victoria Park and in St James's Park.

The London Olympics was course a fabulous success, which brought the whole country together. We all rejoiced in our sportsmen and women breaking records and doing so awfully well. The brilliant opening ceremony is still talked about, nearly a decade later, and our memories still glow of our all-round niceness and those lovely volunteers welcoming foreign visitors. We were happy and proud and united then as a nation, little knowing that Brexit and then a pandemic was around the corner.

I was in the Lake District for most of the London Olympics in the summer of 2012 but I came back just towards the end, and found that all tickets for anything at the Olympic Stadium had long gone. All I could get was a ticket for some women's boxing held at place in Docklands I had never heard of called the ExCeL centre. I have no interest in boxing, but it turned out so exciting. Our girl Nicola Adams won a gold medal – and I was there. Ever since, I have boasted about it, feeling part of the London Olympics family.

London had won the rights in 2005 to host the games, and

almost from the beginning, they were planning on creating a sustainable development. The architects, designers and planners realised that it was the sort of chance that only comes up once a century, to work on such a large, public space and create something new from scratch.

All around the world, in cities that once hosted the Olympics, there are white elephant buildings rotting away, no longer having any purpose in life. We didn't want that to happen in London, did we?

The London Legacy Development Corporation (LLDC) was created in order to make use of Olympic structures and spaces they were acquiring, most of which had previously been dead land.

I remember driving along the North Circular on the way to Cambridge to visit our son in the 1980s and being amazed at all the dirty, stagnant stretches of water and canals around the Lea Valley which I had never known were there.

In preparation for the Olympics, and what they hoped would come afterwards, the Government started buying up otherwise redundant land, canals and derelict industrial sites, and ended up with 560 acres. That is an area bigger than Hyde Park or any of the other inner London Royal Parks. The total cost of acquiring all the land plus the cost of installing power and roads was around half a billion, though I don't think anyone has ever worked out the true costs, as some land was expensively bought on compulsory purchase orders and some was free, in the sense that it was already in the ownership of local councils.

The work of clearing the 560 acres was enormous. It included getting rid of fifty-two electric pylons, then washing the soil, most of which was polluted. Five miles of waterways were cleaned up. Over 4,300 new trees were planted, plus 10,000 shrubs and 120,000 flowers. Nature trails and paths were laid. Then at the Stratford end all the new sporting arenas and stadiums were erected. In total, 80,000 people were employed to make ready the site, creating stadiums fit for the Olympics, and at the same time providing a brand new park.

Then there was the cost of the Olympic Stadium and other sports arenas, plus the media centre to house 20,000 journalists and broadcasters and a village for the athletes. And the work was done on time and, so they say, on budget – but it was a pretty generous budget.

After a lot of faffing, thinking and map reading, I caught the Overground train from Gospel Oak to Stratford. Overground railways are my favourite form of transport in London. You can see out all the time, get sneaky views right into back gardens and back bedrooms. You also get a mobile phone connection, unlike on the Tube. Driving, huh, forget it. The Tube – ugh, horrible, being encased in that underground prison, full of stale air. One of my ambitions in life is never to go on the Tube again. I do like the bus – you can see fresh air, and sometimes even talk to people, which you never do on the Tube. Londoners take an unspoken, unacknowledged vow of silence the moment they enter a Tube station. But buses are slow in the rush hour and roadworks in London never cease.

I have been using the Overground a lot since meeting my girlfriend, going direct from Gospel Oak to Clapham Common where she usually picks me up in her car. I can walk to her house in ten minutes, but come on, I am in a hurry. In over two years of our romance, visiting her at least once a week, the Overground has never once been late.

I came out of the Overground at Stratford station, and found myself at the entrance to Westfield, the biggest shopping mall in the whole of London, if not England, or the globe, a place I had hoped never in this life to visit. I walked on quickly, past some smart-looking high-rise office blocks, and came to a sign saying Welcome to the Olympic Village.

I could see the outline of the Olympic Stadium, familiar to all the billions who watched the Olympics on TV, and now to millions of football fans as it is the home of West Ham United.

I had an appointment with Mark Camley, executive director of Park Operations and Venues at the LLDC. Wow, what a title, must need a rather big visiting card. He is clearly a big boss, though not as big as the overall big boss, the chief executive, whom I was due to meet later in the day.

The appointments had been arranged by the Olympics Park's PR, Helen Holman. I mention her name and position because it is unusual for any individual London park to have their own designated PR on the staff. The best you can hope for with parks owned by local councils is to find someone who is supposed to help the media in general, but they are likely to be stuck in the depths of a town hall and it is often impossible to locate them.

The Olympic Park, fortunately, has had a lot of money to spend from the very beginning and has a proper organisation running it. Hence there is a full-time staff of 150 working for the Olympic Park, under the umbrella title of London Legacy Development Corporation. That is even bigger than at Hampstead Heath, which is a much bigger park, but then the Olympic Park is still a work in progress, with more developments to come.

Helen had sent me a large bundle of booklets and maps, which arrived with a massive thump through my letterbox. I spent ages admiring the glossy prose, the high-quality paper, the trendy photos, the arty design and layout, the hip headlines and on-message slogans, before I actually read all the words. But I did eventually, so I had done a bit of homework before I met Mark Camley.

Mark turned out to be a down-to-earth Scotsman with a long list of impressive jobs. He went to Edinburgh University, read economics, and joined the Cabinet Office in London as a statistician. He was a little bit worried that his Scottish accent might keep him back in elitist Whitehall, but it never did.

He became director of the Supreme Court Group for England and Wales, looking after lots of our courts – not the legal side, but the buildings, workers, health and safety – and had a staff of 1,800.

In 2005 he became chief executive of the Royal Parks. Parks don't always look for horticultural experts any more. They like to have someone who knows how government and the Civil Service works. 'Though as a student I did work in a park for three summers,' he said.

He came to the Olympic Park in 2012, at the time of the Games. I had imagined that running the Royal Parks was a plum job, with more status and prestige than working on an unmade park in the unfashionable East End of London. And he is not even the big boss. He is in fact just one of five exec-utive directors who report to the chief executive.

'But I have a lot of autonomy here. At the Royal Parks, I probably could only change 10 per cent. So much in the Royal Parks has to be done as it has always been done. Here I have 90 per cent freedom, at least in my field, because it is all new. We are creating new things all the time. It will be years before the Olympic Park is completed. I like to think I will be involved in most of the new innovations and developments between now and then.'

One of which is residential housing and new offices: actually building them, using their own money, then finding the tenants, not handing the work over to property developers. He also looks after events, visitors, maintenance, health and safety and contracting out.

Having a Premiership football club use the park means getting 60,000 people in and out of a Saturday afternoon. There are also thousands who come for other leisure and sporting activities, including families and children who come to swim in the Olympic pool.

I stood on a bridge with Mark, just inside the park, the River Lea trickling away down below us and the canal winding its weary way round towards a lock. He pointed out on the horizon where the International Cultural Quarter was soon going to be situated. You what?

Yup, the Victoria and Albert Museum is moving here with its archives, Sadler's Wells is coming, University College London is opening a campus and lots more arts and education institutions are lined up for the future.

In the park itself, there is already a vast building which is used by BT Sport, plus other buildings which house the British Council, the London College of Fashion, Ford Moors, the FCA (Financial Control Authority) and Cancer Research UK. It really is an urban park – filled with famous institutions, in brand new buildings, yet set in a green and rural-looking space with streams and little woods.

So far, the park does not have a Friends of the Park – a

society of local residents – which is not surprising, as they don't yet have many residents nearby.

The Royal Parks are often perceived as off-putting for people who feel it is mostly for a social elite. The Olympic Park has a different problem – some people assume it exists only for those with sporting prowess.

'But anyone can come,' said Mark. 'Anyone can swim in the Olympic pool, the real one, as used in the Olympics.

'We still have to break that image down a bit, let everyone see that this is a park for all the locals and is totally democratic.'

All the same, the Olympic Park has been very successful in a short time, now attracting six million visitors a year.

This impressive figure is slightly massaged, by including the 60,000 who come each game during the season to watch West Ham. But the Olympic Stadium is inside the park so, technically, it's not cheating.

As well as all the new residential and office blocks soon to go up, Mark is hoping to create more green space. At the moment, the proportion of green is just a quarter of the whole – 120 out of the 560 acres.

The land is almost all flat – there are no hills to break up the landscape or the views. And there are no existing woods. But there is a river and the canal does have boats and big plastic swans for the kiddies. One thing Mark is hoping to do soon is put up a rope ladder across the river. Hmm, not sure about that, Mark, it's always a bit gimmicky when parks introduce that sort of stuff. But he assured me families will love it.

We then set off on a tour of the park, with Mark leading the way, which meant we didn't have to pay whenever there was an entrance fee – hurrah.

I didn't go into the London Stadium, formerly the Olympic Stadium, as I have been in monster football stadiums before, from Wembley to Camp Nou in Barcelona. And anyway, it is not open to the general, park-walking public. It just stands there, dominating all its surroundings, and can be seen from almost every corner of the park. But I did admire a massive display of daffodils, which I thought at first were plastic, and a big iron bell, outside the stadium. It used to be inside, and was ceremonially rung by Bradley Wiggins to signify the grand opening of the Games.

Our first stop was the Olympic pool, now the London Aquatics Centre. It is much bigger than it seemed when I was watching Olympic swimming on TV. It was mid-morning, a weekday, and filled with schoolchildren and clubs, all busy. Some were training hard, others mucking around. The pool attracts one million swimmers a year. It was so warm and welcoming inside, whereas outside the day was drizzling and cloudy. The whole interior gleamed. It must cost a fortune to heat and keep so clean.

The seating capacity has been reduced since the Olympics, when it could hold 17,500. Now it takes just 2,500, but it didn't look diminished by the loss of seating.

We then went to the Copper Box Arena, an auditorium I had never heard of, and a name that was meaningless to me. During the Olympics this was where basketball, handball and wheelchair rugby was held. Today it is still used for various sports and can hold 7,500. The week before, the England women's netball team had played Australia – and won.

The Velodrome, where all the Olympic cycling took place, is still there, inside today's Olympic Park, but not owned by it.

The next excitement was the ArcelorMittal Orbit – again

a name and words I did not understand. When I got near, I did recognise the structure from watching the Olympics: it's that funny, brownish-red spiral tower, all tubes and twisted, bendy pipes. It looks as if a drunk had had a go at assembling a monster Meccano set and got all the instructions wrong. It is of course a well-known work of modern art, designed by the Turner Prize-winning artist Sir Anish Kapoor.

It is Britain's largest piece of public art, some 376 feet high, which makes it higher than St Paul's Cathedral, Big Ben or the Statue of Liberty.

Although it looked quite small on TV, once again it was pretty big in real life.

I had assumed, not having been to the Olympic Park before, that it had been taken down after the Olympics, just as Skylon, another chunk of modern structural art, was taken down in 1953 after the Festival of Britain (see p.289). It does look a bit strange, not to say weird, so I would have understood if it had been dismantled.

The then mayor of London, Boris Johnson, and the Olympics minister, Tessa Jowell, had decided that the Olympics site needed 'something extra'. A competition was held for sculptors and artists to suggest ideas, and this was won by Kapoor. His other headline-grabbing claim to fame has been to buy the rights to the world's blackest paint, Vantablack S-VIS, so only he can use it. Another artist, Stuart Semple, retaliated by making an even blacker one, Better Black, and prohibited Kapoor from having any. Since then Semple has pioneered Black 2.0 followed by Black 3.0. He asks customers to sign a declaration on entry to his London art shop that their purchases will not be shared with Kapoor.

Back to the ArcelorMittal Orbit slide, with its black, black tunnel. Its name comes from Lakshmi Mittal, the steel tycoon, one of Britain's richest people. His involvement came about after a chance meeting with Boris Johnson in a cloakroom in Davos in January 2009, as they were on their way to separate dinner engagements. In a conversation that reportedly lasted forty-five seconds, Johnson pitched the idea to Mittal, who immediately agreed to supply the steel.

'I never expected that this was going to be such a huge project,' Mittal later said. 'I thought it was just the supply of some steel, a thousand tonnes or so, and that would be it. But then we started working with artists and I realised that the object was not just to supply steel but to complete the whole artistic project.'

The total cost was £22 million, of which £10 million was donated by Mittal's company, ArcelorMittal, plus a loan of £9 million, which only gets paid back when the attraction turns a profit. The LLDC put in £3 million.

At the entrance, I picked up a leaflet that said the ArcelorMittal Orbit slide has 35,000 bolts and enough steel in it to make 265 double decker London buses. During the Games it attracted 130,000 visitors. Afterwards it closed, and then reopened in April 2014 as an attraction for the general public.

The entrance hall, at the base of the Orbit, or Tower, as it is more commonly now known, is all very modern and cool. You enter under a sort of dark canopy, as Anish Kapoor wanted to give the impression of darkness, then you would progress from the dark to the light.

You can walk up all the way to the top, some 455 stairs.

I declined the offer. Just the week before, I'd had a hernia operation, and so didn't want to tempt my stitches. I took one of the lifts instead.

At the top, there was an excellent view and on a clear day you can see twenty miles. I managed to make out the London Eye, the arch of Wembley Stadium and Alexandra Palace.

On the very top platform, there was a young man being equipped and made ready as if off to outer space, perhaps to the moon. His helmet was being strapped on and he was fixed into a very narrow stretcher. He was then pushed into a tube, hardly bigger than himself, and whoosh, off he went.

He was going down the slide, which is 178 metres long, the world's longest tunnel slide. I had never been aware that inside the Tower was a slide. From outside, I had noticed a lot of plastic tubing, bending and twisting round the whole tower, but I could not see anything happening inside the tubing.

I had not realised that people were paying good money to slide down inside it.

People must be potty.

The trussed-up man had disappeared, into the void, and I found myself wondering what it would be like to go down the Tower, all the way, on the slide. To my own surprise, I found myself putting my hand up. Me, sir, I will have a go, can I be next, please, sir.

I stood waiting till the person ahead was safely at the bottom, some 376 feet below as the crow flies. Only one person is allowed down at a time, as it is so narrow. If you get stuck, you don't want someone crashing into your back.

The cost that day to go down the slide was £8. Sounds a lot, but I can't see them making any profit as so few can go down each day. It's not like a water slide at a big outdoor swimming pool, where a dozen can go down at a time, one after the other, banging into each other – which is part of the fun.

Eventually, when the person ahead had landed, I got securely strapped in and made to lie flat, like a body in a morgue. I couldn't get started at first, till I realised you don't just lie there. You have to haul yourself slightly forward till you start descending. I am so weak in the arms these days, I could not move the weight of my own body. So an attendant had to crawl in behind and give me a slight push. And then I was off. *Whoosh, whee!*

Would I be sick? I had had breakfast but, luckily, not yet any lunch. Would I pass out? Would my hernia stitches burst? Bit late thinking about that. Once you start the downward slide, that is it, no way off, no way out.

It reminded me of two things. Firstly it was like having an MRI scan at the Royal Free, where you are put into a similar enclosed space, moved slowly forward, and then bombarded with X-rays. I always hate having an MRI. It is so claustrophobic, the noise is appalling, you can't see anything, and you feel totally trapped and want to scream.

The other was a childhood memory from the post-war years, running messages to the shops for my mother. There were no supermarkets, just well-stocked grocery stores, such as Lipton's and the Home and Colonial. Inside the shops there was a sequence of overhead tubes that whizzed round just under the ceiling, ending up at the cashier's desk. The shop assistant would take the money and the bill, put them into a tube, and send them whizzing up the line. A cashier would then take the money, put back any change, and send it rapidly back. It always seemed a most cumbersome, complicated system, but as a little boy I was fascinated by it, watching all these little capsules flying overhead as you queued to buy your tin of Spam. I often wondered what it would be like to be in one, flying in the air.

Now I was finding out, enclosed in a dark tunnel, very like a capsule, thundering towards the ground.

I was surprised I didn't feel scared, even though I was clearly trapped and had no escape. I felt protected, swaddled, in good hands. They must know what they are doing. I suppose if I had been able to see out, see the ground rising up and realise how fast I was going, I might have been more scared. But it was all dark and mysterious, like a dream.

Except there was no chance of a snooze, not at the speed I was going. The scary bit was at each bend. They came so suddenly, not when or how I expected, throwing me to one side. You are strapped in, so feel safe, but fear your stomach has been left behind and will be following later.

Some of the bends were double and triple bends, so you could not relax.

I seemed to be whizzing down for ages, thrown round endless bends, but I suppose it all took little more than a couple of minutes. Like dreams, or nightmares, you think you have been having them all night, but they last only seconds.

And then I got stuck. Luckily I was now at the end. The slide ends on a flat bit – and, once again, I couldn't propel myself forward. I could see an attendant's face about 10 feet ahead, at the very end of the tunnel, in the light, peering in to see where I was. I shouted out to him that I was stuck.

He had to crawl up towards me, like Alice down the rabbit hole, though not as agile because he was a big burly bloke. He then managed to haul me out.

On terra firma, I felt so proud of myself that I went mad and spent another £8 on a photo of myself from the reception desk. They asked if they could put it on Twitter and I said certainly, I want the world to know what I have done and can you add that I am eighty-three. Am I the oldest person ever to go down the slide?

In fact my children were appalled. And so was my girlfriend when she found out. They all pointed out that it had been only ten days since my hernia operation, and just three months since a triple bypass.

It was quite a relief to get out into the green bits of the park, away from all the modern buildings, hulking stadiums and ever so arty structures and creations.

The Olympic Park, even on the quarter which is green, is still rather barren and raw, but then it has only been fairly recently created. Stuff still has to grow.

I asked Mark about the wildlife: had they got any yet? He didn't manage to show me any in the flesh but he proudly got out his mobile phone and showed me what looked like a baby deer, though he said was a muntjac. I accused him of fiddling it, downloading it from the internet. But he said no, he really had filmed here, in the park.

Muntjacs are a type of deer, though a bit smaller than the wild ones in Scotland, more like a big dog. They were introduced from China into Woburn Safari Park in Bedfordshire several decades ago and have now spread to many parts of the south-east of England.

On the watery bits, the canal and river, which are being improved and cleaned up all the time, there are some ducks, herons and swans. Bat boxes have been established under all the bridges.

Unlike every other London park I have ever walked in, or any public park anywhere, I saw no dog walkers all day, or, for that matter, any parents with prams. It was a bad day weatherwise, but I assume it is mainly because there are so few established residential streets nearby, with ordinary people living in them. Most of the buildings in and around are modern office blocks or sports facilities. There is no tradition of locals walking in the park each day for the simple reason that there was no park till recently and no locals living locally.

Queen Elizabeth Olympic Park, to give it its full and official title, straddles four different London boroughs – Newham, Tower Hamlets, Hackney and Waltham Forest. Each borough has its own bylaws. When this was first discovered, to make it easy and simple, it was decided to adopt in the whole park the bylaws of Newham Council, as 60 per cent of the park is in its borough. The three other boroughs complained. They wanted their bits of the park in their borough to be subject to their rules. This mostly does not matter, as it is just a matter of principle. Bylaws are not always enforced and, usually, most boroughs have fairly similar ones.

But, aha, it turned out there were slight differences. In Hackney, the rules allow dog walkers to have up to five dogs on one lead. In Newham, the law is four dogs max. So if you came in with five dogs at one of one of the entrances in Hackney, and wandered, innocently, onto Newham territory, you would in theory be breaking the bylaw. Possibly shot at dawn. Or at least fined £20. This has not happened so far. No one has been apprehended. The security services have better things to do.

There is a team of security staff working round the clock to patrol the whole park. Their main concerns are protecting the buildings, the stadium and other arenas, which of course normal parks do not have, as well as valuable national works of art, such as the slide I had just come down on. They would not like that vandalised. It did cost £19 million.

There are also of course the more normal park problems for security to contend with. Rough sleeping has so far not been much of a problem. The park is so flat and open, with no hidden woods, and hardly any bushes behind which to lay out a tent or ground sheet.

I didn't notice many joggers, either, I presume for the same reason as the lack of dog walkers and prams, but Mark had recently introduced a new attraction which could bring in new people – electric scooters. In theory, they were not yet allowed in London on public roads or pavements, a rule which appears mostly to be ignored, so the Olympic Park will be about the only place they can legally be ridden.

I had seen no sign of them so far, and had forgotten what Mark had told me, when suddenly two boys on scooters whizzed past me from behind. What a fright I got. You have to hire them, of course – put money or cards in a slot, like all the coloured bikes now all over London. So far the provision of electric scooters had been a trial run, their future not certain.

There are no memorial benches, which is something I always look out for. Not surprising, really. How can there be touching reminders of Joe and Jane Bloggs, who loved this spot, when this spot has only just been created and the Bloggs have yet to appear? They will come, in the future, when the Olympic Park has established itself in the minds and lives of the generations to come. But there is one well-known person commemorated – Tessa Jowell, the Labour politician who died in 2018. She played a big part in securing and encouraging the London Olympics of 2012. They have named one of the riverside paths after her – the Tessa Jowell Walk.

There is a rather horrid busy main road, the A12, cutting across the park. I found an access area for crossing it, but the lights were not working properly so I had to make a mad dash. But then I always do. My children are always saying my end will come crossing Highgate Road in the rush hour, ignoring all the traffic.

The prettiest part of the Olympic Park – comparatively speaking, as of course none of it can so far be compared with the ancient and sylvan glories of the Royal Parks – is at the north end. This is the bit furthest away from the football stadium, following the River Lea. There is even a bit of a river valley. It's not very deep or extensive, but when you walk along the riverside path, you are lower than the rest of the park, so can't see any buildings towering over you. For about twenty minutes, half closing my eyes, I imagined I was in the countryside (of a sort). Overall, there are 6.5 km of waterways in the park, so when they are all landscaped and planted, you will have a half-decent riverside walk.

I came out at a rather pretty stretch of recently landscaped garden, the first I had seen, called Timber Lodge. It has a little restaurant and a very attractive children's play area called

Tumbling Bay Playground. That's one thing about creating a new park: it might take a while to create attractive features, but you can instantly create attractive-sounding names.

In the confines of the park I counted four schools, newly built, including the Bobby Moore Academy. Now that is a name known long before the park was created – England's 1966 World Cup-winning captain, who had 108 international caps for his country, and a local lad who played for West Ham more than 600 times, widely hailed as one of the best defenders of all time.

As I headed back towards the stadium, and the entrance where I had begun, I came across a little fleet of electric buggies filled with jolly-looking people in dinky pink anoraks. These were the park volunteers, who had just done a shift – middle-aged to elderly men and women, by the look of them.

All London parks these days rely on volunteer workers, who agree to do a few hours a week, clearing up litter, or helping the full-time parkies. In the Olympic Park there are already 600 volunteers, which amazed me, considering it is a brand new park with few nearby residents.

This again is one the many fortunate residues of the 2012 London Olympics. It got such enormous publicity, created such goodwill, that thousands of people came forward to be volunteers, helping visitors enjoy the Olympics and London. They always looked so cheerful, and felt useful and valued. Afterwards, a lot of them wanted to carry on, once they heard about the new park opening. They don't get paid, though if they're employed at one of the public events they get a free meal. They aren't called park volunteers; their title is park champions. The notion is that they are ambassadors for the park, not just little helpers. Names – they do matter.'

The chief executive of the Olympic Park has her office outside the main entrance, near Stratford Tube station, in a big plush block of offices which has a very trendily designed ONE at the front entrance. But I still couldn't decide if I had come to the right block as there was no sign of a street name.

The 150 staff are spread out in a huge open-plan office, covering the tenth floor, and officially they all work for the LLDC. It is a bit more grand and modern and whizzy than your normal park superintendent's office, which is often hidden away behind some bushes.

Lyn Garner is in her mid–fifties and comes from Liverpool. She still has a recognisable Liverpudlian accent and, like Mark the Scotsman, feared this might hold back her progress in the capital. It clearly hasn't, despite the fact that she left school at sixteen and never went to university. She worked first for the local council in Liverpool, then came to London and joined Islington Council, working as a neighbourhood quality manager – whatever that it is (though I am sure she explained it to me).

'I didn't like the job. Islington was very political, and very small, compared with Liverpool Council. There were always arguments and nothing ever seems to get decided. So I packed it in then went off to Slough. Yes, that does show you how much I must have disliked it . . .'

She eventually returned to London, still in local government, this time with Hammersmith. Then she moved to Haringey, looking after Regeneration and Development. 'It was just post the Tottenham riots, so there were a lot of problems.'

She landed the Olympic Park job in 2018. She was just a year into her new position when I met her, so it seemed a bit unfair to expect her to tell me too much about the problems, but she was very forthcoming. Clearly, she is well experienced at handling politicians at all levels, and understands how local politics works, which is presumably one reason she got the job, with its four invested boroughs.

But her biggest surprise has been just how many other stakeholders she has to deal with as well. By stakeholders, she means all the big firms with premises or enterprises inside the park. The LLDC is in most instances their landlord, and responsible for facilities and infrastructure, security and other services, so she has constantly to administrate and often placate the likes of the BBC, BT, UK Athletics, West Ham United, plus all the new institutions, like the V&A and UCL, which are currently about to move in. Some of them can get a bit stroppy and demanding.

'Yes, I have to look after some very big beasts.'

The biggest current beast would appear to be West Ham United and the formidable Baroness Brady, their chief executive. Long before Lyn Garner arrived as chief executive, the London media was reporting various sources of aggravation concerning West Ham's move to the Olympic Stadium. Some of West Ham's Premiership rivals considered West Ham had got an exceedingly good deal, with lots of financial inducements to take it over. The government was of course stuck, wanting the stadium to be used as soon as possible.

'We still run it at a loss. It costs us £20 million a year,' says Lyn. 'We hope in the years ahead it will be a lot less. West Ham of course can't be blamed, just because they negotiated a very good deal. We just have to live with it and try our best to increase our revenue.'

Going round the park and all the attractions, money did not appear to be much of a problem. In the Royal Parks, there's a feeling of affluence because of all the history, the buildings and immaculate landscaping. In many lesser-known, less glamorous London parks, you can see the bits which have become worn and tatty and need money spent.

The Olympic Park gleams like a City slicker, with all its glossy offices and polished spaces. But it does run at a loss. In many ways, it is still a vanity project, though of course that would be roundly denied. The official line is that the Olympic Park is one of the biggest new revenue-generating projects in the whole of London, bringing wealth, work, tourism and energy to a neighbourhood that had become run-down.

The point of all parks, after all, is not to make a profit but to provide a service for the community. From Hampstead Heath and Victoria Park to the Royal Parks, they have to be financially supported. The Olympic Park certainly does generate a large amount of money, and jobs, and excitement, with more to come. In all its expensive publicity literature, it continually boasts that 'The centre of gravity in London is moving east.' That is also fairly true. In my lifetime, I have seen the East End of London totally transformed.

Lyn does seem temperamentally suited to the job, with no airs or graces, and calm, approachable and smiley. She is slender and fit-looking, despite a very exhausting, draining job. She lives part of the week at her home in Berkshire and the rest of the week in London – handier for her job. She has two grown-up children.

She is hopeful that in ten years the park will be finished and the whole of London will see, appreciate and rejoice in its wonders. By which time, another 3,000 new homes will have been built, bringing the number of new homes inside the park boundary to 25,000. A total of 40,000 new jobs will also have been created.

By 2031, it's estimated that there will be 55,000 people living inside or just around the park. They will be connected to a low-carbon emissions heating system and all be within a 400-metre walk of public transport. Up to 100,000 will be going in and out of the park to work every day.

Lyn hopes by then to have found more tenants and uses for the Olympic Stadium, apart from West Ham – perhaps for boxing and baseball – and that the East Bank, the so-called cultural village, where the V&A will live, will be completed. More than half a billion pounds of public money is going into the East Bank, as the LLDC is doing all the building work itself. It is a large investment, but the hope and expectation is that there will be handsome income for decades to come.

Annually, it is costing roughly £16 million each year to run the Park and the structures. But London gains. The World Athletics Championships were held in the Olympic Park in 2017, and it was reckoned to have brought in £100 million, with so many people coming to watch it, and staying and spending time in London.

'I do love the job, love the variety, dealing with so many different sorts of people and businesses. All the stakeholders have been welcoming and friendly. By definition, they are optimistic and hopeful, or they would not have decided to come here, and base part of their empires here. They are used to change, and want change, so are helpful and forward-looking.

'In a traditional park, you will always get local residents and bodies who are against change, who don't want it to happen, who like things as they are. We like to think we can offer global exposure for people who bring their business here.'

Er, how come it has global exposure, Lyn? Stretching the PR a bit?

'As long as West Ham is in the Premier League, there are billions around the world watching the team on TV each week in the Olympic Stadium, knowing there is such a vibrant place in London. That's what I mean by global exposure.'

Good one, Lyn.

I came away with my head reeling. It could have been from all the facts and figures, the size and ambitions and scale of it all, the wonders of an utterly modern park like no other park, anywhere.

Or it could have been coming down that slide at my age . . .

Best Things About the Olympic Park

1. The whole story, how it is a wonderful legacy of the wonderful London Olympic Games of 2012. How, for ever, visitors to the park will be following in the footsteps of giants who once ran, swam, played and competed here.

2. There is also an industrial recovery story –
how this semi-derelict, polluted wilderness,
with old canals and river, has been
transformed, cleaned up, revitalised, reborn.
And a lot of it is now green and pleasant.

3. You can admire the Olympic structures
still standing and being used, such as
the Olympic Stadium, now the London
Stadium, home of West Ham United,
and the London Aquatics Centre, where
swimming still takes place.

4. The ArcelorMittal Orbit – that strange,
spirally tower, designed by Anish Kapoor,
inside of which is the world's longest tunnel
slide, some 178 metres long. Be brave,
be swift and go down it. Even elderly
gentlemen have done it.

5. What is still to come in the next few
years: a Cultural and Educational District,
which will house branches of the V&A,
Sadler's Wells, London College of Fashion,
University College London.

5

HYDE PARK

I decided to shelter from the rain at Marble Arch. I don't mean Marble Arch, the general area, roughly at the west end of Oxford Street, or that horrible maelstrom of a roundabout. And certainly not Marble Arch underground station, as I hate the Tube.

I was sheltering under Marble Arch itself, the big white marble classical three-bayed arch which was designed by our old friend John Nash in 1827 to act as a grand entrance to the approach to Buckingham Palace and built at a cost of £80,000. It got moved to its present site in 1851. Then in the 1960s, when some road widening was being done in Park Lane, it got isolated, still standing on the same spot but somehow left behind, on its own, like some magnificent chunk of debris deposited by a long-forgotten tsunami. Only senior members of the royal family and the King's Troop Royal Horse Artillery are permitted go through it but it's unlikely any of them would want to, given its present position.

As I stood there, I realised I was not quite alone. Behind me, with Hyde Park in the background, two elderly women wearing burkas were having their photograph taken by a man standing under the Arch itself. He was directing what sort of picture he wanted, getting them to stand still and smile. Yes, you can tell if someone is smiling, even under a burka. The eyes give it away.

Then I became aware of someone else, a police motorcyclist in full leather gear. He was sitting so still and quiet that I hadn't noticed him at first, till suddenly his radio started crackling. He was staring out intently into the swirling ocean of traffic roaring round the Marble Arch roundabout, just a few yards in front of us. His gaze, locked on the nose-to-tail vehicles, was hungry and expectant, like a snake staking a rat. I couldn't see what the motorcycle policeman was waiting for.

Just sitting. Eventually I said hello, and asked if this was his regular spot, for whatever he did.

He said he was a traffic policeman, covering from Westminster up to Camden Town. He had regular routes, and this was one of them.

Was he checking speeding? No, he did not have the technology for that on his particular bike. He was looking out for people using a mobile phone while driving and for anyone driving a defective car. By defective, he meant cars with damaged lights or broken windscreens.

This morning so far he had caught two people on their mobiles phones.

'Men or women?'

'Does it matter?' he said.

'Not really,' I said. 'Just asking.'

I wondered if he gets abuse when he rushes out and stops them? He said no. Anyone he pulls over realises they are at fault. He issues them with a summons and in due course they will be called to a court appearance, or they can pay a fine. He does not issue on-the-spot fines.

I suggested he gets little abuse because they must be stunned and shocked at his sudden appearance, not knowing where he has come from. They can't possibly see him lurking under the Arch, till he is roaring up behind them, forcing them to stop.

The mobile phone users are usually talking while driving, but some are actually sending text messages. I asked if he had ever stopped a bus, as so many were roaring by. He said just one. It was a coach, from out of town, not a London bus. How about a police car?

'Not so far. But if I had to, I would.'

He had been doing the job for four years, and absolutely loved it. I can see the attractions, for a certain sort. You get to ride a powerful bike, out in the fresh air, as long as you don't mind the car fumes. You get to roar out, as fast as you can, siren blaring, and frighten the life out of some poor sod.

In fact, that very spot where he was parked has long been associated with law and order in this country. Gather round . . .

Very close to this point there stood a public scaffold known as the Tyburn Tree, on which as many as 50,000 people lost their lives. The first recorded execution at Tyburn was in 1196, although it had probably been used for capital punishment for the best part of a century even by then.

In 1571, the business of death became altogether more efficient with the construction of what's become known as 'the triple tree', with an ordinary gallows replaced by a triangle of beams perched on 18-foot pillars, capable of accommodating eight men or women on each length, or twenty-four in total.

In addition to hangings, women were burned there, and soldiers shot for military offences. Oliver Cromwell's body was disinterred from Westminster Abbey three years after his death, when the royal family had been reinstated, and hung in chains at Tyburn. His headless corpse was buried beneath the scaffold, while his head with its sightless eyes looked out from a pole in the walls of Westminster Hall for twenty-four years.

Hangings became a macabre focal point for the expanding population of London in the sixteenth, seventeenth and eighteenth centuries. With execution days declared a public holiday, people gathered in numbers amid a carnival atmosphere.

Men and women who had been sentenced to death made a final trip from Newgate Prison, somewhere near today's

Old Bailey, to Tyburn, roughly where Oxford Street meets Park Lane, some three bumpy miles by cart. Before setting out, their iron fetters were removed and their hands tied in a position of prayer. With a noose put around their neck, they sat on their coffins on the cartbed for their slow final ride, behind a detachment of marching soldiers. There were stops scheduled along the way, the first being St Sepulchre's Church in Holborn, where a bell would toll mournfully and a glum prayer was bellowed out. It was where prisoners were given a nosegay by weeping relatives. After that there were several stops for the prisoners to sup wine at public houses, meaning they were quite often drunk by the time they reached Tyburn.

Crowds lined the route. In the eighteenth century, philosopher and satirist Bernard Mandeville noted: 'All the Way, from Newgate to Tyburn, is one continued Fair, for Whores and Rogues of the meaner sort ... Where the Crowd is the least, which, among the Itinerants, is no where very thin, the Mob is the rudest; and here, jostling one another, and kicking Dirt about, are the most innocent Pastimes.'

The crowds were sometimes mean, hurling insults or worse. But if the prisoner was believed to be hard done by or even heroic, then there were cheers, and every effort was made to disrupt proceedings. Jostling and shoving hampered the execution team as the cart was reversed beneath the beam and the rope slung over it.

Those who died here were not always quickly despatched. The rope had a slip knot, which meant a slow, lingering death by strangulation. They were turned off the cart when the horses were driven forward, left with their feet paddling the air helplessly. To hasten the process, the executioner or even relatives sometimes pulled the knot round the neck.

Well-heeled victims wore their finest clothes, which were afterwards sold by the executioner, who also made 'money for old rope' by selling the noose – and a cliché was born.

In 1447, five men who were cut down alive had already been stripped and marked out for quartering when their pardon arrived. As the hangman had purloined the garments and refused to return them, they were compelled to walk home naked. The bodies of murderers and many others found their way onto the anatomists' slab.

It wasn't merely murderers and traitors who met a grisly end at Tyburn. As capitalism expanded, so did the penal code, with wealthy people wanting greater punishments for those who tried to take their riches. Enter the Bloody Code in the eighteenth century, which had people condemned to death for comparatively trifling thefts. Even the collecting of firewood became an offence, although not one punishable by death. There was always a chance of a reprieve, with sentences often changed to transportation to Australia in a lengthy bureaucratic process. Conditions in jails were so poor that the prisoners often perished before hearing the good news.

The triple tree was gone before the dawn of the nineteenth century, although a mobile gallows was still towed into position when needed. Coach traffic was increasing and the neighbourhood was going up in the world. Also, the prevailing public attitude towards hanging changed, albeit at glacial pace, and residents no longer wanted to have such vulgar displays so close to home. Not everyone was in agreement about the changes. Samuel Johnson pointed out that executions were intended to attract an audience. 'If they don't draw spectators they don't answer their purpose,' he insisted.

While it's thought the actual site was obscured by the building of the nearby Connaught Square, a plaque set into the pavement at the Marble Arch island reveals that this is as close as we can get to Tyburn Tree.

The rain was starting to lessen so I decided to get started on my walk around the park.

My first stop was going to be Speakers' Corner, just a few steps from Marble Arch. Most Brits have heard that this is the traditional spot where anyone can sound off about politicians, the queen, God, the England football manager, anything that is upsetting them, without being arrested.

The tradition of free speech had already been established at Tyburn Tree. Before they met their miserable end, the condemned were given a chance to speak – sometimes at length – without boundaries. So, for example, Catholics who were hanged here for their faith had a final opportunity to expound their religious views to the gathered crowds.

Speakers' Corner was established by an Act of Parliament in 1872 after there had been noisy demonstrations in Hyde Park calling for an expansion in the number of people who could vote. (At the time it was mostly only landowners.) Karl Marx, George Orwell and any number of suffragettes have broadcast their views from here. Speakers' Corner has been viewed as a cornerstone in the foundation of our liberal democracy.

Alas, I couldn't find it. I had been there about sixty years ago when I first came to London. I do remember standing and listening, but never went back. I decided the speakers were all unhinged.

I noticed a small, circular tea house and ordered a coffee and asked the girl serving where Speakers' Corner was. She gestured behind me. I said what? Over there, she said, pointing nowhere except towards a bit of grass. They usually stand in that corner over there, she said, but only on a Sunday.

She was born in London of Kosovan parents and had just come back from visiting her grandparents in Kosovo. She planned to save enough to go to Roehampton University to do Business Studies.

'Visitors to the park ask me the same three questions all day – where is Harrods, where is Speakers' Corner, and where are the toilets.'

I paid for my coffee and sat down at an outside table. A woman appeared at the coffee stall, tall and blonde, wearing a short skirt and high, clumpy heels. I could only see her from the back, ordering something to eat, so could not guess her age.

She got her coffee and a Danish pastry and sat at the end of my table. She opened her bag and did not take out her make-up, as I expected, or her mobile phone, but produced a solid and serious-looking paperback and started reading it. She was younger than I had imagined – about eighteen, fresh-faced and healthy-looking. She sat reading just a few feet away. I tried to see the title of the book. When she realised what I was doing, she gave me a smile. So I asked her what she was reading.

It was a *New York Times* bestseller, so it said on a sticker, called *This is Where it Ends* by Marieke Nijkamp. I said it looks a bit scary. Yes, she said. It's about a high-school gunman, murdering fellow pupils. Ah, the fascination with violence that fuelled the Tyburn crowds is still in evidence.

'I don't usually read such books,' she said. 'But I was bored reading romances and wanted a change. I bought it in the airport at Amsterdam.'

She was American, from Orange County, California, and had been travelling for three months round Europe – all on her own.

I am always amazed and admiring when I come across young women going around the world on their own. When my wife and I were in Samoa, many years ago, a young American woman booked into the same hotel as us. She was travelling the world, on her own, but said she never went out anywhere in the evening, not in the dark. She always stayed in her hotel. We were going out that evening to a local restaurant, so invited her to join us. She did, but would not let me pay for her meal.

I asked my new friend with the book if her parents were worried about her.

'My father hasn't taken much interest but my mom rings me most days. She helped me plan my itinerary.'

What's been the best place so far?

'Oh, Edinburgh – I loved it. I felt immediately at home. I have decided that is where I want to study. I have just finished high school and wanted a gap year to decide what to do. Now I know. I want to study fashion – and I want to do it in Edinburgh. I don't like California. I have done California. Edinburgh is my idea of heaven.'

Good choice, I said. I wished her good luck and set off across the wide-open, rather empty spaces of Hyde Park.

At this end of the park, cutting across towards the Serpentine, it is flat and rather barren. A lot of the grass had been flattened and made yellow and still had the markings where some sort of big open-air event had recently taken place.

The early-morning joggers and horse riders had done their

morning routines. The cyclists who cut through the park to work had gone. The tourists and visitors had yet to arrive, still having breakfast in their bed and breakfast places, studying their guidebooks. I stood for a while, looking up in the air.

The sky seemed enormous. There were almost 360 degrees of open heavens, something you don't normally see in the middle of busy, urban London. It was like being in the Lake District. At our Loweswater home, I used to go outside in the morning and stare at the open sky, with unhindered views of the fells and lakes all around us. All things lovely, as far as the eye could see.

Looking out from Hyde Park is not exactly lovely. You can hear traffic, you know monster modern blocks are not far away and the horizon always has giant cranes. But if you get into the middle of the park, find a spot with only grass and trees and focus your eyes upwards, you can imagine yourself in some wilderness, cut off from all urban life.

How did that ever happen – a park of 350 acres, right in the heart of not just the busiest, but one of the richest, parts of London? Think of the trillions of pounds you could make if you got the rights to build on it. Yet it is open to all, no entrance fee, not even a fence round it. You can go in at any time, though technically it does close at dusk.

Hyde Park, as a Royal Park, was created by Henry VIII. In 1536, six years after he had sorted out St James's Park for his own amusements, he decided that 600 or so acres belonging to the Abbot of Westminster would do him nicely as a deer park. Enhancing his personal wealth by impounding property like this was one of many perks of the dissolution of the monasteries that King Henry orchestrated, the greatest of which was to legitimise his divorce from Catherine of Aragon. His aim was to give himself a continuous stretch of hunting ground all the way from Westminster up to the heights of Hampstead. He never quite managed that, but Hyde Park remained a private Royal Park for another century.

After it was opened to the public it became a fashionable location, particularly on May Days. But as the country tumbled into civil war, fortifications were built in the park to see off Royalist attacks, and armies were encamped.

Once in power, Oliver Cromwell sold off Hyde Park in three chunks, raising £17,000, an unthinkably large sum at the time. In 1653, a furious John Evelyn wrote in his diary, 'I went to take air in Hyde Park when every coach was made to pay a shilling, and a horse sixpence, by the sordid fellow who purchased it off the state.'

It returned to royal control under the Restoration, with King Charles II using a brick wall to enclose its hefty acreage. In 1663, Samuel Pepys observed how it had become a popular meeting place once again, although his plans to impress the king by 'promenading' were ruined on May Day that year because he couldn't control the horse he had hired for the purpose.

For horse riders, Rotten Row was established by William III as a route between his home at Kensington Palace and St James's Palace, where state business was done. Officially it was the 'Route du Roi', but its name was soon corrupted. By 1690 the broad avenue was lit with 300 oil lamps – the first artificially lit highway in the UK – to improve safety for users.

Nonetheless, Hyde Park remained the haunt of highwaymen, many of whom met their end close by on the Tyburn Tree. It was also a popular duelling ground, where gentlemen settled their differences with a contest involving swords or, later, pistols. In 1772, poet and playwright Richard Sheridan learned to his cost that the sword is mightier than the pen when he was grievously injured by a blade wielded by Captain Thomas Matthews. Sheridan had taken exception to an article written about his wife by Matthews, as singer and artists' muse Elizabeth Linley noted, and the two clashed.

Seven years later, firebrand politician Charles James Fox faced Scottish advocate and Tory MP William Adam in Hyde Park in a pistol duel. At the time Fox was the leader of the Whigs in Parliament. When his assistant suggested he should stand side-on to make himself less of a target, chubby Fox spluttered: 'Why man, I'm as thick one way as the other!' He ended the day slightly injured but the erstwhile opponents became friends in later life.

Queen Caroline, wife of George II, did most to create the look of Hyde Park as we see it today. Her most ambitious project was a long lake, right through Hyde Park and into Kensington Gardens, to replace six natural ponds. This is now known as the Long Water in Kensington Gardens and the Serpentine in Hyde Park. Over 200 workmen were employed to dig out the lake and there was a grand opening ceremony on 1 May 1731. Two yachts were launched for the amusement of the king and queen and their children, plus assorted royal guests from Europe. Today there's an urn on a plinth at the east end of the Serpentine dedicated to Caroline.

A mock battle was held on the Serpentine in 1814 to celebrate the end of the Napoleonic Wars and Napoleon's exile to Elba. Every spare inch of grass was filled with stalls and booths, swings and roundabouts, with attractions that included fire-eaters and 'fat ladies'. Fireworks exploded and the 'enemy' ship was ceremonially sunk, with the strains of the national anthem just audible over the hubbub.

The park also witnessed some more poignant, private moments. When a later Caroline, the estranged wife of George IV, saw her daughter Charlotte's carriage across the greenery after the pair had been forbidden to have contact, Caroline urged her coachmen into pursuit and there was a brief reunion between mother and daughter, observed by parkgoers.

The body of Harriet Shelley, abandoned wife of the poet, was hauled out of the Serpentine in 1816 after she apparently committed suicide. A last letter to her sister Eliza contained the moving line, 'The remembrance of all your kindness which I have so unworthily repaid has often made my heart ache.'

Harriet and Percy Bysshe Shelley had been teenage sweethearts but he grew bored with her company and frustrated by the perpetual presence of Eliza at their home. He sought solace with the sixteen-year-old daughter of a friend even while Harriet was pregnant with one of their two children. She was expecting another child when she died. 'I was unworthy of your love & care,' she wrote. 'Be happy all of you. So shall my spirit find rest & forgiveness. God bless you all is the last prayer of the unfortunate.'

By Victorian times, Hyde Park was central to the throbbing rhythm of London life and was chosen mid-century as the venue for the Great Exhibition of 1851. This was Prince Albert's idea, not only to promote the British Empire but also to celebrate technological achievements throughout the world. Among the exhibits was the Koh-i-Noor diamond from India, a giant telescope, a huge hydraulic press, a rapid printer, early bicycles and public toilets that cost a penny to use. More than six million people flocked to see it, providing a profit of £165,000, enough to set up the splendid museums in South Kensington.

The Exhibition itself centred on the magnificent Crystal Palace designed by Sir Joseph Paxton. After it was all over, the Palace was dismantled and rebuilt in Sydenham in south London, the area now known as Crystal Palace, and also the name of its football team. There is not much to be seen of the Crystal Palace itself today as much of it was destroyed in a fire in 1936.

Hyde Park continued to be a focus of the capital's life. Mrs Ethel Alec-Tweedie, author of a 1908 book about it, wrote, 'And thus from generation to generation Hyde Park has been the playground of London's rich and poor, the wide theatre upon which their tragedies and comedies have been enacted, the forum in which many public liberties have been demanded, the scene where national triumphs have been celebrated.'

Hyde Park has retained its popularity as a public space, where the nation can assemble to protest or praise, to exercise or to enjoy themselves. In the 1970s, CND marches ended there and attracted crowds of 20,000. Today, it is the venue for massive pop concerts and festivals, such as Bob Geldof's 2005 Live 8 event, part of which was held there.

Hyde Park is the most public of all the Royal Parks. St James's Park, by comparison, is awfully discreet, more like a royal garden than a royal park. Hyde Park is of course much bigger and can accommodate vast gatherings all the year round. Victoria Park likes to think it is the People's Park, but Hyde Park probably deserves that title more today, if only by the number of people it attracts during the year while still remaining, in name at least, a Royal Park.

There are not all that many local residents to form a supportive association, being in central London with the local streets mainly filled with posh hotels and shops. This must cut down the number of angry residents complaining about the noise, which might explain why it can get away with having so many pop concerts and mass events. I can't see that happening on Hampstead Heath.

There isn't a lot of antisocial behaviour, local kids looking for mischief. Hyde Park is a destination park, for foreigners and Brits. They come to admire, not wreck the joint. Visitors don't leave as much litter as they do in other parks. They take it upon themselves not to drop stuff, or to tidy up.

Most public parks serve a social and exercise purpose for the locals – for dog walkers, joggers, parents with prams, people wanting to escape their high-rise blocks, the elderly wanting a nice sit down. Hyde Park, like Kensington Gardens, the Royal Park next door, is for passing through, to appreciate and respect, not for daily use.

There are countless statues and monuments, many of which I am sure get ignored by most visitors – from home or abroad. Some are, in fact, pretty meaningless today, even to native-born Brits.

The statue of Achilles, on top of the Wellington Monument, is a whopper, visible as you come into the park from the Hyde Park Corner end. The sculptor was Sir Richard Westmacott, who created a massive bronze statue of the Greek god standing over 30 feet tall, counting the base on which he stands. It shows a naked young man, with rippling muscles, holding up his sword and shield. His genital area is not quite as well endowed as the rest of his body. Westmacott added a small fig leaf, but even so, there is clearly very little there that needed covering.

It was put up in 1822 and is now considered to be our first-ever public monument of a nude male. The money for it was collected by a group of ladies who were disgusted by the antics of a woman who stripped off naked and decided to have a swim in the Serpentine Lake during celebrations in honour of Wellington and his victories. They wanted a suitably impressive statue to honour their military hero properly. The more ribald commentators of the time referred to it as the 'Ladies' Trophy', which is probably not what they'd hoped for.

There's more nudity with the Rima memorial, not far from the nursery, which was put up in 1924 and shows a naked lady doing something strange with birds. It is in memory of a long-forgotten naturalist and writer, W. H. Hudson. The sculptor was Sir Jacob Epstein, another household name in his day. The lady is clearly naked, but in a classical, neo-modernistic, pose. The *Daily Mail* in 1925 welcomed the statue by saying, 'Take this horror out of our park.'

Few see the discreet dogs' cemetery behind the lodge near Victoria Gate. The first canine laid to rest here in 1881 was Cherry, a Maltese terrier who was a frequent visitor to the park. When she died, her owners asked the lodge keeper if she could be buried in what was her favourite spot. The second was Prince, a Yorkshire terrier owned by the Duke of Cambridge, who met the same sticky end as many dogs of the era, under horses' hooves and carriage wheels. The obliging park keeper found himself burying 300 pets before the facility was closed in 1903. Among the jumble of tombstones there are memorials for a cat, three small monkeys and some birds as well. As it's costly to get into the pet cemetery, most people look through the railings from Bayswater Road.

Among other public monuments, there's the 7 July Memorial, for those who died when terrorists went to work on London's transport infrastructure in 2005, the Cavalry Memorial, made from the bronze of captured First World War guns, and the nation's first Holocaust Memorial was sited here.

A relatively recent arrival, which I was keen to see, was the Princess Diana Memorial Fountain. I had not been in Hyde Park for a long time but I had read loads about it when it was created. For some reason, when I first read about in the newspapers, I assumed it was in Kensington Gardens, near the palace near where she once lived.

It is in fact in Hyde Park near the Serpentine Bridge, albeit fairly close to Kensington Gardens. I am sure most tourists and even natives are hardly aware of the division between Hyde Park and Kensington Gardens, or conscious of when they move from one to another.

Despite holding the map up in front of me as I walked, I still nearly missed the fountain. I was looking for a traditional fountain – you know, one that goes up into the air, spurts water, lots of gargoyles. I walked past it twice, not realising it was at ground level, a flat fountain, so to speak. There is no spurting in the air and no cherubs or spires. Honestly, it's more of a pond than a fountain.

It covers quite a large area, about half the size of a football pitch, is surrounded by grass and mainly consists of a stone channel for water which twists round and round. Water inside gurgles away, as there is a pump hidden underground, taking water from a bore. The channel is slightly raised at one end, whence the water flows in two directions, which adds to the swirls and bubbles.

The sun came out as I was standing there, and the water glistened as it flowed. On closer inspection, I could see the fountain is made of very light-coloured granite, from Cornwall actually, which reflected the sun. From a distance, it looks like a necklace of moving water.

A pretty unusual design, for a fountain. It was opened by the queen on 6 July 2004 and designed by the accomplished American landscape designer Kathryn Gustafson. It is meant to reflect Diana's life, though I wouldn't have thought of that if I hadn't read the explanation. Diana's quality of openness is symbolised, apparently, by three little bridges going over the water. Still water and the contrasting gurgling bits are meant to suggest both sides of her character, from happiness to turmoil. Hmm. Not sure about that, but it is a most attractive and unusual fountain.

A couple of young lovers were sitting on one of the little bridges, arm in arm, locked together, and not moving. From time to time, they dipped their bare feet in the water.

During the summer holidays, when the schools are off and a heatwave is on, which today often happens, 5,000 people have been known to gather there, sitting around, with kids paddling. This is according to one of the parkies I spoke to. He was working nearby, picking leaves out of the water. He corrected me, saying he was not a parky but a steward.

In the summer there are two full-time stewards attending to the fountain, keeping it clean and making sure none of the families leave litter, especially glass bottles. Broken glass could of course be lethal. The fountain was not meant originally for children to play in, but this is what it has become – a giant paddling pool for kids. And lovers.

In the first few months there were several accidents, with children taken to hospital after being upended on the slippery granite. The fountain was then closed while some scouring and scratching of the surface of the granite was done to make it rougher and safer to walk on.

There was another drama during some winter storms, when the grass around the fountain got flooded, turning into a bog. New drainage had to be installed. But now it all seems to be okay, and very popular in fine weather. People can enjoy this memorial to the People's Princess. After all, she did like children, and it is true, things did not run smoothly in her life.

Next I came to a surprisingly wild bit of Hyde Park, which somehow you don't expect, bang in the middle of central London. You feel it would be impossible to hide for long in Hyde Park – despite its name, har har.

'Hyde', by the way, comes from the fact that there was a Manor of Hyde, long before the royals took it over in the sixteenth century. The word Hyde is pretty ancient, and occurs in place names all over the UK, generally referring to a piece of land.

In a far corner of the park, towards the Bayswater Road, there is a stretch which on the map is called The Meadow. It has been left nicely overgrown, with bushes and wild grasses and small trees, probably much as it looked when it was the Manor of Hyde.

I stood for a while, enjoying the peace, positioning myself

so it was impossible to see any buildings on the skyline or hear the roar from Bayswater Road. Hyde Park is bordered by three major roads: Bayswater Road, Park Lane and Knightsbridge. I wonder why where there was never a Monopoly board featuring the names of the Royal Parks instead of all the roads and railway stations? I must suggest it to the Royal Parks marketing department.

The quietest spot in the whole of Hyde Park is the Dell, at the far end of the Serpentine. You can't actually get into it, hence why it is so quiet. I had never visited it before and my first reaction was – how daft. What is the point of creating such immaculate lawns, a lovely little lake, tumbling waterfalls, unusual trees and bushes, if you can't actually enter or walk round any of it?

That, of course, is the point. It's designed for you to admire from afar, standing behind an iron fence. It was created purely as a view, a piece of scenery, not a destination to explore or experience. It reminded me of the picturesque stations on eighteenth-century maps of the Lake District, places you were directed to in order to stand and admire what was before you, possibly with your Claude glass, like those used by artists to simplify the view of a landscape, held to your eye the better to frame the view.

Sure enough, there were quite a few people standing behind the fence, quietly ogling the Dell. They seemed to be mainly young men in their thirties – Polish, by the sounds of it. I assumed they must be in some sort of party. All of them were taking photographs, so I did not want to disturb their concentration by asking them dopey questions.

I went back along the Serpentine and had a coffee at a stall.

Next door to it I noticed another, similar, hut. I wandered over, holding my coffee, and saw a sign saying 'Liberty Drives'. Could it be something to do with horses, for the riders on Rotten Row? I stuck my nose against the window and rather surprised two middle-aged women inside, studying bits of paper and looking awfully important. I was trying to work out what they might be doing when an electric buggy pulled up beside me. The driver got out, another middle-aged, middle-class-looking woman. She was followed out of the buggy by a cheerful sixty-something lady who beamed and thanked her driver profusely. From her accent, I guessed the passenger was Canadian.

Liberty Drives turned out to be a charity which helps people with limited mobility enjoy the Royal Parks, taking them on conducted tours or giving them lifts. Mostly it is by arrangement, with parties from various organisations booking an advance tour. But people can be picked up randomly, if they are having trouble walking.

The Canadian explained that she had been resting, feeling rather tired as she has a sore knee. A buggy had stopped and asked if she would like a lift. She jumped in and asked how much. The answer was nothing. They don't charge – but are delighted to receive donations. All staff are volunteers. Deirdre, who had been driving the Canadian, said that 99 per cent of people are generous. It is very rare for someone, having been given a lift, to give nothing.

My final Hyde Park appointment was not till much later. The crowds were thinning, with tourists going back to their digs or their coaches, so I went for a coffee at the Serpentine Bar. Yes, I had just had one, but that never stops me. Anyway,

I had passed the bar several times during the day and it had always been so busy. Now it looked quieter.

I sat with my coffee outside, looking down to the end of the lake. Such a brilliant idea by Queen Caroline, those two centuries ago, to create a lake – a proper lake, long and winding. Not a pond or paddling puddle, but a lake big enough to take proper yachts.

I half closed my eyes and imagined I was sitting outside at the Sharrow Bay Hotel, looking down Ullswater. The evening sun was still strong and I realised this view could almost be from Cobblers Cove in Barbados at sunset, looking out at the Caribbean. Then I thought, steady on, Hunter old boy – too much caffeine.

I began writing up my notes on the day so far when I realised a young woman was sitting beside me on her own, reading a book. I did not ask what her book was this time. I did not need to because she began the conversation, asking me what I was writing. This is one of the many joys of being old. As long as you are vaguely clean and roughly respectable, women do not see you as a threat.

I told her what I was doing, my parks book, and she insisted on taking a picture of me on her mobile. Then she took another, asking me this time to look as if I was studying my notebook. She said she was a nanny, working locally in Bayswater. She had two charges, nine and ten, both at primary school. She had brought them home from school, given them tea, then when their mother came home, she was free. Mostly, if it was reasonable weather, she crossed Bayswater Road and walked round Hyde Park.

I detected a Welsh lilt and she said yes, she was from Swansea. She had never realised that the Royal Parks were, you know, royal. She never knew where they were, or their history, till she started walking them.

'You know they are all part of Buckingham Palace? The queen owns them. That's why they are Royal.'

Not quite, I replied, but their history is connected. The royal family did own them once.

Then I asked what her book was and she held it up – *This is Going to Hurt* by Adam Kay, a junior doctor. It seemed an interesting choice for a nanny.

'Well I am not really a nanny, not for ever. I did it during the summers when I was at Newcastle University, now I am using it as a chance to live for free in London.'

She had graduated in civil engineering. I was most impressed. According to reports, these are among the most desired graduates. Graduate engineers can always get jobs.

'I did get a job, but then decided I didn't like civil engineering after all, not if it means working for one of the big international conglomerates. They always have jobs available. I want to work for a charity, help them with their engineering projects in some deprived region. That's why I spend so much time in libraries, looking at job adverts.'

I wished her luck with her career and her life and she wished me the same with my book and with my life. I explained that I was a widower, but I now had a girlfriend. She asked if it was going well and I said great, so far . . .

'Do you want to know the best playground in the whole of the Royal Parks?' she said as I got up to go. 'Pass me your map. It's in Kensington Gardens. Here, look. It's gated and secure and interactive and has a big boat. Children can play musical instruments. Parents and all nannies love it.'

I did not intend to do Kensington Gardens, as I had decided four Royal Parks would be quite enough, but I thanked her kindly for her advice. Top tip.

My last proper appointment in Hyde Park, as opposed to random ones, was with the manager of the park itself, Jason Taylor. He and his staff have their office in what is called the Ranger's Lodge, a handsome building, with lawns and wooden tables scattered around where the staff have lunch and events.

Jason, aged forty-eight, had only been in the post for three months. He was new to London, as well, never having lived or worked here. He felt he was still learning.

'There are twenty-five gates into Hyde Park and I still haven't memorised all the names and where each of them is. The only one I know for certain is Ice-Cream Gate, because there is an ice-cream van outside. Though I am not sure if Ice-Cream Gate is the official name ...'

Jason comes from Sussex, near Eastbourne, and left school at sixteen to work on a golf course as a green keeper. He then moved on to public parks in Maidstone. He went to college as a mature student and got a degree, then became manager of Maidstone Parks.

It was in his trade paper – *Horticultural Weekly*, of course, which I never miss – that he saw the advert for the job as manager of Hyde Park.

'It was my dream job to manage Hyde Park but I did not for a moment expect to get it. I don't have a horticultural qualification, and have no high-quality horticulturalist experience, which most of the applicants had. My degree is in business management. This turned out to be an asset.

They wanted more of a business manager than a high horticultural expert.

'My first interview was done on Skype. I had gone off to New Zealand to visit my son, never thinking for one moment I would get any sort of interview.

'When I was offered the job, I still could not believe it. For a couple of days I was in a dream. I was constantly looking at my mobile, to check that yes, I was being offered it. And then I just stood there, smiling at the screen.'

He still lives in his family home in Maidstone so has an awkward commute each day, which normally takes him one and a half hours. He had just bought a sleeping bag, in case he is ever working so late he can't get home.

'I had to work late the other week and then have an early start, so my wife went online and booked me a place in Bayswater for the night. It was horrible, a right dump. I am not staying there again. With my sleeping bag, I should be able to sleep on the floor of my office, if I have to.'

His team numbers thirty-four – a lot more than his previous park. There are nine management staff members assisting him. Then there are twenty-five gardeners and maintenance people, who are technically subcontractors.

His most frequent problems, day to day, are what most park managers have to face – litter and conflicts between cyclists, walkers and dog owners.

A new problem is the dumping of the dockless bikes, which people now just abandon. Hyde Park, being so central and so flat, attracts lots of visitors who decide to hire bikes. When they have finished pedalling, bikes are left without consideration to other park users, which greatly upsets Jason and his staff, who have worked so hard on the landscape and aesthetics of the park. Each morning they spend a lot of time collecting up the bikes and putting them in a central storage place, waiting for them to be collected.

'When I got the job, I did worry about what I could possibly do here. I mean, how could I improve things, how will I make a difference? It seemed to be running so smoothly, everything looked so wonderful, all the facilities worked so well. That was my first image.

'Now I know, of course, that things don't always work as well. Hyde Park makes the most money for the Royal Parks, and attracts the most people. So the work is constant, all the year round.

'When I arrived and looked at the map, I saw that Kensington Gardens was right next door, with just a road dividing us. I had this image that over there was the badlands. We would meet on the border and have a shootout, like in the cowboy films. We would be rivals, perhaps even enemies.

'In reality, of course, we all get on really well. We always help each other. I have now met the managers of all the other seven Royal Parks and know I can always call them for help or advice.'

That day he had an unusual worry, the sort he never faced at Maidstone Park. For the previous three months, a creation by the internationally known artist Christo had been floating in the middle of the lake. It was 7,500 brightly painted oil barrels, stacked like a pyramid, so they were towering 100 feet high.

I had noticed them several times during the day, admiring the daftness of it all, the huge size and complicated structure, and wondering how they had been erected, and why, and also how they would be taken down.

That was Jason's current worry – what to do with them next, now the exhibition was officially about to end.

The installation had proved of enormous interest to tourists and Londoners since it had been erected three months earlier. Most of the newspapers had covered it, and millions of snaps and selfies had been taken.

'Next week, when it is due to go, I don't want 7,500 oil barrels just left floating there. I have looked at the original plans, but couldn't find what the future intentions were for them. However, we have had an approach from the Glastonbury Festival people. They are interested in using them as litter bins. I hope that works out. It will be one worry less.'

Jason kindly offered to drive me in a Royal Parks buggy back across the park to where I had come in, at Marble Arch.

'I know you are not a Londoner, Jason, and have only just taken over, but tell me, where exactly is Speakers' Corner? Have you worked it out yet?'

'Don't you worry,' he replied. 'That struck me as well when I arrived, that there was no sign or indication of where it is.'

He took me to a fence where a little area was closed off with red plastic barriers. I could see some holes in the ground where fresh concrete had been laid that very day, while I had been wandering the park. I could see they were getting ready to create some sort of foundation base.

'A plaque is going up next week. It will tell you all about Speakers' Corner. So the world from now on will know exactly where it is and its history.'

Well done, Jason. You are making a difference already.

Best Things About Hyde Park

1. The Serpentine, a man-made lake, created in 1731, but big enough to have yachts and mock battles. It continues on into Kensington Gardens where it is called the Long Water –which it is.

2. Hyde Park events – there have been national events, performances and displays held there for centuries. Hyde Park is like an open-air Albert Hall. It still gets mega pop concerts and Winter Wonderland.

3. Achilles' statue on the Wellington Monument – the first nude public statue in the UK. Its erection, hmm, was in 1822. Today he's probably not endowed enough to get on Love Island.

4. Princess Diana Memorial Fountain – a more modern creation from 2004, which isn't erect like a normal fountain, but flat. Very cool, moody and atmospheric. And you can paddle.

5. The Dell – a sylvan idyll, near the end of the Serpentine, but you can't enter it or walk around. It is a created pretty rural scene. Look upon it as a photo opportunity.

6

THE ROYAL PARKS AND
THEIR CHIEF EXECUTIVE

It so happens that the overall boss of the Royal Parks, the person who runs them all today – the chief executive of the Royal Parks – is based in Hyde Park. So I returned next day in order to talk to him.

It's a shame about his title. Chief executive sounds so commercial, bureaucratic and faceless. For centuries the boss of the Royal Parks was known as the royal bailiff – much grander and more splendid-sounding.

I interviewed the then royal bailiff back in 1982. At that time, his office was in a horrible modern government block on Marsham Street, Westminster. Today the boss might have lost his glamorous title, but at least he has a stunning office, right in the middle of Hyde Park, the Old Police House, whence he runs his royal empire.

Andrew Scattergood is in his forties. He was rather serious and preoccupied the day I met him, but it was a busy day for him, with lots of meetings.

He went to Bristol University to read history, then joined the Civil Service on their fast-track scheme, rising up the ladder in the Department of Culture and Sport. He played an important part in drawing up the successful bid for the 2012 London Olympics, working with Tessa Jowell. Preparatory work among civil servants began nine years before the games actually took place. In that capacity, he had linked up with various London parks during his time in Whitehall. Several of the Olympic events were of course held in the Royal Parks.

When the position as chief executive of the Royal Parks came up in 2012, he applied for it, but didn't get it. Not that first time. A woman was chosen who went on to leave after three years. It was second time lucky for Andrew, and he took over in 2015.

There are eight Royal Parks in all. Five are in inner London – St James's, The Green Park, Regent's Park, Kensington Gardens and Hyde Park. Then there are three outer ones – Greenwich, Richmond and Bushey. Hampton Court Park is legally a Royal Park, but it is now administered by another body.

In 2017, all the Royal Parks ceased to be totally government controlled, no longer run by the Civil Service. They became instead a charity – interesting news I had somehow missed. I suggested, being cynical, that this must have been for the tax advantages, to make the most of their incomes without having to pay VAT. But Andrew said no.

The tax situation remains roughly the same. The main point of becoming a charity was so that the Royal Parks could immediately become a totally independent body for the first time. It is now a bit like the National Trust, raising money, making decisions. Best of all, it can now plan for the long term, building up a reserve rather than having to budget annually, and can also seek charitable donations.

Even so, 25 per cent of its income still currently comes from the government. In recent years, this government money has been going down by about £500,000 every year – another reason why those at the charity feel they are better off raising money and being self-reliant. Thirty-five years ago, 95 per cent of funding for the Royal Parks came from the government and the annual budget came to £5.5 million. Today, the annual budget is £40 million, three-quarters of which is raised by the parks themselves.

'Gardens and open spaces are the treasures of London,' said Andrew. 'No other city in the world has quite as many. They are not just good for the residents but are a huge attraction for all visitors. The government knows this. I think they and everyone else appreciates the beauty and value of the Royal Parks. But they are not cheap to run.

'The Royal Parks get 77.8 million visitors every year, which is an enormous number. A very large number of visitors are from abroad, bringing income to the nation. We did a recent survey and we found that Kensington Gardens has most foreign visitors – about 47 per cent of all their visitors.'

This particular survey also gauged visitor satisfaction: 98 per cent reported that the parks were either 'excellent' or 'good'.

There are 150 full-time staff members employed directly by the Royal Parks, spread across all eight parks. Landscape, gardening and maintenance are these days mainly contracted out, but most contract workers work full time in the parks and ultimately report to the chief executive. Counting them all, the total number of people working each day in the Royal Parks comes to about 500.

They include eighty-one police officers, who are part of the Metropolitan Police. The police headquarters are in the same building in Hyde Park where Andrew and his senior management have their office, The Old Police House. The police are at the back, where they also have stables for their horses. I had a look later and saw the horses being exercised in a large yard.

At busy times of the year, when big events are on, several thousand people come each day to work in Hyde Park. In the summer, the restaurants take on extra catering staff. In the winter, there can be 3,000 extra workers brought in to create and run Winter Wonderland.

Andrew finds there are always people with horticultural and landscape experience working in ordinary parks all over the country who are keen to work in the Royal Parks. His problem is finding people with financial, business and technology experience. These are the folks he needs today because so much of the work is concerned with raising money or planning future projects.

This explains why Jason turned out to be fortunate with his timing when he applied to be the Hyde Park manager.

'The people with those business and technical qualifications don't want to or never consider working in the Royal Parks. We can't of course pay them the money they might make in the City. But the work is fascinating and satisfying and worthwhile.'

I noticed in the corner of his large handsome office, right at the front of the Old Police House, that he had a sofa bed. Surely he didn't use it for the odd kip? Oh yes. He has been known to sleep on it when he can't get home for the night.

He lives in Surrey with his wife and three young children, commuting by train from his home to Waterloo. But often there is a late-night engagement, such as the Lord Mayor's Banquet, to which he gets invited as chief executive of the Royal Parks.

Then there are times when he has to have a very early start, when a big event is imminent, such as a pop concert, or Winter Wonderland. He needs to be on the premises by seven because there can often be unforeseen overnight problems that have to be sorted.

I am sure that, back in the grand old days of the Royals Park, the royal bailiff never had to doss down in his own office. He probably had valets, and his own coach and horses to transport him to the handsome bailiff's lodge that went with the job.

These days, there are still twelve staff lodges scattered across the Royal Parks, where staff live, but not all senior staff want tied accommodation. If you have young children, as Andrew has, and you are settled in a family home before you get the job, you know that having a tied house is not necessarily all that wonderful. You still may have to pay tax on the benefit, and if you are unwise enough to sell your existing house, you might not be able to afford any thing half decent when you come to retire.

He is exceedingly proud of working for the Royal Parks, aware of the status and prestige that goes with the name. I wondered if that made Royal Parks managers feel rather superior to their counterparts working away in less glamorous parks, such as, say, Burgess Park, my next destination park. So far, no one I had mentioned Burgess Park to had ever been or knew where it was. Even Andrew seemed unsure of its location.

While Royal Parks employees like to feel proud, he said, there's no arrogance attached. They always know how much they still have to achieve.

His main satisfaction comes from restoration work – improving something which is run-down and has become an eyesore – such as a new playground near Gloucester Gate. This was due to be unveiled the following week, after a great deal of work.

The single biggest change in any of the Royal Parks since he took over four years ago is probably the removal of the Regent's Park nursery. All plants, trees and bushes for the Royal Parks will now be grown on one site, the nursery here in Hyde Park. It is hidden away, unseen by the general public, but I had a quick peek and it is enormous.

To have just one nursery for all the Royal Parks cuts costs and releases a valuable plot of land which can be used for something better, possibly more lucrative. The Regent's Park nursery was on prime land, covering well over an acre.

So what will happen to the Regent's Park nursery? It's already been demolished and the ground was currently being cleared. There's a plan to ask for tenders from potential developers, though of course it will all be subject to planning and building regulations.

'We want whatever we decide upon to be in tune with the Royal Parks, so it must have a cultural, artistic, educational or horticultural interest.'

One likely possibility, among several, is for the new building to look like a conservatory, like one of those at Kew Gardens, which would be an attraction in itself. He showed me a glossy brochure of the possible design, and it looks most attractive. It would then be rented out, and provide an income.

Andrew makes a point of visiting all eight Royal Parks at least once a month. His personal favourite is Greenwich Park, where he likes to stand in the Rose Garden, in Rangers' Field, looking out at the cricket ground. 'It's always so quiet. I like looking at the roses, and also watching any cricket that is on, but you still can't help being aware of all the history and historic buildings which are all around.'

As chief executive, looking after the heritage and quality of the eight Royal Parks, he has three areas of constant concern.

Firstly, there is health and safety – ensuring that cyclists are not making it dangerous for walkers, that dogs are not a danger to cyclists or walkers. This is the same for all park managers, really, of even the smallest, most modest park.

All the Royal Parks are patrolled by police. The worst incident since Andrew arrived was a battle between gangs and police in Hyde Park. There were several injuries in the fight, but no one got killed. There have been four suicides in the Royal Parks since he took over.

'You would not believe the dangerous things some people do. One of our rangers in Richmond has just let me see some CCTV of someone putting a baby on the back of a two-ton deer. These deer, at certain times of the year, can seriously injure.' And they have, over the years.

His second major concern is any environmental impact that changes in policy might bring.

Then there is finance, making sure the Royal Parks are financially viable. During my chat with him in his office, money matters did seem to be the most frequent topic to come up.

A large part of the £30 million needed each year comes from pop music events, especially from Hyde Park. Over the years, stars who have performed here have included Paul McCartney, Bono and Bruce Springsteen. There is now an agreement with Westminster and Chelsea councils not to put on more than nine large events a year. Council licences always have to be issued for such public events.

In addition, each year a Royal Park hosts the BBC's

Outdoor Proms. But the biggest single money-making event is the annual Winter Wonderland in Hyde Park. This is a huge Christmas Fair, complete with fairground, shows, concerts, stalls, displays and events, which lasts for six weeks.

Andrew wouldn't reveal the precise income from Winter Wonderland. As a charity, the Royal Parks don't need to make public all their finances.

Then there is income from catering. In Hyde Park, there are two very successful restaurants, at either end of the Serpentine, plus four small tea houses. In all the Royal Parks, money is generated by parking charges. So income comes from varied sources.

I had so far not noticed many memorial seats in Hyde Park, nor in St James's Park. Andrew told me there were quite a few. I must have missed them. How much do they cost?

The answer was £10,000 in Hyde Park. I was astounded. I thought £2,000 on Hampstead Heath was such a lot. I suppose being situated in a wealthy part of central London means it's possible to charge those high prices.

I wonder if I should create another memorial bench in my own honour, this time in a Royal Park? Wouldn't that be fun? Wouldn't that be posh?

Now, which Royal Park would I choose? I will have to think about that, talk to my girlfriend. By the end of the book, I might have decided ...

7

BURGESS PARK

I feared I was going to be late for my appointment at Burgess Park, which is not like me these days. When my wife was alive I was always late for things, relying on her to get us there on time. Now I am always early, especially when I am going into foreign and strange lands, which is how I always look upon south London. I was very early, but somehow I missed the stop I meant to get off at, Elephant and Castle, and found myself at the Tube terminus at Kennington.

There was no escalator so I had to queue for one of those massive archaic lifts. A sign above one of the two lift doors was flashing away 'No. 1 lift shall be the next lift'.

I wrote it down, this ponderous wording, wondering why they did not say 'will be' the next lift, or, even simpler, 'Next lift . . .' The word 'shall' made it sound biblical, as if some great god of the Underground had issued a blessing, commanding the lift to obey and bow to his wishes.

I had arrived at the wrong station because I'd got engrossed reading something absolutely fascinating, so well written and informative – a piece by me. I wrote it back in 1983, the last time I'd visited Burgess Park. Not been back to it since.

People who move to London from the north tend to arrive at Euston or King's Cross and look for somewhere relatively nearby in north London to live. They think it will be handy when they visit the old folks in the north. Once you settle in north London, you never leave. I assume it is the same with people from other parts of the UK. I know lots of people from Wales and the West Country who first arrived at Paddington, then end up living their lives in west London. That's my excuse for so rarely having ventured south of the river – at least until the last year. I now do so regularly for romantic reasons.

Once out of Kennington Underground, I jumped out and got a bus back to Elephant and Castle. I then caught another bus down Walworth Road to Albany Road.

On the old map I was clutching, photocopied from an ancient A–Z, there was no clue to any greenery beginning so close to the main road. Burgess Park was marked, but still looked fairly small, which was how I remembered it from almost forty years ago.

I came to a park entrance. A man was drinking from a bottle of beer, right beside a notice saying, 'Alcohol Control Area'. I continued along a long strip of grass – just a path, rather than a park. There was a tennis court with a large notice which said there was a cafe, open every day, entrance at the back. I was still early for my appointment, so I went round the back to investigate. Everything was locked up.

I walked on and eventually came to a proper cafe, the Park Life Cafe, which was open. I had a coffee while waiting for my interviewee to arrive, and picked up a copy of the local paper, the *Southwark News*. I do love local papers. Wherever I am in the world, I always read whatever the local rag is, whether it is the *Gleaner* in Jamaica, the *Advocate* in Barbados, the *Bulletin* in Mallorca, or the *Cumberland News* in Lakeland.

The *Southwark News*, the 'Independent Voice of the Borough', boasts that it is 'the only independent paid-for newspaper in London'. I thought about that for a few moments, wondering if it was true. In my borough, Camden, the long-established *Ham & High* is part of a group, and still has a cover price. The excellent *Camden New Journal* is independent but is free. So the *Southwark News* boast, carefully worded, might well be true.

There has been such a change in my lifetime in the local press – so many newspapers have gone, yet so many are now free. Free papers were traditionally just advertising sheets, with nothing worth reading. So it's good that the *Southwark News* is both independent and has a modest cover price, just 50p. Long may it thrive.

The paper reported a call for a weapons ban in Camberwell because of the growing number of fatal stabbings. For some reason I thought Camberwell was fairly upmarket, though I have never been there. I should have recalled that this was the neighbourhood ruled by the Richardson gang in the 1960s, renowned for drug dealing, pornography, police corruption and sadistic torture. Charlie and Eddie Richardson began a turf war with Ronnie and Reggie Kray, although all four notorious convicted gangsters ultimately survived those brutal times, which is more than can be said for their mutilated victims.

Gang culture lives on in London and one story in the paper that day revealed that Southwark now has the second-highest murder rate in London, after Haringey, which is where one of my daughters and her family live. It's frightening, really. Almost all of the victims seemed to be teenage boys, killed either by rival gangs or by their own gang exerting some sort of punishment.

Another news story was about youngsters stealing yellow dockless hire bikes, the ones which get dumped all over London. Young people have been riding them around Peckham, mugging innocent pedestrians and then dumping the bikes.

While Southwark appears to be riding high in the crime statistics, it is clearly doing well as regards having a social conscience. According to the paper, Southwark has the highest amount of social housing of any London borough and is always top at trying to deal with homelessness. The council had just been awarded £650,000 of government funding to resolve homelessness.

Reading the local paper and seeing all the problems highlighted even more the need for local parks, everywhere, especially in areas which had been deprived in some way. This is the main reason I have come to Burgess Park, to see if it is indeed the jewel in Southwark's crown.

Like the cafe in Victoria Park, the one in Burgess Park turned out to be agonisingly smart, modern and tasteful, with couches, and homemade dishes available every day. On Hampstead Heath, supposedly in an upmarket area, the cafe I go to, known as the summer cafe, beside the bandstand, is still stuck in the 1950s.

I talked to a waitress, who was Argentinian, and the chef, who was Italian. The couple who run the cafe were not there that day. They took on the lease a year ago and have done an excellent job, turning it into a place where locals come to eat and have coffee and chats. No alcohol, I noticed. Again, modern London, alas. I do like a drink whenever I have a meal.

My date was with Rebecca Towers, head of Parks and Leisure for Southwark Council. She arrived bang on time at 11 a.m., looking very spruce and efficient. She comes originally from Reading, and did various uninspiring jobs in sales after university, before moving into charity. Then she started in local council work, ending up in Parks.

Since 2015 she has been head of Parks and Leisure in Southwark and is responsible for 130 different parks across the borough, many of them pretty small, some little more than patches of grass. She assured me that some of the small ones are really lovely, such as Cherry Gardens by the river and the David Copperfield Park, off the New Kent Road, which is really only a sliver of green.

She has a staff of seventy working across Parks and Leisure, plus another ninety-six who are contract staff dedicated to maintaining parks. As we all know, the government and local authorities seem to have contracted out almost everything.

Southwark has spent £20 million on its parks since 2009. It seemed to me an amazingly high amount, considering the total acreage of their parks is scarcely 1,000 acres. Burgess Park, at 140 acres, is the biggest, more than twice the size of Southwark Park.

I said she must be under pressure all the time to raise money from the parks themselves, to cover their costs.

'No, not all the time, because Southwark's parks are well funded. But there is a need to use assets within our parks wisely and generate income where possible.

'We are very fortunate here. Southwark is a wonderful borough and the council believes in the value of parks. Some local residents have in the past been concerned that we were planning to spend £6 million on new paths and grass, which we did in Burgess Park, saying it could be spent on more useful facilities. Everyone acknowledges the value of parks – and of this park in particular.

'Don't forget, this park was created within living memory from what were streets, factories and houses, where no park existed. After the initial creation of the space, it was left somewhat unfinished and the recent investment has enabled the park to fulfil its potential and live up to the original vision.

Every local person knows and appreciates what has been done. We had a master plan, which we have stuck to. And there still is more to come.'

She suggested I study the current master plan, which is not printed but is available online. She gave me the reference.

At my age, I find it so hard reading stuff online. It's part laziness but part being brought up always having stuff printed. This was becoming one of my problems in all the London parks today. So few now have printed leaflets and maps, or even printed lists of events, assuming everyone lives online. Plus, of course, they want to save paper, help the planet, so they say.

I said all this and Rebecca immediately whipped out her mobile to show me some of the master plan. It seemed to go on for thousands of words, with loads of graphs and diagrams. I said lovely. How kind. Looks great. I will look at it all when I get home. Possibly, maybe.

The original master plan for Burgess Park was an incredible creation, something that will probably never be done again, either in London or anywhere else on the planet. Burgess Park is an urban vision created in the post-war years, which was why I wanted to write about it, back in 1982, by which time it was beginning to take some sort of shape.

The story of Burgess Park begins in the war years, at the height of the London bombing. Some town planners who were sheltering in an air-raid shelter made a promise to themselves and each other. 'When this is all over, we'll make the world a better place to live in. We will give some greenery to people who haven't got any, making up for what they have been through.'

There was no existing public park in the immediate area,

no football pitches, not even any greenery. It was one long industrial sprawl, at intervals being increasingly decimated by the Luftwaffe.

As a result, the 1943 Abercrombie Plan was drawn up with the opening line: 'Adequate open space for both recreation and rest is a vital factor in maintaining and improving the health of the people.'

Once the war had ended, the plan swung into action. This was post-war optimism at full throttle. It was named after Sir Patrick Abercrombie, an ambitious visionary who saw opportunity in smouldering bomb sites, to create a green corridor so that hard-pressed city dwellers could enjoy the benefits of wide-open spaces.

He walked readers through his plan, explaining how people would get from doorstep to open country 'through an easy flow of open space from garden to park, from park to parkway, from parkway to green wedge and from green wedge to Green Belt'.

His working equation was four acres of green for every thousand people. Even before the war ended the LCC, as it was then, started buying up bomb sites, factories, disused railways, slums, abandoned churches and old industrial buildings between the Old Kent Road and Camberwell Road. The original concept was for a 135-acre park, to be completed in fifty years. Amazingly, it has more or less kept to plan, although now it is 140 acres.

Along the way, thirty streets were knocked down, wiped from the A–Z map, hundreds of houses obliterated and the old canal filled in. Factories that were flattened included one owned by soft-drink makers R. White's, Watkins Bible Factory, Newby's Ice Store and a commercial bakery.

From today's perspective, the plan for a park sounds perfectly logical but it wasn't entirely plain sailing. When the war ended there was an immediate demand for housing and jobs, rather than recreation facilities. The process of compulsory purchase used to acquire the land sometimes took ages, leaving boarded-up buildings in situ while unhappy neighbours looked on. In 1965, three London boroughs become one as Bermondsey and Camberwell were subsumed by Southwark. This was a vital moment in pushing the plans forward. Nonetheless, there remained a piecemeal approach, with some land grassed here and there as time and space permitted, to hide the bomb-site blight.

There were other challenges in store, too, not least with the foetid waterway running through the proposed park. When digging had first begun in 1807, the Surrey Canal was intended to bring produce from Croydon's market gardens into London. In fact, by the time it reached Camberwell in 1809, its basin in the Thames at Rotherhithe proved much more profitable than the canal proper, so digging came to an end.

When it came to filling in the canal in 1971, the banks were found to be polluted with creosote, carried down from the timber yards at Greenland Dock, once part of the Surrey Commercial Docks. Worse still, the factory where luminous dials had been manufactured left the ground radioactive.

Nonetheless, a brand new park was well under way, created from scratch, where nothing had been green. It's a feat that will probably never be repeated. The Olympic Park in the East End – a much bigger, more recent concept costing billions – took advantage of a lot of existing canals, rivers and green spaces. And it had the glamour of the Olympics and the whole government onside, able to throw billions at the project, determined to create a legacy.

Burgess was and still is a local council park. No council, anywhere, is ever likely to have the money, energy or power to compulsorily buy up 135 acres from scratch, raze it to the ground and create a sylvan oasis in what had always been one of the most overcrowded, neglected, impoverished areas of London.

Burgess Park was named after Jessie Burgess, an alderwoman, who finished the war as the first female mayor of Camberwell. She was a hard-working Labour councillor who at one time served on forty committees. She always supported the project and did much to get it established. So when it came to naming the park in 1972, her surname was a popular choice.

When I first visited Burgess Park a decade later, I was taken around by the then park manager, Dave Sadler. Although work had begun, imposing the park on the industrial hinterland, today's rolling grasslands were a distant dream. Camberwell born and bred, Dave had been tempted out of a job with Kensington and Chelsea's parks department to take this on. One of his first memories of the job was entering a newly acquired factory near Christmas-time to find the locks had been cut off and there were vehicles parked inside, filled with stolen whisky.

It was just as well he was there to guide me around for at that time the park still appeared to be a bomb site. He led me through piles of rubble, half-demolished buildings, roads being dug up and houses being knocked down. I couldn't actually see any greenery at all. He took me carefully through scaffolding and diggers, walls half knocked down, an army of workmen bashing away, but as we progressed, now and again he stopped to show me with great delight definite little patches of new green grass, struggling to establish themselves.

His biggest triumph, just completed, was the brand new lake. He stood back, waiting for me to exclaim, which I did. Fish were being put in and, most surprising of all, the day I was with him, some sailing dinghy boats had just arrived, compete with sails. Canoes would soon be joining them.

I said it seemed a little bit, er, upmarket, if not pretentious, having a proper sailing club on a sterile new lake, still surrounded by the bomb sites. Did he really think there would be a demand for sailing in Peckham? The toffs, if he ever got any, would think it ridiculous, sailing in such a small, artificial space. The locals might be mystified.

Mr Sadler was convinced it was worth introducing. If it is good enough for the public schools, it would be good enough for their local council schools. 'I can see local schools sailing here every day,' he beamed.

He himself was going on a course to learn how to sail the following week, feeling that as his park was going to offer sailing, he should know how to do it himself.

One of the problems Mr Sadler had to put up with back in 1982 was that there were fourteen different resident associations in the local adjoining streets, not all of whom were as convinced of the need of a park as he, Southwark Council and the planners were. These residents were fed up with the lorries and dirt and dust and noise, claiming it had ruined their views, ruined their lives.

As I was walking round the lake with Mr Sadler in 1982, an elderly woman in an apron waved to him from her house.

Grace, as she was called, had lived there for sixty-four years. I admired her neat lawn and said it must be lovely for her to have a view of the lake. That started it. She hardly paused for breath for the next twenty minutes. 'I hate it! I wish it had never been built. It might look nice to you, but when it's sunny the noise and swearing is dreadful, these hooligans, they just climb over, chuck each other in. I get kept awake all night. Then in the morning, your speed boat, Mr Sadler – must it go round the lake joyriding every morning . . .?'

Mr Sadler slowly explained it was a new boat, and that they were not used to it yet, but had been told it had to burn petrol every morning, which meant riding it fast. It was not joyriding. He was very sorry . . .

He was closely liaising with local schools and had organised a wildlife area for the benefit of children, many of whom came from tower blocks.

Mr Sadler has long since retired. Since 2009, the park has had a major overhaul to widen its vistas.

The manager today is a young woman called Louise Wilcox. She comes from Peterborough and read business studies at Loughborough University. For a time she was a tennis coach, then she worked in Peterborough City Council, working her way up to managing parks and recreation facilities.

'When I saw the job advert for Burgess Park in 2014, it looked fascinating. It was my dream to manage a large, vibrant urban park. Burgess Park is large but also a destination park – I mean people come to it specially, to walk or cycle or join in events. It's now much more than just a park known to the local residents.'

Not only is she thrilled by the park, and the wonderfulness

of Southwark Council, she also reckons she has one of the best offices of any park manager in London.

I waited to be convinced, having seen quite a few managers' offices by then. Hampstead Heath and Olympic Park bosses could be anywhere, in their boring modern blocks. Victoria Park's was new and functional, but quite cosy. Royal Parks, well they know how to treat their guys – and girls, if they ever have any running the show.

Louise took me behind the cafe into Chumleigh Gardens. I never knew such a place existed, and I don't remember hearing about it back in 1982. It is something out of Old England – immaculate period cottages clustered round a lush square garden, carefully tended. The houses were originally almshouses, dating from the early nineteenth century, once home to the Friendly Female Asylum for elderly ladies. The almshouses had escaped the wrecker's ball and survived the park creation, one of several relics to endure. All of the alms-houses are used today, with the South Almshouse occupied by Louise and her staff. I counted eleven bijou cottages, or at least what had been separate cottages. Most are connected together these days, though the front doors remain.

Previously, one or two served as accommodation for park-ies, but now they are used by the staff as offices, meeting rooms, storage and the Park Life Cafe.

Louise took me to her upstairs office, flung open the window and invited me to look down into the gardens, breathe it all in, while she continued to exclaim about how jolly lucky she was.

Louise is responsible for a full-time staff of twenty, who work from Chumleigh Gardens. Most are not directly on the

Southwark payroll, but are contract staff, such as the twelve gardeners. They work for Quadron Idverde, a French-owned company which does contract garden and landscape work all over the UK.

Her team consists of contract management staff, park attendants and park wardens. The wardens patrol the park on bikes, making sure the bylaws are being obeyed. They can issue a fixed penalty notice fine of £150 should anybody seriously transgress, such as not clearing up after their dog.

She then took me, along with the council's ecology expert Jon Best, to look at the World Garden. This looked surprisingly well established, with palm trees and exotic plants, considering it was all begun from scratch just twenty-four years ago. The idea is that park visitors can come and admire and enjoy the sort of vegetation they might have remembered from their childhood, or been told about by their families. So they have an Asian garden, which contains Japanese and Chinese plants; a Middle Eastern garden, with a jelly palm in the middle and a Persian ironwood tree; a Mediterranean garden, with some luscious black grapes hanging over an archway. I tried some. Not quite ready, but much sweeter and more advanced than the ones in my garden at home.

The World Garden is rather hidden away. I don't think I would have found it without Louise. It leads into a little square and a courtyard, equally attractive and well kept. All of it was totally empty. It was by now mid-morning but, even so, I suspect many visitors don't know it is there.

Jon, the ecologist, told me what the ethnic trees were, which I could not have named otherwise. There were no plaques or signs in front of the trees and plants telling you their names and origins. Louise said there used to be signs, but they had gone for some reason. She would investigate.

Next we went to St George's Garden, long and open this time and hard to miss, as it is beside one of the main paths. It is a wildflower garden and all the plants were sown from seed as recently as 2013. Everything was in full bloom. I could see a mass of tall yellow flowers, waving away at me, huge and flapping, about ten feet in the air. When the ground was first prepared and planted, a lot of sand was added to stop the soil from dehydrating. The garden now self-seeds. Nothing has been added since and yet there are still flowers blooming for ten months of the year. So the gardener said.

Once a year, in early February, the whole garden is cut right down, so that it can rejuvenate come spring. No chemicals or fertilisers are added. The idea is that you should feel like you are walking through a prairie.

Good things have followed. The park's sparrow population has made a recovery, with at least thirty making their homes there compared with a single pair a decade previously. There are starlings (as numbers drop these sleek, shiny birds are classed as endangered), whitethroats and reed warblers. On one July day someone recorded 160 butterflies, including a comma, small tortoiseshell, speckled wood and a lofty flier, the white-letter hairstreak.

In Burgess Park as a whole, sixty species of birds, four different bats and eighteen types of butterflies have been observed. Isn't nature clever, given a little nudge from its human friends?

We walked a bit further and came to a large mosaic on the side of a building, made out of painted tiles. It depicted a large butterfly, the Camberwell Beauty, about 20 feet across. This time there was a sign, saying it was a Camberwell Beauty. That's how I knew.

Jon the ecologist explained that the Camberwell Beauty does not live in Britain. And it doesn't come from Camberwell, anyway, or even England. It is a Scandinavian butterfly, mainly seen in Norway, which every so often makes appearances in the British Isles. In 1748 one was spotted in Coldharbour Lane, Camberwell. It has rich chestnut wings measuring no more than 3.5 inches across, peppered with sky-blue markings and bordered with a lacy-looking frill. It was so unusual and exotic that people flocked to see it, thus it became known as the Camberwell Beauty. Presumably in Norway it has a Norwegian name. Only periodically does it come to the UK, about every four decades or so. I suggested that all this should be included on the sign.

Louise explained that future plans include some nature trails through the park, with explanations. Jolly good, I said. Alas, her plans seemed to involve downloading the information from the internet on an app on your mobile. Ugh, what a faff. So many museums these days have also gone too hi-tech and audiovisual for my liking. They get carried away with their own technical cleverness, showing off new kit, just because they can.

The park has an outdoor gym with around twenty pieces of equipment, none with fancy technology or electricity. There is a football pitch, a rugby pitch and a splendid cricket square.

Louise is amply supported by the Friends of Burgess Park, which has a motto that sums up the group's reason for being: 'Protect, promote, enhance'. With all its activities, organisations and clubs operating, the park is busy from dawn until dusk. On summer weekends, an estimated 4,000 pay a visit.

I watched a groundsman doing something. I do like to watch people working. He was putting down what looked like sand. The sports fields are at the end of the park, towards Camberwell and a busy road. I imagine the ball sometimes goes over the fence and hits one of the cars. That day there was work being done on demolishing an old tarmac road elsewhere inside the park, digging it up in order to create another garden and woodland.

I came to a rather attractive cobbled area. Two men were busy spraying the cobbles from a huge pipe attached to a large van announcing, 'Foam Stream'. I watched for a while. One of the workmen stopped and explained with pride that they were killing the weeds. Drowning them, you mean? No, killing them, but without using chemicals or insecticides. They were using organic foam, which was boiling hot. Once it hits the weeds, they give up and die. They then either sweep the dead leaves up or leave them to blow away. Environmentally good, he added, rather smugly, which of course every right-on parkie in the land is trying to be these days.

What about the hot water? You have to heat that up, so aren't you using energy? He sighed. I'm sure they get fed up with clever clogs asking questions. He pointed to a diesel engine, which boiled the water. Then you are consuming diesel fuel? Tut tut. Diesel is now bad, so we are being told. You want solar power, I said. I didn't wait for his reply but walked away quickly, in case he hit me.

In the park are various listed buildings, none of them quite on a level with some of the famous monuments in the Royal Parks, but surprising all the same for a park created from bomb sites.

The kiln, dating from 1816, is still there, standing a bit less proud than in its industrial heyday. Open-topped barges filled with either coal or limestone were towed there by horses and the cargo unloaded into the kiln. Limestone was burned to make quicklime, used as mortar in houses and agricultural fertiliser.

Another listed building is the Passmore Edwards Library, Baths and Wash-house, built in 1901. The building has some fine stone engraved letters and other ornaments. At present it houses a boxing club and a creative arts venue, the Deli Theatre. I looked at a poster of forthcoming attractions and lots of well-known stand-up comedians were about to appear, such as Romesh Ranganathan. Coming soon was an evening of women wrestling. All tickets had already been sold. Curses.

The basement of the building was empty at the time, and all of it was due to be renovated, so it was hoped. It belongs to the council.

Burgess Park, being a random, rather higgledy-piggledy creation, has not got a tall fence or gates round its borders, so it is always open. The wardens don't generally work after dusk so in theory anyone could arrive and doss down.

The borough has dedicated officers and organisations providing support and services for rough sleepers. Park wardens will speak to a rough sleeper and can make referrals to services and signpost local shelters. John, one of the park wardens, explained that in severe weather conditions the council has what is known as SWEP. Councils do love acronyms. It stands for Severe Weather Emergency Protocol and it is a system for quickly transporting people to shelter.

One of the proudest, most popular creations in the park is the

BMX bike park. It is enormous, about the size of a small football stadium, and is up to Olympic standards. Yes, BMX racing has been an Olympic sport since 2008. People come from all over the country to the Burgess Park BMX track and big events can attract crowds of up to 5,000. It is perpetually busy, with youngsters clad in helmets and protective clothing cycling hard up slopes and pelting down the other side. 'It has put us on the national map,' said Louise. Well, a national map for BMX fans.

Next to it, an urban games park is planned. A Lido for swimming, however, is out of the question, budget-wise.

The whole park, all 140 acres, is on the flat, but they have created what they call sculptured mounds, really just titchy hills, the biggest of which is known as the Mound.

The Mound is a mere hummock, about 30 feet high. It was created from a great pile of soil, which would have cost good money to transport out of the park. A membrane was laid and some good topsoil put over it. It looks rather convincing. And from the top, which takes about a minute to reach, you do get some reasonably nice views, such as a sighting of the Shard, supposedly, in the far distance towards the City. I failed to spot it. Nearby, there is a fairly decent-sized stretch of grass known as the Great Lawn.

Signposting, posters, branding, snazzy titles and cool headlines are all part of the work of a modern council. Around Burgess Park, I had noticed some attractive, nicely coloured art nouveau-style posters. I wanted to buy one, or at least some postcards to send to friends saying, 'Where am I? Bet you can't guess.' But they aren't for sale.

I took a picture of one on my mobile that said, 'Come two or five minutes early and ride in the park.' This is clearly to encourage cyclists, as all paths and routes are open to them. Then I took a snap of another poster, equally pretty, warning cyclists to slow down.

Burgess Park has a barbecue area, actively encouraging barbecues – which not all parks do – as long as they are restricted to a certain area. From afar, I thought it was a playground. It has numerous permanent barbecue grills, made of steel, created specially by the council's in-house fabricators, who also produce signs, gates and fences. There was, however, a temporary ban on barbecues, imposed at the request of the London Fire Brigade, because there had been lots of fires in public places.

Louise explained how their barbecue area was extremely popular in the summer, but could cause problems. Hundreds of people cram into a small place and there can be a risk of fire spreading, or people getting rowdy after drinking too much.

'We sometimes get people coming in at five in the morning to reserve their grill. They leave things like a bottle of water to show it is theirs.

'They come from all over the borough and beyond. It's very popular for birthdays and weddings and other celebrations. If they have invited dozens of guests, sometimes up to a hundred, they want to be sure they will get a grill.

'We have had people setting up a stall and selling their own hamburgers and beers, but we do stop that. That is against the park bylaws.

'We do like the barbecues being used, though we ask that groups try to stop cooking after nine in the evening.'

Burgess Park clearly has a barbecue culture of its own, which it has created to serve the needs of the locals, from all countries. Stuck in your crowded tower block, there are not many opportunities for open-air cooking. London parks do reflect London life today.

I finally made it to the Burgess Park lake, which was about the only feature I could remember clearly from forty years ago. It is now about a third bigger, and looks more natural, but it is still rather concrete and brutal and exposed. It was very windy, just as I remembered it then. Good day for sailing, I thought – sailors do like a bit of wind. No sign of any yachts or dinghies. I asked Louise if she had heard of any sailing on the lake, but she said not in her time as manager. Perhaps it never happened.

At one end was a footbridge across the lake. As we were about to walk on it, I noticed a large hole in the tarmac.

'Rats,' said Louise. 'We are plagued with them in the summer. They live here beside the water. I am not sure if they actually dug a hole in the tarmac, or just burrowed underneath causing the tarmac to cave in.

'Jon, you know what to do with them, don't you, Jon. In two words?'

Jon Best the ecologist was still with us. 'Sweet potatoes,' he said, smiling.

What? I'd never heard of that. I once had rats in our back garden under some wooden decking. What a mistake. I had to get Camden Council to poison them.

'They like sweet potatoes,' explained Jon, 'but their stomachs don't. They can't digest them. It then turns to a form of poison, a bit like cyanide. I am told it works. So that is the next method we are going to try.'

There is a small island in the middle of the lake and on it I noticed a heron, standing tall, important and regal.

'Oh look, a heron,' I said.

'I think you'll find it is a cormorant,' said Jon, who went on to point out some great crested grebes, plus some other ducks and birds fluttering around, whose names I didn't catch.

Fishing is allowed in the lake, all year round, unlike at Hampstead Heath, which has a strict fishing season. The charge is £4.40 a day, paid online before downloading a receipt to a mobile, which can be shown to a park warden, if asked. Good job I don't fish – I would never be able to cope with all that.

In the lake there are carp, tench, bream, roach, rudd, perch, dace and catfish – some pretty large specimens. A 22-pound carp was once hooked out of the water. But fishermen are asked to throw their catches back, once the obligatory photograph has been taken.

There were two elderly fishermen at one end of the lake, silently staring, while at the other end, near the back of Cobourg Primary School, I could see saw a lone young fisherman wearing a hoodie. He was standing on a dinky little concrete fishing platform, with his umbrella up and his supplies for the day set out beside him.

I excused myself from Louise and Jon, asked them to wait a bit, and said I must talk to the lone fisherman. I suppose lone fishermen everywhere must be driven mad by nosy strangers asking if they have caught anything.

He looked at me rather suspiciously. I don't think he feared I might be from the council, wanting to see his permit, but that I might be an elderly idiot, the sort who wanders round parks talking to people.

I explained I was doing a book about parks, and was with the park manager, look, that's her over there. He continued to look suspicious, but eventually, having clocked Louise in the distance, he relaxed and put his hood down.

No, he had not caught anything all day. He had started at seven and it was now one o'clock. He was hoping to catch a perch. He was originally from Bristol and lived in a nearby flat with his girlfriend. He did have a job, working in 'high-end retail', but would not elaborate on what that meant. On the counter at Harrods?

'No,' he said. 'Does it matter?'

I said sorry, and then asked about his girlfriend: was she in high-end retail as well? He said she was a designer, an artist really, who did a lot of drawings.

He comes here fishing two days a week, up to seven hours each time, yet rarely catches anything.

It seemed a bit sort of eccentric, not to say mad – spending all day on such a windy lake, just standing here. In the winter, he must freeze.

'It's Zen,' he said. 'I can stand here on my own and think deep thoughts.'

Isn't your girl resentful, that you spend your days off fishing, and catch nothing?

'Sometimes she comes as well, to have a sleep and get a free meal.'

I thought that meant he must take her to the nice cafe in the park. He said, oh no. She stays with him while he fishes, then gets to share his sandwiches when he has his break. He has to come at seven in the morning to bag this good spot on the little platform.

'There is an unwritten rule that if someone has it, you don't try to barge in. It only really holds one fisherman.'

Sounds lovely, I said. Then I went back to join Louise and Jon, who were talking to some groundsmen working on the football pitch.

Walking round the whole 140 acres of the park, which is long and thin, comes to almost two miles and took me about an hour. Not once did I come across a memorial bench, not even near the flower gardens or pretty spots.

Over a late lunch with Louise, in the nice cafe, I asked her about this. Was it deliberate, perhaps to keep the park wild and natural? This would be hard to do when every local must know Burgess Park has been artificially created, out of nothing that was green. Or did they not want to look like all those traditional municipal parks, with their regimented flower beds and rows of memorial seats dedicated to long-gone park lovers?

'No, none of that. We have no memorial benches because no one has ever asked for one.'

I suppose this is a result of being a fairly new park, like the Olympic Park, and still not fully completed. Long-time locals have not yet established deeply rooted affections for their local park, passed down through the generations. It does take time.

When today's granddads or grandmas eventually die, their families will think, oh, they loved this park, they were always so happy here, let's have a seat in the park in their name. Then we will always visit it.

In many areas, park benches have taken over from graveyards as a remembering place for our dearly beloved.

I asked Louise where she lived. To my surprise, she still lives in Peterborough, her hometown, where she used to work. She stays in London from Monday to Friday, then on Friday goes home to Peterborough.

Today was a Friday, so she would soon be catching the train home. Her round journey, door to door, takes her three hours. Sounds horrendous to me, but she's used to it after five years.

I asked what she would be doing this coming weekend, back home in Peterborough.

She said she would be attending a 1940s festival, dressing up in period clothing, either as a wartime land girl or a member of the wartime WVS – Women's Voluntary Service. She and her partner are keen members of a re-enactment group and go to lots of fairs and gatherings. I had heard of the Sealed Knot, when people re-enact the Civil War of the seventeenth century, dressing up as Roundheads or Royalists, but I had never heard of people dressing up as if it were the 1940s. To me, that is not history. That is my childhood.

I asked if she had any wartime ration books. She said just one, so I promised to send her one from my collection. I do like to help.

I asked if she would like to stay as manager of Burgess Park till she retired. Or perhaps she was still ambitious for further progress and promotion, possibly to a bigger, more famous park?

She paused and thought for some time. I was clearly pushing her into an answer, on a topic I sensed she had not thought about before.

'I think a Royal Park would be nice. I think I would only leave here if I was moving to a Royal Park.'

I said I now had some jolly contacts in the Royal Parks. I promised to put in a good word for her, if she ever applied.

Best Things About Burgess Park

1. History – that it exists, its inspiring story, a post-war fantasy, dreamt up in an air-raid shelter, so that when all the bombing was over, local people would have some green space in a deprived area with no parks.

2. Chumleigh Gardens – old almshouses, round the Old English Garden, so sweet, where the parkies have their office, lucky things.

3. Park Life Cafe – beside Chumleigh Gardens, delightful cafe, nice décor, in an otherwise fairly drab area for cafes.

4. World Garden – different trees and plants from all over world – as are so many local residents.

5. Lake – not quite as yummy as a Lake District lake, but come on, admire how they have created it out of bomb sites.

8

GREENWICH PARK

Greenwich has such a rich maritime history that it seemed only fitting to arrive there by boat. Greenwich is on the Thames and is the home of the National Maritime Museum, the Royal Naval College, *Cutty Sark* and other significant chunks of our nautical past. It would be rude to go by Tube.

The last time I visited Greenwich, some forty years ago, I went by boat, but I remember it being hard to get a time-table and find a suitable boat. When I did, it turned out to be a rather small launch and the captain, who was doing the steering, was also our guide, using a microphone to point out London highlights along the way.

For most of my lifetime in London there have been plans to turn the Thames into a superhighway. It is such a natural communication system, so broad and navigable – why can't it be used more, the way it was in the past, when the Romans were here? Yes, it does bend and twist a bit, does not always appear to go quite the way you want, but it is such a convenient route, going physically right through the heart of London from east to west and metaphorically right through our history, joining all the important bits together. Why don't we sail serenely along the Thames instead of sitting at traffic lights till we get poisoned by the fumes?

I have heard these sorts of moans and comments since the 1960s, yet I don't think I have consciously been aware of any massive increase in river traffic. But when I arrived at the Embankment pier, blow me, there was a queue of superboats, long and sleek, waiting to disembark hundreds of passengers. Minutes later, hardly pausing for breath, they had loaded up again and whoosh, were off and away. While I haven't been look or paying attention, the Thames has become a superhighway. I'd got it all wrong.

The boat I got was called *Aurora*. It was run by Thames Clippers and held 220 passengers. The archaic launch I had last been on held about twenty. It had no facilities and wheezed along ever so slowly. *Aurora* was like a marine version of the Eurostar train from St Pancras, so modern and smooth, so fast, so big, so well appointed.

There were proper seats and sofas in black leather, or what looked like black leather, not rickety old slatted wooded benches as in ye olden days. There was a proper cafe with meals and drinks and a big TV screen, presumably telling us fascinating stuff about the Thames, though when I got close and watched for a bit it was showing commercials.

In the very near future, even bigger passenger boats are planned for the Thames. Sailings by the Dutch-owned *Ocean Diva*, longer than a football pitch and with a capacity for 1,500 passengers, are in the pipeline. For now, the smaller big boats would have to do.

This one was full of mostly British families. I had forgotten the summer holidays had just started. Instead of being surrounded by bemused and solemn foreign tourists with little idea of where they were going or why, sitting quietly taking it all in, there were screaming kids rushing up and down the gangways on their scooters, mums with pushchairs pushing to find space. But all of them were clearly thrilled and excited to be on a superboat.

I got the last vacant seat, at the very front. I sat down and had a good view of all the sights coming up and the various bridges we glided under. Beside me was a young family – mum and dad and two boys of about five and seven.

'Is that London Bridge, Dad?' asked the younger boy.

He had already asked this question twice, as we went under different bridges. Perhaps he thought London Bridge was a generic title for all London bridges. His father patiently identified each one, in the correct order. I was most impressed. Despite living in London for so long, I am still hazy about the bridges. I know the names, roughly, but not in the correct order.

The dad also pointed out and named all the amazing new skyscraper buildings, which was helpful. The one that looks like a piece of broken glass, that's Europe's tallest building, the Shard. And the one that looks a bit like a mobile phone, that's the Walkie-Talkie.

From the Thames today, London appears to be a sea of skyscrapers, each bigger and weirder than the last, like an army of giants competing for attention. Look at me, am I not the biggest, the newest, the greatest? There seems no pattern or design, no uniform plan, thanks to unbridled capitalism and enormous wealth. It seems as if everyone has been able to build just what they please.

The views into central London from surrounding areas are of course subject to control, particularly those in the same frame as the dome of St Paul's Cathedral. Policy states that any development in the vicinity should be 'subordinate to the cathedral'. But the new buildings still seem a jumble. When you arrive by sea into New York harbour, the skyline appears somehow shaped and regulated; the skyscrapers are impressive, but conform to some sort of pattern. Paris has stayed resolutely low rise around its Arc de Triomphe. Yet the modern London skyline is like a playground for mad architects, given a box of Lego and told to get on with it, be as crazy as you can. So many look half finished, with slices yet to be added, or missing, but they turn out to be complete. Construction isn't finished yet. In the spring of 2019 an extraordinary 541 skyscrapers were awaiting creation or completion. Alas, this race for the city's summit doesn't mean a new supply of housing for hard-pressed Londoners, battling with sky-high rents.

I don't think I had really been aware of the tremendous amount of new buildings in London till I was on that boat trip to Greenwich. Yes, I have often stood at the top of Parliament Hill on Hampstead Heath and tried to identify the towers in Canary Wharf, but they are far way, blobs on the horizon, and you are roughly looking down at them. On the Thames itself, you are on the flat, surrounded by them, towering over you.

In a way it felt reassuring. London must be rich, prosperous, vibrant, optimistic and hopeful, otherwise there would not be all this activity. For the last 500 years, the capital has constantly been growing and reinventing itself, creating new wonders. Where will it end, people have always thought? The pace today does seem much quicker than it was, certainly in the post-war years.

William Wordsworth, standing on Westminster Bridge on 31 July 1802, looking down the river towards St Paul's and the City, was half amazed and half appalled. He felt that earth 'had not anything to show more fair', yet in another sonnet composed that same year, he mourned that 'getting and spending we lay waste our powers'.

I got talking to the mother of the two young boys beside me. She turned out to be a Brazilian called Priscilla, who has lived here for twenty years. I showed off my twenty words of kitchen Portuguese, which amused her. She was very friendly and outgoing. Her husband Steve, who worked in some sort of IT job, was more reticent. They lived out in Essex, near Harlow. He had taken a week off to coincide with the school holidays, so he could take them somewhere in London each day. Today they were going to North Greenwich to go across the river on the cable car, the Emirates Air Line, opened in 2012 for the Olympics. I had assumed it was a no longer working, having been derided as a white elephant, one of Boris's vanity projects, but apparently it was still going. They had been to Greenwich Park the previous week.

Steve was sent by Priscilla to get coffees and soft drinks for the children – and came back with coffee for me as well, which was kind. I hadn't even asked. And he would not accept any money.

The atmosphere on the boat was jolly, a happy-holidays feeling, all the families excited by the adventure of being on a boat, the parents hoping their kids would learn something about London history and have a memory of this day for ever. I know from the experience of my own children that they don't always remember the event you thought was really good at the time, but instead remember something trivial and piddling.

I got off the boat at Greenwich Pier, said cheerio to my new friends and had a quick glance at the *Cutty Sark*, a streamlined beauty. Her name comes from a line written by Robert Burns in his famous poem, 'Tam O'Shanter'. Cutty sark meant a short shift or shirt, a corruption of the French *courte chemise*. You can see that the lady on the figurehead of the ship is wearing one. I remember telling my own children where the name came from. I was born in Scotland and lived not far from Clyde when I was very young, so I liked to pass on my Scottish heritage – which I am sure they have totally forgotten, even if they took it in at the time.

The clipper was built in 1869 and cost £16,150. It could travel at some 17.5 knots, or 20 mph, when her six-decker sails billowed in a steady wind. She brought back tons of tea from Shanghai within a speedy 120 days or less and later broke records in trips to and from Australia. But *Cutty Sark* launched the same year as the Suez Canal was opened to powered vessels, providing a continental short cut. Compelled to travel the long way around via the Cape of Good Hope at the bottom of Africa, her speed suddenly became secondary and steamships continued to erode her vital statistics. Although she barely made any money for successive owners and last set sail in 1938, she has since been highly prized for her elegant rigging, although she still costs a lot to maintain.

I was a bit confused at first seeing reference to the Royal Museums – which is now the joint name for Greenwich's local museums – the *Cutty Sark*, the Royal Observatory, the Maritime Museum and the Queen's House. Along with Greenwich Park itself, they are now collectively classed as a World Heritage Site. Really, this is a park that is all about its buildings.

So on this occasion I skipped a proper visit to *Cutty Sark*, wanting to get into Greenwich Park itself. As you walk up the hill towards the beginning of the park proper, you are confronted by so many massive, handsome impressive buildings and squares and courtyards it is hard to work out which is which.

Originally there was a Tudor palace on the site, the favourite residence of the kings and queens. Four monarchs were born here, at what was called the Palace of Placentia – the pleasant place. These were Henry VIII, Edward VI, Queen Mary and Elizabeth I. It became Henry's favourite palace, somewhere he could indulge in the sports he loved like wrestling, hunting and hawking then wander to the palace entrance on the Thames to watch ships leave London with wool and metal aboard, or return laden with spices, silk and gold.

Elizabeth made the palace her principle summer residence when she was queen and it was here that Sir Walter Raleigh is said to have thrown down his cloak over a puddle for her, so that her shoes would not get dirty as she walked. Here too Elizabeth finally signed the death warrant for her cousin Mary, Queen of Scots. The Tudor palace has long gone, but it is thanks to its presence that Greenwich Park can boast that it was the first Royal Park. The royal family enclosed some 200 acres on the hillside outside their palace as early as 1433. St James's Park was not enclosed and fenced off till 1530 – a newcomer, really.

Greenwich remained a deer park for about four centuries, until it was thrown open to the public in the 1850s. By then the London & Greenwich line, the country's first urban railway service, had been operating some fifteen years, bringing people out of an increasingly smoky city across 878 brick-built arches into the area's green, rolling hills.

Before the palace's demise, the Queen's House was built nearby, designed by Inigo Jones at the start of the seventeenth century in a Palladian style, long before it was fashionable. Tree-lined avenues splayed from it, giving it a continental feeling.

Queen's House and the park remain but the palace has been replaced by some grand baroque buildings, first earmarked as a hospital and later the Royal Naval College building. It was designed by Sir Christopher Wren at the end of the seventeenth century, with additional bits and pieces by Nicholas Hawksmoor, who began his career as Wren's clerk, and Sir John Vanbrugh, architect and playwright.

By instruction of Queen Mary II, the Royal Hospital had been built to house naval veterans, with 2,700 living there at its peak. She also made sure the design of this new building didn't block the view from the Queen's House, which is why there's a gap in its edifices. These men were without means and likely injured, either physically or mentally, by the interminable series of sea battles that erupted as Britain waged wars to establish pre-eminence, putting out the first foundations of empire. They were quite literally cannon fodder, as the Royal Navy found itself lined up variously against the Spanish, Dutch, Americans and, on many occasions, the French, as well as minor players like the Barbary pirates. Without this grand refuge we can suppose most would have been condemned to a workhouse.

At first the men wore grey frock coats with brass buttons, breeches and a tricorn hat, until the Royal Navy became defined by its love of blue. Food was plentiful, as was tobacco and ale. There was discipline, too, including a yellow punishment coat worn by transgressors for a set period, as a way of shaming them. Among those retired sailors was John Worley, with a full head of white hair and a shaggy beard, who remarkably lived until the age of ninety-seven after a career at sea lasting seventy years. He was not overawed by his new surroundings and more than once was punished for coarse language and drunkenness. (Bread and water for a week, loss of allowance for two weeks and no leaving the premises for a month.) As it happens, we know what he looks like because he is among the images in the Royal Hospital's Painted Hall, our nation's answer to Rome's Sistine Chapel.

Architecturally, the Painted Hall was part of Wren's design and is the size of a small football pitch and as stately as a cathedral. But that's not why it is so striking. Its ceilings and walls are a canvas containing bodies heavenly, fashionable and fantastical, all in awesome proportions. The Hall was decorated by artist Sir James Thornhill, who began in 1707 and took nineteen years to complete the project. He was paid a pound for every square yard on the walls, with the amount rising to £3 for the ceiling. By 1726 he had earned £6,685.

Thornhill included Worley in the mix, as well as a self-portrait, both being safe ground for an artist at the time, whose work was like a commentary. But, as I discovered, he had to take account of the shifting sands of politics in the first quarter of the eighteenth century.

When I arrived in the Painted Hall it looked empty. Then I noticed some red day beds in the middle on which some human bodies seemed to have been abandoned. I moved nearer, not wishing to disturb anyone who was dead, or simply asleep. There were four people – two men and two women – flat out on their backs on the day beds, staring up at the ceiling, completely motionless. It would clearly make you dizzy if you stood for too long, cricking your neck to stare up and study the whole ceiling. Better to lie down flat, take the weight off your neck. I stood quietly, not wanting to disturb them. They were silent and still, not talking to each other, or even showing much sign of life. Perhaps they had passed out, or were in a trance.

I heard some talking coming from the far end of the Hall, so I walked over slowly to investigate. The rear wall was also totally painted, but studying it was easier than having to look up at the overhead painting.

A guide aged about fifty was addressing a party of some ten very attentive visitors. I loitered at the back, eavesdropping. On the back of his jacket were the words REVEALING THE CEILING. Catchy, huh? He was identifying people in the painting, revealing the extended family of George I in 1714 when he succeeded to the throne, the first of the Hanoverians. Although his claim was a distant one, he was a Protestant, and that counted for something. Even at his death in 1727 he barely spoke any English. Anyway, the painting included his children and relations, all of them stunning and beautiful and so well dressed. This was to indicate how good they were going to be for the country, that they were going to be here for ever, and would reign over us through the generations – which they did, until the death of George IV in 1830. The guide went on to point out many symbols of peace and prosperity in the painting, such as fruit and food, as well as gods and angels and art, all of which were there to indicate that the Hanoverians were going to bring peace and civilisation to the rough old English.

He then put his hand behind his back and produced from a pocket a torch, which he proceeded to shine on some of the individual figures and scenes as he described the contents. Not just a verbal tour de force, he had lighting as well.

'What about the king's wife?' he asked. But he clearly wasn't going to stop to wait for an answer as it was patently a practised rhetorical gesture. 'She is not in the painting. Where do you think she is? Hmm?'

There was silence. Before I could stop, I found myself suggesting: 'In the kitchen! Making his supper?'

He did have the grace to laugh, perhaps pleased that someone was really listening, at least. He switched on his torch again, revealing a hand – the queen's. I personally couldn't see a hand, and thought our guide was seeing things, or making it up, but most of the tour party nodded their heads wisely.

The queen, he went on, had been swept under the carpet, metaphorically, because she'd been unfaithful, having had an affair with a Swedish count. The marriage between George and his cousin Sophia in 1682 was rooted in her dowry rather than any mutual affection. When the engagement was announced she is supposed to have cried, 'I will not marry that pig snout.' The marriage was a miserable one and both sought solace elsewhere. On at least one occasion the future king tried to throttle her. The unfortunate dashing count was murdered while Sophia was exiled to a remote castle, where she was kept under house arrest and never permitted to see her two children again. That hand under the carpet, so our guide informed us, was a nod to people in the know, about her miserable fate.

The Painted Hall was intended as a dining room for old matelots. Quite what the salty old sea dogs would have made of it, no one knows. In 1806 it was the eminently more fitting location for Horatio Nelson's body when it was lying in state, and some seventy years later the veterans were moved out and it became the Royal Naval College. It gave sterling service through the twentieth century, training young officers from both home and abroad, until the site became a tourist attraction in time for the dawning of the Millennium.

The Royal Naval College buildings still stand square and imposing, always to attention, but today they house the University of Greenwich. You can still get into some areas, notably the Painted Hall.

Across the road is the National Maritime Museum, which has, among two million treasures, the coat worn by Nelson when he was fatally shot at Trafalgar.

Afterwards, I walked up the slopes of Greenwich Park proper, looking back all the time at the buildings below, and beyond to the expanse of the Thames and in the distance the City skyscrapers I had sailed past that morning.

I also looked across the park, sideways, to Crooms Hill, which borders Greenwich Park and snakes up to Blackheath. It is one of the handsomest, most desirable roads in all London – as nice inside as outside, for I once visited two people who lived there, though not together.

One was Cecil Day-Lewis, the Poet Laureate. I went to interview him for the *Sunday Times* back in the 1960s. His wife was the actress Jill Balcon, a screen goddess in the 1940s, theatre actor from the 1950s and popular radio voice. I remember some very lively and attractive blonde-haired little children running around, one of whom turned out to be Daniel Day-Lewis, the multi-award-winning actor.

The other person I knew who lived there was my friend and fellow journalist Nicholas Tomalin and his wife Claire Tomalin, an eminent writer. For a while, Nick was my boss on the *Times* Atticus column. It was no secret that there were difficulties in the marriage, although it endured until he was killed by a Syrian missile in the Golan Heights in 1973 while reporting on the Yom Kippur War. Claire wrote movingly about how the death made it feel like the sun had been eclipsed.

Greenwich Park contains another complex of ancient and historic buildings of significance, this time right in the middle of the park itself. It is clustered around the Royal Observatory, which was founded in 1675 by Charles II. At the time it was built, the Tudor palace still existed, as did the Queen's House, but it preceded the Royal Naval College buildings.

Astronomy is considered the oldest science. From its study came pressing questions on space, place and time. Until the middle of the sixteenth century, it was generally thought that the earth was at the centre of the universe, a theory in which the Catholic Church was heavily invested. Poland's Nicolaus Copernicus believed the planets circulated around the sun but wisely kept this a secret until he was on his deathbed, to avoid ecclesiastical punishment.

Other scientists took note, including Italy's Galileo Galilei, who then ran up against the church and its inquisitors before his death in 1642. The cold, dead hand of faith put the brakes on the idea across the Catholic world, but in Britain Charles II, who favoured broad religious tolerance, was less cowed. With better understanding of the stars would come a greater ability to accurately navigate at sea. Like other European rulers with an eye on the burgeoning maritime trade routes, Charles II was keen to nail the issue of longitude.

He appointed the Rev John Flamsteed as the first Astronomer Royal, 'to apply himself with the most exact Care and Diligence to the rectifying the Tables of the Motions of the Heavens, and the places of the fixed Stars, so as to find out the so much desired Longitude of Places for perfecting the art of Navigation'. Flamsteed's legacy included a painstakingly achieved 3,000-star catalogue.

The second Astronomer Royal was Edmond Halley in 1720, after whom Halley's Comet – visible from earth every seventy-five years or so – was named. With new, improved telescopes, better mathematical equipment, clock pendulums and a bit of free thinking, knowledge about celestial motions gathered like moss on a stone.

By the 1760s, there were rival methods of measuring longitude. There was a chronometer, which worked like a clock at sea, and the *Nautical Almanac*, drawn up by another Astronomer Royal, Nevil Maskelyne. Initially, the almanacs were a far less costly option. By 1767 the Greenwich Meridian, the standard line from which longitude is measured, was being used by British sailors and mapmakers. It established the time of day: when the sun was at its highest point above the prime meridian, it was deemed to be noon.

Accurate time-keeping became increasingly important, especially as railways developed. On 1 November 1884, GMT was adopted universally at the International Meridian Conference in the USA and from that, twenty-four time zones were created (every 15 degrees longitude representing one hour's time difference).

Today the Meridian Line is just a little nondescript line of cobbles on the ground, but it never fails to intrigue, amuse, entertain and presumably even inspire visitors from all over the world. It is now more photographed than it has ever been in its long history. This is the age of the selfie. Everyone has a mobile phone. Everyone can take themselves, or have themselves taken, all in a second, and immediately send it pinging round the world to show off to folks back home.

It is strange to realise that this rather modest if ancient building, stuck out on its own in the middle of a London park, should have dictated two global principles. Not just the Greenwich Meridian but Greenwich Mean Time, the time by which other time zones around the world measure themselves.

I didn't go in. It looked too busy already. I did take my children many years ago, when I think it was free, but I might have made that up. Now it is £8 just to get inside the gate, and stand on the Meridian line and have your photo taken – what a rip-off. But then you can caption it by saying you had one foot in the Western hemisphere, one in the Eastern hemisphere.

The best view in Greenwich Park is from the Wolfe statue, near the Royal Observatory, towards the river and London. General James Wolfe lived in McCartney House, right beside the park, for a few short childhood years before joining the Royal Navy aged thirteen. He won popularity with fighting men when he refused to shoot an injured Scots Highlander during clashes north of the border, saying his honour was worth more than his commission. This innate sense of fair play was clearly tested by the French, as it wasn't long afterwards that he threatened to lay waste to Quebec during a siege. In what's known as Wolfe's manifesto, he stated, 'We must teach these scoundrels to make war in a more gentleman like manner.' In 1759 he perished in the process, and his body was shipped back to Britain and put in the family vault at St

Alfege's Church in Greenwich. The statue was erected and paid for by the people of Canada in 1930.

There's lots in Greenwich Park you can no longer see, including a first-century Roman temple and a sixth-century Anglo-Saxon cemetery. Even these days, the park yields surprises. In 2019 an archaeological dig manned by volunteers uncovered a Second World War air-raid shelter in the park grounds, containing a toy soldier made of lead.

The superintendent of the park, sorry, park manager – I keep forgetting – has his office on the far side, the south side, beside Blackheath Gate. There is an old lodge nearby, beside the gate, once lived in by park keepers, but now let privately in order to produce an income.

Graham Dear has been manager of Greenwich Park for ten years. The main attraction of the job was not the obvious ones – all that landscape, all those views, all those amazing buildings, all that royal history. His sole motivation at the time he was looking for a new job, back in 2009, was sport. He wanted his next job to be somehow involved with sport of some sort.

He had always loved playing and watching all forms of sport, so naturally, in 2009 he knew, as we all did, that the Olympics were coming to London. Lots of plans and preparations had already begun, and he reckoned there must be a job he could land with some sort of Olympics connection. His first thought was finding work at the Olympic Park, even if just as a park keeper – anything that might give him a ringside view of some of the Olympic events.

He is fifty-eight, comes from Harlow in Essex and took a degree in botany at Southampton University, after which he worked in a nature reserve, and then did a diploma at Kew Gardens. He moved for a while to Wolverhampton to work for the Council Parks Department, then back to Kent to run country parks. So he had come with twenty years' experience of parks and nature.

As a runner, he had taken part in the London Marathon, which has been going since 1981. He ran it in 2003, and managed a commendable time of three hours, thirty minutes – considering he was dressed as a rat. His young son had been very ill and Graham was raising money for a local hospital, dressed as a cartoon figure called Reggae Rat, loved by his poorly son, who did go on to recover.

So imagine Graham's delight when, while looking around for a sport-related job, the manager's job at Greenwich Park came up. He knew by then that Greenwich was going to feature in two Olympic events – equestrian and modern pentathlon.

Once he got the job, he was involved in the massive preparations, having to build from scratch a stadium holding 23,000, the biggest of the Olympic stadiums, apart from the Olympic Stadium itself.

During the busiest period of the Olympics, he did not live at home for several weeks, living instead with some of the other managers in the lodge by the gate at Greenwich. Every time they returned to the lodge in the evening, to get into their beds, they had to go through security: 'All Olympic venues had heavy security, because of the fear of terrorism.'

It is now almost ten years since the London Olympics, but he can still go into raptures about the excitement of it all, even though it was a one-off event.

Still, he has had a big sporting event to get excited about every year – the London Marathon. Today, it still starts at Greenwich Park.

Over 17,000 runners – the ones running for charity, as opposed to the professionals – start from Greenwich Park, beside the Wolfe statue. They are joined there by another 13,000 who have started from nearby Blackheath. It means there are 30,000 runners, all running through his park. Much to his pleasure, oh yes.

This army of runners does of course cause certain logistical problems. The main one is what to do each year with at least 30,000 items of discarded clothing. What happens, particularly if it is a wet or cold day, is that the runners keep themselves wrapped up in old clothes while standing around waiting, which can take some time while they are being organised. Then suddenly they are off, tearing off their top garments and chucking away loads of empty water bottles. Disgusting – what a mess. They have deliberately put on old gear, stuff they know they probably won't ever need again or will come back to collect. In just a few moments there is a veritable mountain of old clothes. Each year, it takes twenty staff about three hours to clear it all up.

Earlier on, before coming to the start, they have taken off their more valuable street clothes and personal possessions and been given a bag which goes on one of six articulated lorries that take all the bags to the finish line. But their old stuff, put on to keep warm while they hang around and wait, will almost always get dumped. Among the dumped rubbish, stolen supermarket trolleys are often found, which a few have used to trundle their gear to the start.

Graham just smiles indulgently at the memory of the annual scene. The sight of all this rubbish does not seem to upset him. Anything half decent is given to local charities, while the rest is recycled.

'Oh, it is a lovely atmosphere. I love it every year. People are so happy and expectant. There is an air of such joy and camaraderie. It is a one-off experience, just to say they have done it. So before they even start, they know they will always remember it.'

Graham's immediate management staff consists of only five members, all directly employed by the Royal Parks. As in most other parks today, the rest are contract staff, in this case twenty-five park keepers, mainly gardeners, who are full time and have their own yard and staff quarters elsewhere in the park.

Graham and his five parkies have their office opposite the lodge at the Blackheath Gate, discreetly hidden away. Inside it is ever so comfy and attractive, with its own sitting room, kitchen and sofas, as well as their desks and offices.

In all the private parkies' quarters I managed to visit on my tour of the London parks, I was always impressed by how they'd managed to organise their lairs, making themselves comfy, creating a personal space for themselves, unseen by the public. They build their own nests, not some sterile habitat created by some distant management or HR department. I am surprised they ever go outside into their park. I would be tempted to pull up the drawbridge and lock the door whenever some irate member of the public was approaching, incensed because their dog/bicycle/pushchair/dignity had been offended.

Of course, I know they are all working jolly hard, not skulking inside or skiving. They do need some privacy and comfort, plus their own kettle and fridge and bickies and chair. They have to do far more work with far fewer workers than ever before. Just thirty years ago, there were fifty gardeners working full time at Greenwich. Today it is twenty-five, while the annual number of visitors has increased from three million to five million in the last twenty-five years.

It is now a World Heritage Site, a Grade I-listed park, with a history that goes back 570 years, but it can still feel seriously under threat for want of resources. Our national lottery has come to the rescue, with a £4.5 million grant to help future-proof the park, so it can be enjoyed for generations to come. Greenwich was recently voted the happiest borough in all London. The population in the local borough is predicted to increase by 20 per cent in the next ten years, with more and more high-rise blocks eating up more and more open space. The local community needs the greenery of Greenwich Park more than ever.

There's a wish list that includes improving biodiversity in the whole park, building a new educational centre for the local community, a bigger restaurant and helping to protect ancient trees.

The latter appeared to be Graham's biggest current worry that day. Some 340 ancient horse chestnuts have got a nasty lurgy, known as bleeding canker. 'There's no cure. They will all be dead in twenty years. You can't breed new ones. When it spreads, as it will, it is likely that eventually there will be no conkers left in the whole country.

'Sweet chestnuts have also got a fungus. Ours have been

here since the 1660, but they are under threat. It is terribly depressing. I hope I am not still working here when they all die.'

But cherry trees are doing very well. During cherry blossom time, there are about 100 visitors each day from Japan and China, taking photos of each other standing in front of the cherry trees.

'There are in fact only twenty cherry trees, but they are in a neat row and they all come out at the same time. Last year the Japan embassy in London offered to pay for another twenty, which we thought was very generous.'

Alas, the generous gesture did not come to pass. 'Our cherry trees are Pink Perfection, which is an English variety. They wanted to plant some Japanese ones. So it never happened. But they are donating trees to the playground instead.'

Like most of the best-known parks in London, money is made from film and TV crews, either filming in the park or paying to set up their caravans and trailers while they film nearby.

'We have had loads of films shot here. When they eventually come round locally, the five of us in the office always have a meal out, usually Pizza Express, then go to the cinema and watch the film. They like to spot the places they recognise. We have seen such rubbish films over the years, but we always go and see them. The only one I ever enjoyed was *Bridget Jones 3*.'

The Friends of Greenwich Park organise quite a few facilities, which they finance and run, such as the bandstand concerts. They book the bands for the season and pay them; the concerts are free to the public.

There's no problem with rough sleepers as the whole park is

enclosed and is shut each evening at dusk. The park has its own Metropolitan Police station, with officers who regularly patrol.

As always, there is a running battle between cyclists, runners and dog walkers, each group thinking the park should be organised for their benefit. Greenwich Park has an extra complication in that there is a road through the park, used by commuters, limited to the morning and evening rush hour.

The park is relatively small, just under 200 acres – about a quarter of the size of Hampstead Heath – so it doesn't take long to walk round. It doesn't have a lake, but has quite a variety of landscape – a big hill, a flat bit, some groups of grand buildings, then hidden away are some empty hollows.

Graham is very fond of a section called Lovers' Walk, which has had that name for centuries. 'I have this fantasy of holding a picnic in Lovers' Walk and inviting people who might have courted there, or got engaged there. We would have a giant picnic, all of them together. Not got round to doing it yet. But I still think it would be a nice idea one day.'

Graham likes being in the park in the dark, when they turn on a laser beam which shines out from the Observatory, right along the meridian, sending a beam across London. He also likes the view from One Tree Hill, very popular with locals and regulars, and the Queen's Oak.

The Queen's Oak is a fallen tree, lying like a large dead whale behind a fence. Graham was thrilled recently to get a tree expert – a dendrologist – to come and examine samples. The dendrologist confirmed that the oak had been there since 1292. It had actually died in 1900, but continued to be supported by ivy. The hollow of the trunk may even have once been used as a cage for miscreants. Like other oaks bearing a monarch's name, it has its own legends. King Henry VIII and Elizabeth's mother Anne Boleyn are said to have danced around it in that narrow window when their relationship was happy.

Graham was standing near the Queen's Oak one day when a stranger came up to him and told him that one of his ancestors had lived in a lodge in the park. His ancestor had been a park keeper, until he committed suicide.

'He told me his name, Eaglestone, and I realised at once who his ancestor must have been – Rob Eaglestone, who died in 1848. His story has been handed down verbally through generations of Greenwich park keepers. He was supposed to deliver some Royal Park venison to Queen Victoria, but he didn't. He might well have been drunk. There were lots of rumours about his behaviour. Anyway, the queen called for him, in order to tell him off. He was so ashamed, couldn't bear the disgrace, so he killed himself.

'Isn't it amazing, these stories being passed on. It must have been handed down in his family, which is how this descendant knew it.'

Eaglestone's former home, Keeper's Cottage, was excavated by volunteers in 2014.

Graham loves all the history of the park, and was very pleased recently to have found what he thought was a piece of Roman pottery. It has now been identified as a Roman tile, which is much rarer. He has it on the shelf in his office.

He offered to take me to the site of an Anglo-Saxon cemetery, but we never got there – he was distracted along the way, insisting we look at the tennis court.

I didn't see much copy in a tennis court – from afar it

just looked like any other public tennis court – till Graham explained that the Meridian lines goes straight through the middle of it. It is marked with a blue painted line.

'One year, when Federer and Nadal were playing not far away at the O2, I thought what a good idea to have them play an exhibition game on our tennis court – one of them playing in the Western hemisphere, one in the East. They would serve the ball from West to East. I did try to make contact, but I was told they had no spare time.'

Next, Graham took me to the gardeners' yard, which at one time contained a large glass nursery. The chief executive of the Royal Parks had earlier told me about this – how the nurseries in the Royal Parks were being closed, leaving just one, in Hyde Park.

The Greenwich Park nursery had already been demolished. It has left a lot of spare space, which they were using that day to do recycling, using a monster machine, which crushed up old leaves, dead wood and plants. It then spreads it all out again in the park. These days, you don't want anything organic to get wasted.

I met Alan, the head gardener, who has a staff of twenty. He has been here for twenty years and has seen an enormous increase in litter.

'People are better educated in many ways today, more aware of their environment. Most people do put their rubbish in the bins provided. But what has happened recently is the arrival of firms like Deliveroo. People sit on benches, decide they would like something to eat, let's have a picnic, so, on their mobile they dial Deliveroo. A meal comes to them quite quickly, on a bike. We are a small park with good roads nearby and good paths inside the park. The meal gets delivered right to the seat where they are sitting.

'On a good day, when loads of people do that, the rubbish bins can't cope, even though we try to empty them all day long.

'When it's a sudden sunny day, there is an explosion of visitors. Instead of going off for the day to Brighton, as in the past, they come into the parks, especially our park. We have so many other local things they can see on the same day.

'We don't like having lorries trundling back and forward in the park all the time emptying the bins, but we have to. In the old days, on a nice weekend, we would pack up on Saturday and not deal with the litter till Monday morning. Now we can't leave it. There is too much.

'No one likes to see lorries in a park. It doesn't look good. Ideally, I would like to get rid of the lorries and use shire horses. Wouldn't that be lovely?'

Oh, they are such romantics, our modern park keepers. And they do all so love their jobs. I don't think I met one all year who complained about the work, about their bosses or even about their pay.

Graham drooled over the urban views from the top of the park, down across the river to Canary Wharf and Docklands.

'It has changed so much since I have been here. Every week the view is slightly different. I am constantly fascinated by it. There is something about the perspective – looking down a hill, across the river, and then up in the air at the skyscrapers. I can't explain it. It's not like looking at them on the flat. On the flat, you have to look up at them. But looking from another height, they stand up in front of you, as if they are closer than they really are.'

One of the advantages, nay joys, of getting to meet a park boss is that they will take you to see something which, even as a regular visitor, you might never see or realise was there. This time it was the Queen's Orchard, which is not marked on any of the maps I had. It is hidden away behind a brick wall in the bottom right-hand corner of the park, down near the Maritime Museum, tucked into a corner near the children's playground and the boating lake.

I laughed aloud when Graham proudly pointed out the boating lake, complete with little boathouse and a few little boats for hire. It was like something from a miniature village, a toy for the kiddies to play with.

Call that a lake, I said. Not exactly the Serpentine. It looks about the size of my back garden. He was rather hurt at my mockery, and explained that the little boating pond, like the tennis court, is crossed by the Greenwich Meridian, something I would never have known. So you can take out a little rowing boat and with a couple of strokes, go from East to West. Exciting – but I will save it for another day.

We walked past the boats, further along the boundary of the park, behind which I could see the gardens and outline of the Maritime Museum. It was like walking along a rural lane. We came to a door in the boundary wall. Graham got out his key to open it but, to his surprise, it was open already. So we went in.

Inside was a youngish woman gardener, working away. Graham introduced himself, saying he was the park manager. She said she was Alex, the new gardener, just started that day.

This ancient orchard behind the wall, about the size of a football pitch, had lain empty for some years. Greenwich

Council owned it, but had never really known what to do with it. They would never of course get permission to build on it – even from their own planning department. So they had recently offered it to Greenwich Park, thus enlarging the park for the first time in centuries, if only by a modest amount. But the Royal Parks did not have the staff or resources to bring it back to life and maintain it as a proper garden for visitors to enjoy.

'But some volunteers agreed to look after it. They have been working on it for over a year and they now plan to open it to the public, every year from about May to October. I didn't think it was open yet.'

And he hadn't met the new gardener, Alex, till that moment. She said she had yet to meet the volunteers, the ones who had done the main work of digging over and laying out the garden. She was formerly a gardener for Greenwich Council but was now employed out of the Park's gardening budget.

We left her to get on with her work while Graham and I walked round the garden, admiring what the volunteers had done so far, creating a sunken rose garden, new trellises and plants. It is a most attractive, hidden-away garden. In the years to come, I can see people coming in for a sit down and a quiet rest – perhaps those who look up at the steep hillside of Greenwich Park and think, hmm, can't manage to slog up all that, I'll just stay down here.

I wondered out loud to Graham how Alex would get on when she finally met the volunteers. Volunteers, from my observations, don't always take easily to being bossed around, and most of all, criticised, not when they are giving their time and labour for free. In all parks, the volunteer groups, the Friend of the Parks, the local Park Society, or whatever name they have, do splendid work and contribute so much to the good of their local park. But they do like praise and gratitude from the professionals. They can also be prone to disagreements, falling out among themselves or with the park officials. It is a delicate balance all round.

The days of the park superintendent as dictator, directing exactly which flower beds go where, and when and what grows where, have gone. Park managers have to be a mediator, listening to all opinions, all interest groups. These days, you need labour and financial support from the volunteer bodies and charities because of all the budget cuts. A sensible manager seeks their approval for almost everything they do. Parkies have to be diplomats. Would Alex cope?

We agreed that as a young modern woman, she would probably handle the volunteers well. An older gardener, male or female, who might be much more experienced, having seen it all, could be set in their ways and might ruffle a few feathers. A young, pleasant, smiley woman would get on well with all them.

Though what do I know? I am only a visitor, passing through another park.

I walked out of Greenwich Park, down the hill, passing the lovely bijou shops and restaurants, and the grand historic buildings, and waited for my Thames Clipper back to central London, which arrived just as I got there. That's the way to do it.

Best Things About Greenwich Park

1. Getting there by boat along the Thames from the middle of London to Greenwich Pier – a stunning experience, not to be missed.

2. All those magnificent buildings you see on arrival, now called the Royal Museums. Feast your eyes on the architecture and the history.

3. Wolfe statue on the top of the hill. A bit corny, as everyone hangs around there, taking snaps of themselves, but great views back towards London.

4. The Greenwich Meridian – equally corny snap, with one foot in the East and one foot in the West, but come on, the folks back home in Cincinnati or China will be well jel.

5. The Queen's Oak. Just a dead tree – you must have seen one before. But one that's been there since 1292? I thought not.

9

LONDON WETLAND CENTRE

It was wet in the Wetlands. I got soaked – the first time on any of my park walks so far, even in the depths of winter when I first started, that I had hit bad weather.

Howling wind and sweeping rain was interrupted by sudden, sneaky, suggestive flashes of bright sun, hinting at what might be round the corner, promising good times, which of course was a come-on, a tease, as the rain immediately came tumbling down again.

It was as if nature knew I was going to walk the Wetlands – let's make it really wet for him, a judgement for deciding to walk round a park which is unlike any other London park.

The London Wetland Centre is different in one vital way: you have to pay to enter. I wondered if that should perhaps exclude it from a book celebrating the glorious, wonderful, open public parks of London?

Then I thought, what is a park anyway? An oasis where the population can go and freely breathe? We would all agree with that definition, though it does not have to be totally green. Modern parks have cycle paths, playgrounds, skateparks, buildings, cafes and lots of attractions for the kiddies that are usually covered in concrete or tarmac.

Ideally a park is not just a green and open space, but broken up with woods, trees, water, possibly a stream and bridges or maybe a decent-sized lake, if the park is big enough. We all like to be able to gaze at water, it's so good for the soul, and perhaps get a boat out and row around it. Municipal parks, since the Victorian era, have traditionally had a boating lake, though it is not mandatory.

We also expect a park to have facilities – not just a nice bit of grass and a dash of water, but some sporting facilities, a playground, events and entertainments, shows and displays. And what about monuments to look at and cafes to sit down in and eat, which have nothing to do with nature? Modern park managers know they must provide a lot of that stuff, otherwise we visitors might never come back.

It must be open to all, not like say a private park, cut off from the public, available only to the posh people and their chums. They might call the grounds of their stately home a park, but we are not allowed to park ourselves there. It is a private park. We are talking public parks, where people can go whenever they like.

The London Wetland Centre scores well on almost all of those counts. There's lots to see and enjoy, which any park worth its name would appreciate – over 100 acres of water, trees, plants, wildlife and assorted, ever-so uplifting attractions. What's not to like?

But does the entry fee disqualify it from being a public park? I don't think so. It is public in the sense that it is open to the public all the time, as long as they pay.

It is not just a park that provides fun for the public and their kiddies. It has a meaning and a message. It likes to think it is helping to save the planet and, as such, it is probably the most uplifting, educational, environmentally worthwhile, right-on park in the whole of London.

The London Wetland Centre, as you might guess, is not a Victorian creation. Nor even a twentieth-century one. It is a twenty-first-century child, a modern park, opened for our delectation in 2000.

Given that it is so unusual and wonderful, it is strange that I was not aware of it until three years ago. I never even knew it existed until I was invited to a sales conference held there in 2017.

It was organised by a very famous publishing house, one that just happens to be the publisher of this very book – Simon & Schuster – and I was asked to address the gathering. There was an organised tour offered afterwards, but I had to rush off, so I never saw anything of the Wetland, except the conference room, which was very nice. And dry.

I suppose my ignorance of its existence these last twenty years is because it is in the depths of south-west London, somewhere near Barnes – wherever Barnes may be. We north Londoners, eh? At it again, imagining that anywhere south of the river is abroad.

Yet pop and rock's greatest figures once trailed to Barnes and its Olympic Sound Studios to make music history. The studios originally began in central London but moved to Barnes in 1966. Over the years, it has hosted Ella Fitzgerald, the Rolling Stones, the Who, David Bowie, Madonna, Prince, the Spice Girls, Queen and Jimi Hendrix. Soundtracks for iconic films including the first *Italian Job*, *The Rocky Horror Show* and *Jesus Christ Superstar* were cut there.

So many legends, including Led Zeppelin, were born in Barnes, and one died there – not in the studios but on a nearby road. That was Marc Bolan, who was killed when a purple Mini driven by his partner Gloria Jones crashed at dawn one September morning in 1977 as the pair returned to their Richmond home. Aged just twenty-nine, he had penned songs like 'Jeepster' and 'Ride a White Swan' and was known for his tousled hair and glam make up. The sycamore tree where the car came to rest is now festooned with memorabilia.

Bolan – real name Mark Feld – was so convinced he would die in a car crash that he never learned to drive.

The studio still exists, although not quite on the same scale, and now contains a cinema as well. But the memories live on.

To get to Barnes, I caught the Overground from Gospel Oak to Clapham Junction, a journey I now know well and always do with my little heart beating. It is the route I take when going to visit my girlfriend, which I do every week. Touch wood.

At Clapham Junction, I had to change to a local train. A few stops later and it was like idyllic countryside. Outside was all sleepy and quiet, while inside the train was practically empty, hardly more than one passenger per carriage, and mostly dozing.

Barnes turned out to be an impressively rural spot, with a village green that has its own pond. Traffic regularly gives way to swans as they plod across the roads. Barnes Common looked awfully pleasant, what I could see of it through the rain. There were lots of affluent-looking country-type houses and extensive playing fields, all well manicured. Several large vehicles went slowly past me, splashing up rain, with trailers behind carrying rowing boats, proper racing skiffs – eights, by the look of them. The Wetland Centre at Barnes is situated in a bend of the Thames where there is a lot of local rowing.

My contact at the Wetland Centre, Maria in marketing, had told me it was just a ten-minute walk from the station. It took me half an hour. I am a slow walker these days, since I had a new knee, but it was the lashing rain that slowed me down. I hate getting wet.

Originally, the London Wetland Centre consisted of four giant reservoirs, dating back to Victorian times, which by the end of the twentieth century were owned by Thames Water and had become surplus to requirements. There are photographs of the old reservoirs in the main entrance building and they look like reservoirs anywhere, stark and concrete, eerily empty and dead, as if they have landed from the moon. Each of them was rigidly rectangular, in a block, like adjoining monster washing-up bowls.

Enter Sir Peter Scott. Everybody of a certain age has heard of him: artist, naturalist and preservationist. His famous father, Robert Falcon Scott, is better known as Scott of the Antarctic, the leader of a doomed expedition to the South Pole. The legend must have loomed large for young Peter.

Already a national hero from previous exploits in Antarctica, Scott senior set out to conquer the South Pole, full of colonial confidence. But due to a series of blunders and quirks of fate, he was beaten there in 1911 by Norwegian Roald Amundsen, by a full thirty-four days. On the desperate trudge back to base, Scott and his men all perished, having written diaries and letters that would later inform the British public about the hopelessness of their plight. Scott was the last of his team to die, in the shelter of a flimsy tent pitched in the most inhospitable arena on earth, with his last written words being, 'For God's Sake, look after our people.' A shocked nation embraced him as an emblem of noble effort rather than infamous failure.

In 1948, a movie, *Scott of the Antarctic*, was made at Ealing Studios depicting the drama, with John Mills in the title role. It was probably the first film that ever had an effect on me. When it was shown in my school hall in 1950, at the end everyone cheered – or cried.

Peter Scott was born in 1909 and wasn't yet three when his

father died. In one of the last letters to his wife, Scott senior instructed her to 'make the boy interested in natural history if you can – it is better than sport'. One of his godfathers was J. M. Barrie, creator of Peter Pan.

Peter went to public school and Cambridge and turned out to be a *Boy's Own*-style hero – good at sports as well as jolly interested in nature, and also a very fine artist. In 1936, he represented Great Britain in the Olympic Games in Berlin, winning a bronze medal for sailing. Arguably, he was somewhat overshadowed by America's Jesse Owens, who single-handedly dismantled Hitler's theories on Aryan superiority by winning four gold medals and becoming an international icon. (Yet again, the Olympic Games seems to crop up somewhere, somehow, in almost every park.)

During the Second World War, Peter Scott was a naval hero, serving on destroyers in the North Atlantic and gunboats in the English Channel, picking up a clutch of bravery awards in the process. In 1945 he stood as a Tory candidate for Wembley North. It was not a good time to be a Tory candidate, as Labour won by a landslide. He then turned his energy to painting and protecting wildlife, creating the Severn Wildfowl Trust. In his younger years, he had mostly been interested in seeing geese through the barrel of a gun. That changed even before the outbreak of war. Despite the depravations of the immediate post-war period, he established a nature reserve at Slimbridge in Gloucestershire in 1946, the parent of the Wetland Centre at Barnes. He also turned to broadcasting, fronting lots of nature programmes for the BBC. In the 1950s and '60s, he was as well known and admired for these as David Attenborough is today.

Today, he is most remembered for helping to found the World Wide Fund for Nature. The panda that signifies the WWF – that was his work, produced in 1961. Thanks in many ways to his work, the globe now realises how we all have to care for and conserve all forms nature and wildlife. If all of this wasn't enough, he was also a champion glider. This bold pioneer and polymath died in 1989, aged almost eighty.

At the entrance to the Wetland Centre in Barnes, there is a large statue of him, plonked in a stretch of water and some reeds. Before he died, Peter Scott had heard of the empty reservoirs in Barnes and immediately thought how it would make a perfect wetland natural reserve. It would not be as big as Slimbridge, which is some nine times larger, but for Scott it wasn't the size that mattered.

He had long had an ambition to create a wetlands environment somewhere near London, for the 20 million folks living in and around the London area. He wanted the Metropolitan masses and their children to learn about nature and conservation without first having to travel to the West Country.

In 1989 he did a painting of the London Wetland Centre – eleven years before it opened to the public. The landscape looks pretty much as it does today. The big difference is that in the far distance, in the painting, you can't pick out the Shard and the London Eye as you can today – if it is not raining and if you put on your best specs.

Slimbridge has spawned many similar wetlands sites around the UK. There are now ten – in England, Scotland, Wales and Northern Ireland, plus several abroad.

It is of course a charity. It is not local council sponsored or funded, hence it has to charge an entrance fee in order to finance all its numerous worthy works. Entrance is not cheap but you can get an annual membership, as many locals do, which allows you to come in every day, all the year round.

Each year they attract around 165,000 visitors. It was higher a few years ago, when it first opened. Now it has settled down. Seven per cent of all visits are by school parties. I could hear them before I could see them, rushing along the paths, dashing into the hides, overexcited. There are forty permanent staff and about 200 volunteers.

I met two of the staff members who have been here from the beginning. In fact they each arrived in the late 1990s, before the site had officially opened. They remembered the work that went on breaking up the concrete reservoirs, replacing all the soil, cleaning all the water and creating paths and islands. All the soil had to be recycled, for fear of pollution from the leftover Victorian stagnant sludge and debris. Over 300,000 plants and 27,000 trees were planted.

The total cost came to around £15 million, which came from various sources. One of them was the house builder Berkeley Homes, who got to build on some of the nearby land around the reservoir that wasn't needed by the Slimbridge people for their new wetlands.

You can look out at practically the whole site from viewing windows in the main building, getting a bird's-eye view of it all. It's hard to appreciate now that until relatively recently it was a man-made, concrete reservoir. It looks so natural, all the reedy waterways and rippling lakes, buzzing with wildlife. It reminded me of Botswana and the Okavango Delta, on a titchy scale, of course. The Okavango Delta, when the annual floods come and the whole delta comes to life, covers about

20,000 square miles and turns into a lush and vast animal habitat. Boats are needed to navigate the waters to avoid the hippos, elephants and crocs. On the sprawling grassy plains and scrubland there are leopards, giraffes, lions and rhinos. Can Barnes compete with all that? We shall see.

The first of the two long-time staff I met was Adam Salmon, the reserve manager. He comes from the West Country and was on the dole when he first volunteered as a helper at Slimbridge. He worked for the RSPB before moving to London when the Barnes Wetland was being created.

I tried to avoid making any corny remarks about his surname being apt for someone working in wildlife. He must have heard them a million times. 'King of the Fish, that's what my name represents.' These days he is king of ducks, of all sorts, and their habitat.

Reserve manager does not mean he runs the staff's reserve football team but looks after all the parts of the wetlands which are not buildings – in other words, not the visitor centre, lecture rooms, conference rooms, restaurant or observatories. His job is to protect and conserve the native birds and all the seasonal feathered visitors.

Looking back over the twenty years or so since he arrived, when they were first working on establishing the site, he wishes they had not planted so many trees. That was a mistake. The trees have grown too well, and too quickly. Wildfowl need grasses, which can support insects, not trees. They now find themselves doing regular coppicing, to give the grasses a better chance.

The water for the Wetland Centre still comes from the Thames, through a pipe which drew river water from

Hampton, upstream. At the pipe's end is a small grille, to make sure only the titchiest fish ever go through. Today the titchy fish which have got in have multiplied and grown, often turning into 4-feet-long pike and whopping eels.

Around 70 per cent of the site is watery, but fishing is not allowed, and neither of course is boating. The Wetland Centre is not a human recreational or sporting park. That would disturb the thousands of wildfowl who have made it their home.

One of the crosses Adam has to bear is New Zealand pigmyweed. Sounds nasty. It's also known as Australian swamp stonecrop and, back in the 1970s, it was freely sold as an oxygenating plant. It's anything but, as it grows in a dense mat to the exclusion of all else. He says it is currently spreading everywhere, all over the country. It is now banned from sale, but there's no way of eradicating its suffocating mass once it has arrived and established itself in the muddy margins.

His other pain in the arse is the Canada geese, the black-necked, white-cheeked birds that arrived from North America a few centuries back and are now widely considered a pest. I am not a bird fan – can't really tell one bird from another – but I do know a Canada goose when I see one. They used to arrive each year near our Lakeland house at Loweswater, massive flocks of huge, ugly, strident honkers that waddle around as if they own the place, scaring away all the little native birds from their regular feeding grounds. Having stuffed their faces, the geese then shit all over the place – horrible, smelly shit which stank long after they had grown bored and flown off, doubtless to cause havoc at another waterhole.

Like every good bird lover should, Adam tried to defend them. He explained that their poo is in fact full of nutrients.

The only problem is that at the Wetland Centre, it is not the sort of nutrient that encourages the sort of grasses which the wildfowl need and like.

Another pesky foreign visitor that can make its presence felt is the American mink. First introduced to Britain in the late 1920s to stock fur farms, they had gone rogue by the mid-1950s, making life very uncomfortable for the water vole, which of course all naturalists and children love. In Kenneth Grahame's *The Wind in the Willows*, Ratty is in fact a water vole. (For reference, there's no such thing as a water rat: there are brown rats, black rats and water voles. You can distinguish the water vole because alone of the trio it has a furry tail.) The Wetland Centre has had a long struggle to protect our sweet little water voles from the American minks, but hurrah, they now have quite a decent colony. Water voles are shy, hard-to-see creatures, presenting quite the challenge to visitors who yearn to observe them.

That can't be said of two other Wetland residents, who are probably the talking point among most who come to the centre. Todd and Honey are affable Asian short-clawed otters who are resident in one of the centre's fenced-off ponds. At feeding times they both make an appearance, doing laps of their enclosure alongside some graceful flip turns in the water, on account of their bendy spines and rudder-like tails. Todd, the male otter, is perpetually busy, dashing from pond to pipe and back, while partner Honey makes more sedate progress. They won't reproduce as Honey has a contraceptive implant. Still, Todd obviously cherishes Honey and passes her food so she doesn't miss out. Between them they talk using a dozen or so different calls signs, including whistling. Most of their diet is unfilleted fish; their strong jaws cope with skin and bone, no problem.

But there's a third person in the relationship, and that's Bob the heron. He turns up every feeding time to snatch some of the grub. Every so often Todd becomes a bit proprietorial and swims threateningly close to Bob's long legs. There's an audible clack of the beak as Bob lashes out. He's not one of the official Wetland residents, more a chancer who turns up in the hope of an easy meal. He makes himself scarce between feeding times.

Just forty years ago, (European) otters were on the brink of extinction in the UK, thanks to hunting and a too-liberal use of pesticides. Happily, their population has expanded and they can now be found across most of the nation, a tribute to the cleanliness of today's waterways. But in the wild they are timid, rarely seen creatures. If you see something that looks like an otter, it's more likely to be the brash mink, darker in colour and narrower of face.

Richard Bullock is the other long-term naturalist I talked to – yes, another vaguely apposite surname for someone working with wildlife. How does it happen so often? Richard is a trained scientist, who read biology and geography at Bristol and is the Wetland's biodiversity officer. I began by asking him how many birds were on the site. Turned out there was no straightforward answer. Did I mean different species or total numbers? And did I mean now or in the middle of the winter? Like human tourists, they all have their seasons.

Of the wild species, they probably have up to 150 different species, the ones which arrive at some point during the year. Of the native breeds, which live here full time, there are forty-three different species. As for total numbers, on any one day there are probably up to a few thousand birds, fluttering, flying or sashaying around, minding their own business, ignoring all the prying eyes and the high-class binoculars.

Most of them are ducks, some diving, some dabbling, which did not sound all that exciting to me, but a number are rare and exotic, if not to say downright strange. Take the small-headed southern screamer, so named because its territorial call can be heard two miles away. The fulvous whistling duck is a paragon of the age, with the males doing most of the egg incubation and duckling care and couples staying faithful to their partners for many years. Bare-faced Muscovy ducks were once kept as pets by native South Americans because they hoovered up insects that invaded rudimentary homes. Female shelducks are blessed not only by a dusky laugh but also with the crèche facilities their community establishes for ducklings.

Ponder for a moment the eider duck, bizarrely the heaviest and, at the same time, the fastest duck in the UK, travelling up to 70 mph at full pelt. That's thanks to its very particular breast-bone shape. Most of us encounter eider in our duvets, rather than in their natural home, on the shoreline. That's because mother ducks pluck warm, light, fleecy down from their bodies to make nests for their young. Threads rather than feathers, it is this that lands up in bed coverings, with forty nests' worth sufficient for just one duvet. In Iceland, farmers cash in by selling the empty nests. But the birds that have given up their down live on, as farmers are all too aware that a mother eider disturbed too soon will discharge a ghastly brown oil on her nest, ruining it. Perhaps the best thing about the eider ducks – titter ye not – is that one of their calls sounds like ooh-err comedian Frankie Howerd.

Then there were the entertaining Egyptian geese that untied the shoelaces of a fellow visitor while foraging around his trouser legs for food.

I wrote down the names of other ducks, which until that day I had never known existed, such as – let me see, where are my notes? – a gadwall, wigeon, Laysan, Javan whistling, falcated and ferruginous ducks alongside canvasbacks, red-crested pochards, Puna teals, garganeys and red shovelers.

The bird population totals can vary not just with the seasons but with the times of each day; it can, for example, depend on the tides. When the nearby Thames, which of course is a tidal river, is low, more gulls arrive locally, looking out for lunch on the mud flats.

There is one man-made irritation that makes life hard for the staff trying to care for and cultivate bird life, and that is the noise of aeroplanes and helicopters. The Wetland Centre is not twenty miles from Heathrow, where there are some 1,300 take-offs and landings each day. Although the airport itself seeks to minimise disruption by alternating the use of its runways, there's still inevitable interference from the metal birds. Low-flying helicopters have also become a menace and, more recently, so have remote-controlled drones.

Birds like peace and quiet, as we all do, but they are more easily disturbed than humans, getting in a flutter when approached, rising up and flying away. Consequently all visitors to the Wetland are advised to keep as quiet as possible so as not alarm any of the wildlife. 'Keep quiet – birds have ears too,' warns one of the many signs around the lakes.

This is why you can't get access to any of the larger lakes or land on any of the islands. You have to stick to the viewing stations, which are scattered around the edges of the lakes and ponds.

No dogs allowed, of course, unlike normal parks, nor bicycles – lucky Wetland managers. That is one running aggravation they don't have to cope with – the constant tension in all normal parks between dogs, bikes and walkers.

There is a security fence all the way round, in case you were thinking of trying to creep in for free. It means that rough sleepers are also not a problem. Not many rough sleepers can afford £13.40 to come in for a kip.

Visitors are not allowed to touch any of the birds or pick any flowers, though all children are desperate to do both. Anyone transgressing is carefully informed of the reasons. It is patiently explained what happens if you pick a rare orchid, for example, which the staff has worked so hard to establish. Dead, that's what happens – unlikely ever to seed and reproduce.

But what about common daisies and buttercups, which young children have traditionally picked for years with no apparent harm to the species, in order to make daisy chains or check if they like butter? Surely buttercups and daisies are not likely to become endangered species? I asked Richard Bullock, one of my two managerial friends, what he thought.

He admitted that some nature reservists are now having second thoughts about banning the picking of all daisies and buttercups. Some now allow it, in moderation. Richard is still on the side of caution and is of the opinion that daisies and buttercups should not be over-picked, whatever the temptation.

In the Wetland Centre, you are not allowed either to pick leaves or berries, or of course feed the birds. That means you don't have to address the thorny issue of whether or not to feed bread to the ducks. (No, because it stops them having a balanced diet or yes, because there's not enough food in the wild.) Here it's simply a no-go.

The whole purpose of the Wetland Centre, which distinguishes it from all other London parks, is conservation and education. The WWT is devoted to the care of wildfowl, native or otherwise, and at the same time strives to teach us to protect all wildlife, for future generations to come, not to harm or destroy it by our wicked human ways and selfishness. This was a message Peter Scott worked out for himself in 1946, when he was very firmly gamekeeper rather than poacher, so to speak. For many years he was looked upon as fairly eccentric, but now the whole world is trying to protect the planet – from ourselves.

The WWT is proud to have a global outreach, with members from as far away as China, who follow all developments and new wildlife arrivals, read all the reports and make annual expeditions to the site. Not all the work of the WWT takes place in Britain, either. It's been instrumental in bringing up numbers of the struggling Madagascan pochard to sustainable levels. Once thought extinct, a tiny colony of twenty was discovered in the Madagascan wetlands in 2006. In association with other conservationists, the WWT collected eggs which were then hatched in a hotel bathroom. At one point a quarter of the world's population – seven chicks – were living in a cardboard box with a plastic ice-cream tub for a swimming pool and balled-up socks as playmates. Later, all that was replaced by a proper breeding facility and now there are more than 100 'Mad Poch' ducks living in and around it.

A shining success story, illustrating the ethos at the heart of everything done by the WWT. Of course, it does have to make money. That involves providing some sort of entertainment as well as education for the visitors, especially the younger ones. Hence they have a playground, cafe, fun events and large souvenir shop.

I walked for a while with Richard along the path beside the main lake. A rather handsome, stocky fellow with a brightly coloured neck, possibly some sort of goose, preened itself on a fence, staring at me, superciliously. I got busy trying to take a selfie with it on my mobile phone, but the rain was still ruining visibility and the goose wandered off.

There was a lot of squawking and squeaking and fluttering of wings from inside a roped-off compound known as the Tundra. Richard explained it was a red-breasted goose telling off a mallard.

I enjoyed seeing some amazing displays of fine feathers, colourful wings and haughty necks, all quite splendid, though I would never have known what they were had they not provided notices.

I stopped to admire a spur-winged goose, which looked a bit fearsome, and apparently in the wild it can be. They feed on certain poisonous insects and it has a spur from which poison can be passed on to humans if you touch it.

I did not see any of the eight species of bat that live in the Wetland Centre, although it's hard not to be pleased on behalf of Daubenton's bat, which likes to live and feed over water. What a paradise.

Still, all this fascinating information and the sighting of unusual species did rather go above my head. I can get excited in parks by their monuments, buildings, construction, desperate to know their history. I get uplifted by lakes and views, hills and woods, and of course always excited by talking to people. An interest in animals and wildlife, alas, has passed me by. When my children were young, we would never let them have a dog or a cat, though they longed for one.

When our first two were aged six and eight, we were driving up to the Lake District when I informed them that something exciting was going to happen to the family.

'A dog,' said Caitlin. 'I want a dog!'

'A cat,' said Jake. 'I do hope we have a cat.'

The answer was another child. We had just discovered that my wife was pregnant with Flora.

We did get a tortoise for them, which is still alive, now fifty years old, and a huge attraction. And I love her dearly. See, I can be an animal lover. Whenever visitors are in our garden, out she trundles. She is now an endangered species. Pet shops can't sell them any more. In fact there are tortoise burglars in our area – they sneak into back gardens and steal them.

Our children are now grown up. You can guess what Caitlin and Jake did when they had their own children. Yep, got a dog – and a cat.

The Wetland Centre does not of course have any tortoises, as they are not exactly wildfowl. Neither do they have any wild rabbits, which surprised me. Almost 100 acres of grass, trees, plants and water, most of it out of bounds and human-free, yet no rabbits. Apparently there are none next door, either, on Barnes Common, though in Richmond Park, not all that far away, there are loads of rabbits.

Once there were some Highland cattle in the Wetland, but

they have now changed to Dexter cows, which are smaller and more adaptable. These are bovine eco-warriors, eating the grass to just the right length for wetland birds to graze. Their dung becomes dinner for the bats, so they serve a double purpose. Isn't nature clever? Even I admit that.

The Wetland Centre is lovely for all locals who want a quiet walk with no bikes or dogs or noisy attractions, but of course the most enthusiastic visitors are birdwatchers, or twitchers, as they are normally called. They flock here from all parts of the country and the globe – just like birds, in fact.

Whenever something unusual makes an appearance, which they hear about instantly on the relevant websites or by word of mouth, they rush here hoping to spot it, to bag it for their collection, like trainspotters. This I can understand, having the collecting instinct myself. In fact I have twenty different collections. I get such pleasure in hunting down new items, studying them, learning from them, caressing them, then filing them away and very often forgetting where I have put them – which means I often buy stuff I already have. So stupid and wasteful.

The Wetland Centre is so popular with twitchers everywhere that it has bagged many prizes and awards. According to the Wetland staff, however, there has been a rise in recent years of regular visitors who are not necessarily ardent birdwatchers, who do not come solely to spot birds. What they come for is well-being and happiness.

They have been given a name – sensualists, here for peace and quiet, that's all. People come to commune with nature and their own thoughts and don't want to be disturbed by other people. Many people use parks to exercise their bodies.

Sensualists use the Wetland Centre to calm their minds. They don't do much walking. They are simply being there, sitting, soaking it all up.

I came across six hides as I walked round the Wetland, which does not take long, as you are restricted to their paths. Mostly you have to watch the wildlife behind fenced areas, though they do wander all over the paths, unable of course to read the notices. In these hides you can sit with your thoughts, or your binoculars if you really want to do some heavy-duty twitching.

I used to have a hide in my fields in the Lake District. Well, what I called a hide. I created it out of a ruined dry-stone wall, building it up again, putting branches on the top, leaving a little peephole from which you could look out and not be seen, handy for spotting red squirrels, deer, rabbits and foxes. My grandchildren loved it, though not as much as they loved my treehouse. The peephole in the hide was mostly used by me, to spot anyone coming to the front door of my house whom I did not want to see. So I was able to hide in the hide.

At the Wetland Centre, the hides are super hides, proper constructions, with all mod cons like electricity and visual displays. Their biggest hide, the Peacock Tower, is three storeys high, a city skyscraper of a hide. It has even got a lift, amazingly, to take those not quite active enough, or to carry heavy equipment, up to the top storey to get an even better view of all the Wetland.

I do tend to use lifts instead of stairs these days, since I had a new knee, which stiffens up on stairs, whereas I can walk on the flat for miles. There was a long queue for the Peacock Tower lift when I approached it, so I headed for another hide, the Headley Discovery Hide, named after one of their sponsors.

It was large and spacious, like a high-class cricket pavilion, facing onto the main lake. Inside there were display units and a long wooden shelf at window height for humans who wanted to perch there.

It was totally silent and seemed entirely empty. I had not seen at first that two people were already there. A woman in a woolly bobble hat was sitting looking out of the window, while further along, about ten yards away, a man was also sitting. Each was motionless, looking out, staring out, at nothing as far as I could see, registering nothing, as if looking inwards, not outwards.

The woman had a pair of binoculars on her lap, but did not appear to be using them. The man had no binoculars. He could have been dead, or a dummy, a statue plonked there years ago and forgotten. Perhaps a human scarecrow, to scare off the more daring wildlife from getting too near.

I did not realise for a while that they were together, a couple. They were seated so far apart, the better, I assumed, to be alone with whatever sensual or visual or mental thoughts and delights they were experiencing.

I observed them quietly for a while, trying to work out if in fact they were observing something out there that I could not see or understand. Then I edged a bit nearer to them, to follow their gaze. I had not wanted to disturb their quasi-religious communing, but my movement had caused the man to turn, suddenly aware of my presence. I coughed, said hello, sorry to intrude, could I ask if you come here often?

The woman turned and stared at me, eyes blank. She did

not appear upset that I had interrupted her idyll, just confused by the strange being that had suddenly appeared in her vision who was clearly not a duck or goose. She stared a bit longer, but said nothing. Then she returned to her silent observations.

The man, however, did take in my presence and eventually said yes, they did come here often. They had come from Sutton in Surrey, an hour away. They came three days a week, staying for around three hours each time. Now that they were retired, transport was free, so they could come and go any time. They often went to the Wetland at Arundel – one of the Wetland empire – but preferred the London Wetland.

So they were keen twitchers?

'Not really. I am a birdwatcher,' said the man. 'My wife is a twitcher. You don't have to pass an exam to be a twitcher, or get a certificate, you just call yourself one. But if there was a test, she would pass with flying colours.'

She looked at me, still a bit confused by my presence, then picked up her binoculars and turned away to look at something.

They were not in a birdwatching club, so he continued, nor ever came in parties or ever went on guided tours of the Wetland. They preferred to come on their own, and sit in this hide. It was always quiet. Perfect for just looking.

'We never go in the Peacock hide. It gets full of clubs. You can't get moving for their tripods. This is always quiet. We are usually alone at this time of day.'

He looked at me, half smiling, half accusing, as if suggesting I was ruining their lone communion, but really, he did not mind.

'She's a very good twitcher,' he continued. 'Knows a lot, but she doesn't show off, not like male twitchers. You hear a male twitcher boasting, "I have just seen a jack snipe." Another male twitcher will say to him, "You idiot, don't you realise that is a common snipe?" And so these twitchers twitter on, arguing with each other, showing off.

'Twitching for men is a competitive sport. Females are much better behaved.'

(For the record, common snipe are, well, common, with long bills used in a sewing-machine action when they feed. Jack snipe are smaller and rarer.)

His wife turned round and gave a half smile to show she had been listening, despite looking through her binocs.

He explained that he always just stared generally, at the birds and at the scenery, towards the horizon and the sky, not looking at anything in particular, or trying to identify what was out there. That was what made him a birdwatcher, not a twitcher.

'The thing about twitching, or even just birdwatching like me, is that people who don't do it can't understand why on earth you do it. We find it relaxing, peaceful, soothing, and hypnotic.

'When you are watching TV at home, or looking at anything close up, you are using both eyes, so a lot more of your brain is active and involved. When you are looking out at ducks on the water, they are far away. So you are really looking at infinity. And when you look at infinity, what do you do? You can relax, your brain turns off. It is very soothing. So much so that I often nod off. It's only later I find I have been asleep.

'But she is always watching. She once came sixteen days in

a row. Sixteen days! She says she found something different to look at every time.'

She looked rather pleased at this praise, if praise it was. I asked if she brought food with her.

'Oh yes, I always bring a little picnic for us,' she said. 'We eat it here, while we are watching.' Then she went back to her binocs.

I asked what he did before he retired. 'I was a BT manager,' he said, blankly. Then he smiled, as if waiting for me to enquire more, ask him what he managed.

I really wanted to know if they had children, and what they might think, but it seemed a bit pushy to ask too many personal questions. I apologised for disturbing them, and thanked him for his wisdom and observations.

Then I went out into the rain and made my way to Barnes railway station, heading for home. By which time I was totally soaked.

But I had had an experience of a park with a purpose, unlike every other park I had visited. And I had met a philosopher . . .

Best Things About the London Wetland Centre

1. The hides, all six of them, plus an observatory, are well-appointed, five-star hides, especially the Peacock Tower, which even has a lift.

2. The peace and quiet, to stroll and stare and ponder, without fear of being run over by a bike or having to listen to dog walkers shouting at their stupid dogs, or each other. They don't allow dogs or bikes – or shouters.

3. The wildlife; obviously, that is the purpose, especially all the ducks and geese. Even if you can't recognise a Madagascan pochard from a McDonalds hamburger, you can read the signs and then boast about it afterwards.

4. For twitchers, it is heavenly; so much to see, so much to fit in, ever changing, ever interesting – one life is not really long enough to know it all.

5. A warm glow, which is almost guaranteed, because you are doing something educational from which you will learn, and something worthwhile, supporting the care and conservation of the planet. Thank you.

10

RICHMOND PARK

Richmond Park is countryside. I don't mean wild countryside, like the Highlands of Scotland, where you can see nothing or nobody for scores of miles, where you can imagine you are the last inhabitant on earth. Richmond Park is after all just ten miles from the centre of London and, although it sits lofty above the nearby town, it is on the whole fairly flat. From most parts you can spot urban life in the far distance – tower blocks and London skyscrapers or, in the nearer distance, posh houses on the banks of the Thames.

But because Richmond Park is so enormous, covering 2,500 acres and measuring two and a half miles across, you do feel you are cut off, away from all that built-up stuff, somewhere cared for and loved despite its wildness – possibly the Cotswolds. So nothing too unkempt, then, or scary, or with people or things which might frighten the horses.

Richmond Park does have lots of folks riding horses, which gives it that Home Counties feel. Inside the park there are four handsome homes, three having evolved from sedate residences to more modern uses. The views are stunning, especially of the river. There is a feeling of affluence and safety.

How can anything nasty ever happen here? It is easy to believe it when they say there are no muggers or flashers lurking in Richmond Park, and no signs of the homeless hanging around, unlike in so many of the inner London parks. It must be about the safest open space anywhere near London, considering its size. At least that's what they say. Can this be true? Or is it all an illusion?

I came out of Richmond railway station and walked down the lovely bijou streets towards the park. You pass one end of Richmond Bridge, a five-span construction in Portland stone completed in 1777 and now the oldest-surviving Thames crossing in London. Then it's a case of climbing Richmond Hill, and finally looking down upon the vast sweep of the meandering Thames, with silent scullers gracefully cutting through the water.

So many people of taste and discernment over the decades have exclaimed in delight: 'Yeah, I could live here, this is lovely, this is like being, well in the countryside, but with all the restaurants, delis and pretty houses.'

It does of course need people with a few bob in their pocket to afford the best houses on Richmond Hill and bag those stunning views, hence locals have included TV and film stars like David Attenborough, Richard E. Grant and actor John Mills and his family, as well as mature pop stars like Pete Townshend and Mick Jagger, who lived there for a long time while married to Jerry Hall. She still has the house.

Even at Richmond Gate, the entrance to the park, the neighbourhood's sense of grandeur is endorsed by the large and imposing Star and Garter building, once a famous hotel which was visited by Queen Victoria, Dickens and Napoleon II. In 1916 the hotel was bought to provide 'a permanent haven' for the young men who were being disabled in their droves during the battles of the First World War. It quickly reached capacity, with both staff and patients struggling to combat the idiosyncrasies of hotel design. When the war ended, the hotel was torn down and replaced with a neoclassical mansion designed by Sir Edwin Cooper, who was also behind Hull's Guildhall, Marylebone Town Hall and the Lloyd's office in Leadenhall Street, London. The hospital was opened in 1924 by King George V and Queen Mary.

Last time I had visited Richmond Park it was still a

hospital, but in 2013 it finally closed. The very day I arrived in Richmond for my walk, the London *Evening Standard* had a whole-page story about one of the flats in the building being sold for £7 million – wow. Developers had taken it over and finally created eighty-six luxury flats. This particular flat has six bedrooms and a fab of view of the Thames – a view that was listed by an Act of Parliament in 1902 which protects the land on Richmond Hill from new development. The very same vista inspired painters Joshua Reynolds in 1780, J. M. W. Turner in 1819 and the poet Wordsworth in 1820.

Deer are the park's best-known and biggest wildlife attraction, resident since the seventeenth century. There are currently two types: around 350 fallow deer and 300 red deer. Fallow deer were introduced to Britain by the Normans, but are now the most widespread species of deer in the UK. Fallow deer are usually spotted and normally come in shades of chestnut, though they can range from white – a true colour, not albino – to dark brown. A fallow deer family consists of a buck, a doe and the fawns. Although there were fallow deer here in Roman times, today's population descends from medieval imports from the eastern Mediterranean. Substantially bigger, red deer are indigenous to Britain and are the country's largest land mammals. In a family group they are known as stags, hinds and calves.

All the males have antlers from their second year, which they shed every year around March or April. Fallow deer antlers are shaped something like a human palm, while red deer antlers extend with age in a series of points. Locals keep an eye out for the antlers falling to take as souvenirs, but it's a race against time. If fallen antlers get collected by the parkies, they are sold.

Thanks to the deer, trees in the park are very specifically

shaped by a browse line, with bottom leaves and branches squared off, having been neatly nibbled. Their grazing also keeps the grassland in trim.

If you've ever wondered which Richmond came first, Richmond in Surrey or Richmond in Yorkshire, it's the northern settlement that wins. Hurrah. We northerners have to stick up for ourselves. Surrey's Richmond was christened by Henry VII when he rebuilt a manor house there in 1497, naming it for his existing earldom in Yorkshire. That manor house became Richmond Palace and was home to a young Henry VIII and, later, two of his six wives. Queen Elizabeth I died there. The proximity of the palace was key to the creation of Richmond Park. Charles I retreated to Richmond in 1625 to avoid an outbreak of the plague in London. A dozen years later he enclosed land, including some of the finest medieval forest remaining in the country, with a wall measuring eight miles in length, to provide a convenient hunting ground between royal palaces at Richmond and Hampton Court.

There was a lot of discontent at what the king called 'New Park', as local people had previously wandered freely there. So the king built six entrances into the park, allowing them to walk through at will. Although considerate to his subjects on this score, this one generous act wasn't enough to prevent his execution in 1649.

Richmond Palace fell into ruin after the English Civil War, although Charles II later renovated part of it for his French mother, Henrietta Maria. The park fared altogether better than the palace as it continued as a popular hunting ground among the great and the good. As they preferred to hunt in private, new rules were imposed down the decades that barred increasing numbers of people. Everything finally came to a head when one Princess Amelia, second daughter of George II, shut the gates to anyone whom she didn't call a friend.

Resentment grew until Richmond brewer John Lewis contrived a showdown at one of the gates, leading to a court case that started in 1755. Three years and a lot of litigation later, he won the action and, thanks to him, ladder stiles were installed over the park walls that meant pedestrians had guaranteed access once more and the stiles remained there until the early 1880s. Carriages needed specially issued tickets for another century, though, until the Crown Lands Act of 1851 ensured full public access.

I thought I would start at the centre of things. At the heart of the park are the Pen Ponds, both built in the eighteenth century – one for anglers, the other for model boats. The last documented evidence of ice skating on Pen Ponds was in 1962. Today, the ponds provide an environment that's strictly for the birds, including a sixteen-year-old arthritic cob swan, whose ungainly waddle on land causes consternation among visitors, although he can swim with ease and grace, like a bird half his age.

The derivation of the ponds' name is not clear. Some think it is because together they are roughly the shape of an old-fashioned fountain-pen nib. Another theory is that they were originally sheep pens, which sounds more likely. The setting is the sort of flat, barren open space where you often find sheep pens, handy for herding large numbers together. Although man-made, the ponds are fed by a stream. I found the Pen Ponds a bit grim and windswept, even on a fairly nice autumn day. When I met a woman walking beside them with her dog, I happened to say as much.

'Oh, you want pretty ponds, do you?' she snorted with contempt. I agreed some of the ponds in the other Royal Parks could be rather twee, such as the one in Hyde Park, but I said I liked the Hampstead Heath ponds for their greenery and interesting shapes.

On Hampstead Heath, you rarely meet lone women, with or without prams, wandering off the beaten track. They stick to the popular, populated paths. Here quite a few women seem to walk alone, sometimes with prams, miles from anywhere. Good for them. I chatted to one woman and asked if she felt safe in Richmond Park. She said certainly, that was one reason she came. Back in Hackney, she would be scared to walk alone in her local parks. So the park's priceless reputation for security seemed justified.

One place I remembered clearly from a previous visit was the Isabella Plantation. I was stunned by it, coming across it by accident years ago. It is not far from Ladderstile Gate, the scene of John Lewis's triumph, but it's easy to miss. And yet it is huge, a park within a park, at 42 acres almost the size of St James's Park.

At the main entrance of the Plantation are some very handsome wrought-iron gates, which lead you to some neatly laid-out paths and well-cared-for trees and bushes. (Without the fences enclosing the area, all this would be just so much deer fodder.) The word plantation has connotations of the slave economy, which of course was still booming when this part of the park was created by Lord Sidmouth in 1831. Sidmouth chose oaks, beeches and sweet chestnuts to stock this newly defined area, along with shrubs from across the globe. Later it was left to become a more natural wood. In the 1950s, the then superintendent George Thomson opened up the wilder bits, created grassy clearings and introduced three ponds and streams, each fed from the Pen Ponds, which are outside the Plantation but not far away.

Spring is the time to see the Isabella Plantation spring into colour. There is a particularly fine collection of Japanese azalea, rhododendrons, acers, gunnera, dogwoods, tulip trees, magnolia and camellia. But it's the azaleas that offer up the most dazzling display, especially around the three ponds – Peg's, Thomson's and Still – whose shimmering water reflect back colours, soft and vivid. In April and May, when they are all in full bloom, you can hardly get moving for azalea fanatics, all with their cameras and movie equipment.

There was just one snapper there on the day I visited. Naturally I said hello, keen to hear where he was from, learn which were his top five azaleas, possibly get his whole life story. He totally ignored me. Well, that happens. He was too preoccupied making infinitesimal alterations to his lenses and minor adjustments to his tripod.

A man using walking poles was more forthcoming. He said he tries to visit the Isabella Plantation every day, all year round. Now that he is not as fit as he was, he often takes the minibus to the park, which runs from the Roehampton estates on Wednesdays in the summer. It goes around the park, he said, so you can pop off and catch it later. The bus service must be a great asset to people in Roehampton, where there are high-rise blocks, in contrast to quaint Richmond. When the minibus is not running, he sometimes drives himself to the park, and parks in one of the car parks.

There's no mystery why photographers or walkers flock to the Isabella Plantation, but no one is certain how the place got its name. Was it inspired by the thirteenth-century Isabella, fourth child of King John, who went on to become the Holy Roman Empress? Or was a French-born Isabella, dubbed the She-Wolf of France, who deposed her husband King Edward II – later murdered at Berkeley Castle in Gloucestershire – the inspiration? Then there was Isabella of Spain, patron of Christopher Columbus's explorations, as well as the later Isabella, Queen of the Spanish Netherlands. The last two are perhaps more significant, thanks to a colour known as Isabelline, which is like the hue of grey-yellow parchment … or the colour of grubby underwear. The Spanish Isabella was said to bathe just twice a year while in the Netherlands. The second Isabella pledged not to change her drawers until the end of the Siege of Orléans that began in 1601, without realising it would be a full three years before that spat ended. No one knows if the soil colour is really 'soiled' colour, and it probably doesn't bear further scrutiny.

When I had last properly visited the Isabella Plantation, in 1983, there were seven designated gardeners working there full time, but at that period they were still creating new views and clearings and ponds. Today there are five gardeners and an apprentice, employed through a contractor.

The Plantation is stunning, so well cared for, with many artistic vistas. It is really an open-air theatre, created for us to experience nature at its best. I think I would put it in my top ten of memorable places to visit and experience in all the London parks. Having made that sweeping statement, I will try to think of what the other nine might be.

By 1908, Richmond Park was being promoted as some-where for 'walking, boating, punting, picnics and other jollities'. The Edwardians valued equality far more than their Victorian predecessors and, at the same time, the mushrooming middle classes looked forward to relaxed weekends. Fences were removed when the king himself had decreed that all parts of the park become 'more accessible than hitherto'. By 1915, sports fields for footballers and rugby players had been marked out near Roehampton Gate.

The impetus to lure Londoners out in their leisure time continued after the First World War, with the railway in its heyday. Richmond Golf Course was opened in 1923 by the future King Edward VIII. According to an *Illustrated London News* of the day, it was a place 'where royalty and artisans are equally welcome'. Two years later his brother, the future George VI, opened a second eighteen-hole course, and both remain in operation today.

Inside Richmond Park, the nation's favourite naturalist Sir David Attenborough advises visitors to 'tread lightly'. Attenborough – who has a pond in the park named after him – knows a thing or two about wildlife.

As well as the 130,000 trees in the park – of which 1,100 are veteran oaks more than three centuries old, some more than 800 years old – there are some sixty types of bird breeding alongside a fascinating array of insects, butterflies, wildflowers and fungi. To safeguard all these, the park has introduced a pretty draconian set of rules. Don't stamp on the anthills, we're told, as these distinctive mounds in the open grassland created by yellow meadow ants are a source of food for green woodpeckers. Ants are a favourite dish of the stocky, red-headed bird, the biggest of our three woodpecker species. Moreover, some of those mounds are a century old. Don't let dog poo linger on the grass, either, because the excessive nutrients in it are damaging. There are forty-five dog waste bins in the park for pooch poo.

Don't move fallen wood, for twigs, branches and even trunks are host to countless insects that themselves become food for other park life. The prince among insects is the stag beetle, whose orange-headed white larvae can live for up to six years buried in bark, while shedding its skin four times. The larvae is something of a neat freak, contentedly eating away at rotten wood, and it's our own desire to clean up parks and gardens that have helped endanger stag beetles. Having emerged from a cocoon into adulthood in the autumn, the beetle – which can measure as much as 7.5 cm in length – stays underground until summer comes, when it must find a mate. The moment it flies off in search of a partner is the moment it becomes vulnerable to hunters like crows and magpies. Rain can also stop play for the stag beetle, whose magnificent mandibles are only ever used to see off love rivals. Stag beetles are among more than 1,350 beetle species to be found in the park.

Don't pick up items from the woodland floor. Leave that to nature's janitors, the jays, who clear up acorns in their beaks, throats and gullets – up to nine at a time – to store them in natural holes, leaf litter or tree bark. These deposits made in the autumn give them a food bank for the winter months and the spring beyond, caches which curiously they can locate no matter how widely distributed they are. But there's always a few that get away. If you see an oak sapling protruding from an area of scrub, with no parent tree in sight, it may well be a jay that's planted it there. The jay, which flashes by with its vivid blue wings, must be in something of a race with grey squirrels, who likewise want to furnish their stores with acorns and also keep an amazing mental map of those food dumps.

Don't harass the deer by getting too close. This is especially true if it's the birthing or rutting season, when the males compete for females, entailing a lot of dramatic barking, roaring and clashing of antlers. A bad situation is inevitably made worse if you have a dog. The park authorities – who like to warn that these are less like Disney creatures and more like safari animals – would like to see a 50-metre rule observed so that no one gets injured.

Don't leave litter as it's harmful to wildlife. Discarded gel packets and their ripped-off tops tossed to one side by runners and cyclists have become a troubling menace in recent years. Don't let dogs trample freely in areas where skylarks nest because it drastically cuts the chances of a tuneful wander in the months that follow. And don't light barbecues anywhere because a raging fire would cause incalculable damage to wildlife and the grasslands it depends upon.

It's a lot of don'ts. But Richmond Park has a lot of visitors – about six million each year. Without some firm boundaries it would be carnage.

Richmond Park is run and administered by the Royal Parks charity. Although it is no longer in royal ownership, there are still royal connections. As I learned earlier, when meeting the chief executive, the Royal Parks are now managed by a charity, and Prince Charles is the charity's patron. One of the four great houses situated in the park is still a royal residence. Thatched House Lodge is home to Princess Alexandra, a cousin of the queen, born in 1936 – the same year as me. So still a young woman.

White Lodge is home to the Royal Ballet Lower School. Lord Sidmouth, the creator of the Isabella Plantation, was one of its illustrious former residents. When he became prime minister in 1801, Sidmouth was gifted the park's White Lodge for a lifetime by George III. Horatio Nelson visited to outline the Battle of Trafalgar plans to him. After a political life marked by peaks and troughs, Sidmouth died there in 1844. Sidmouth is pretty well forgotten today, though I do have his autograph. He is in my collection of letters or signatures from prime ministers, all the way from Walpole in the 1770s to the present age. Lord Sidmouth died at White Lodge in 1844. His name is not totally forgotten locally. On a map of the park, I noticed there is a wood named after him.

When it reverted to her family's possession, Queen Victoria stayed here and it's where her great-grandson, the awkward royal, Edward VIII, was christened in 1894. There's a photo of him in Queen Victoria's lap, with father George V and grandfather Edward VII flanking them.

The lodge you can visit in Richmond Park is Pembroke Lodge, built on the site of a one-roomed mole-catcher's cottage. Over fifty people work in this Georgian centrepiece, which seems an enormous number, till you realise that it has become one of the country's leading wedding venues. Over 300 take place there every year. Pembroke Lodge was at one time the home of prime minister Lord John Russell, an ardent reformer who was twice PM during Victoria's reign but never one of her favourites. His grandson Bertrand Russell, philosopher, mathematician and winner of a Nobel Prize in literature, was brought up in the house. Later he remarked that he grew used to the sight of wide horizons and glorious sunsets while he lived there and said: 'I have never since been able to live happily without both.'

Just inside the gates of Pembroke Lodge there's a headstone in memory of 'Boy', a 'faithful and loving little friend', which I assume was a hound. The headstone bears the initials CED, known to be Georgina Ward, Countess of Dudley and great-great-grandmother of actress Rachel Ward. She was the tenant after the Russells. Her spell in the park inspired her to write a cookery book, *21 Ways of Cooking Venison*.

In the Second World War the lodge was requisitioned as the headquarters of 'the Phantom Squad', an intelligence outfit established in Richmond Park after the Dunkirk evacuation, intended to thwart invading Germans using wireless technology. Later, in the Normandy Landings, its soldiers roamed the fluid front line reporting back the position of Allied troops so RAF pilots and the artillery knew where to unleash their firepower without risking casualties from friendly fire. Draining the Pen Ponds at the time, so eliminating them as a navigational aid, helped keep Pembroke Lodge safe from Luftwaffe bombs.

Pembroke Lodge still feels like a stately home, with wood-panelled walls and period fireplaces, as if those aristocratic Victorian prime ministers were still living there.

There is a splendid restaurant which has become a destination in itself, with people coming just to eat and toddle around the gardens. The creator of all this business is the tenant, Daniel Hearsum, who lives on the premises. He has a fine collection of Pembroke Lodge memorabilia, some of which was on show on the walls the day I was there. It includes a UFO report by the parks police on 17 March 1975, which was a clear, starry night. Two constables saw 'what appeared to be a very large star in the sky'. 'After a few moments the object started to move to the left and turned sideways,' the report says. Although the pair lost sight of it momentarily, they estimate it was hanging in the sky for some ninety minutes at least. There are prints of the park through the ages, as it has inspired numerous artists and photographers, including one of style icon Audrey Hepburn walking her dog here in 1950.

Thanks to the Hearsum Collection, the memory of seventeen-year-old Sylva Boyden, possibly the first woman to make a parachute jump in Britain, lives on. No one locally seemed to have heard about her till they acquired a report about her in a French newspaper. Then they researched her and found she went to Richmond Park in 1919 to watch the Royal Flying Corps test a new parachute. She was so taken with the activity that she lied about her name and age and made three jumps that day from a tethered balloon. During a career that included jumping from aircraft, as well as balloons, she made some 150 jumps and was dubbed 'the famous English airgirl' in the *New York Times*. She appeared in RAF pageants and air shows in Britain and Europe, often as the only female participant.

I walked round the front of Pembroke Lodge, impressed by the carefully manicured lawns and flower beds, the only ones in the whole park. They are, in a way, out of keeping with Richmond Park, but Pembroke Lodge is a wedding venue. Brides like a pretty garden in the background for their wedding photographs. The gardens of the Lodge cover about 14 acres and there are excellent views down and over the Thames. Looking the other way, with your back to the Thames, I discovered a surprising and rather amazing view which takes you right into the middle of London through a shiny telescope sited on a steep mound.

Legend says it's called King Henry's Mound because Henry VIII is said to have stood on it, watching for a rocket being fired at the Tower of London on 19 May 1536 to indicate that his second wife Anne Boleyn had been executed. A day later he was betrothed to Jane Seymour and ten days after that, they married. Historians have poured cold water on this version of events, though, for it seems Henry spent the night of Anne Boleyn's execution elsewhere. A trawl through ancient maps reveals it has also been known as 'The King's Standing' and 'King Henry VII's Mount', among other names. The mound is more likely a burial chamber dating from the Bronze Age that was later used as a platform for falconry.

There was no fee to use the telescope, so I followed instructions and focused it as directed and found myself looking straight at St Paul's Cathedral, a view I had not been able to see with the naked eye. I could not believe it was so distinct and clear, yet all of ten miles away, with a London skyline dominated by office blocks. And of course there are also the surrounding trees in the park, and lots of hills.

St Paul's is of course pretty tall at some 365 feet. It held the record for being London's tallest building from 1710, when it was finally finished, until 1967. That was when those towers in the City started to shoot up. Now St Paul's is dwarfed by so many other buildings, in the City and Docklands, as I saw on my Greenwich boat. There's one pushing up on the cathedral's shoulder, sited in Stratford, that's caused a bit of a stir. London's tallest building today is the Shard, which has held the record since 2010. It is 1,016 feet high, three times the height of St Paul's. Probably by the time this book is published some other monster will have pushed the Shard into second place. Or even by the time I get to the end of this paragraph.

And yet through that telescope, St Paul's is so clear, so beautifully framed, thanks to a bit of careful cutting of some nearby trees and the planning controls that protect the sight lines closer to the capital. Even cleverer, the view through the telescope is framed at the bottom by an iron gateway. This is just a few hundred yards away and was created a couple of years ago – a gate that is a proper work of ironwork art.

The gate, which I walked through later, leads into Sidmouth Wood, and the iron-worked, elaborate lettering on it reads simply 'The Way' – a rather complicated, but cunning, piece of word play. Its first meaning is immediately apparent – this is the way into the wood. But 'The Way' has religious overtones as well, as it is tenet of Daoism (or Taoism), a Chinese philosophy established in the fourth century BC. Additionally, the gateway was created in 2010 to commemorate the 300-year anniversary of the completion of St Paul's. So good Christians will naturally think of Jesus's words – 'I am the Way, the Truth and the Life.'

I wandered further round the Pembroke Lodge gardens and sat down on another bench to admire the view over the river. I was joined by a young Muslim woman wearing a headscarf with a little boy of about four. She said she wanted her little boy to see the views. When she was young, she lived on the Roehampton estates and her parents often took her to Pembroke Lodge to admire the views. Now she lived out in Surrey. She had made the trip specially, to show her son the gardens which had meant so much to her at his age. He looked pretty bored. While she talked to me, he got out a tablet and started playing some sort of computer game.

Holly Lodge is now one of four Royal Parks depots on Richmond Park, as well as being an educational centre. The park is so huge that more than one depot is needed, but Holly Lodge is the main HQ for the park, where most of the senior staff are based. It's also where today's superintendent is based.

I wandered into a yard and thought I had made a mistake. It was full of women in helmets and riding gear, brushing down horses and getting ready to go riding. These are livery stables, rented from the Royal Parks. Nine horses that day were being stabled there, each owned by private individuals who regularly come to ride them. Around the park there are several other livery stables, whose riders use the park, which means there can be up to fifty horses trotting around at any one time. No wonder Richmond Park always looks so frightfully rural.

I had come to see Adam Curtis, who has been working in Richmond Park for fourteen years. He was officially called assistant park manager but would rather be called 'superintendent'.

'Most of the general public call us that anyway, when they ask to see someone in charge,' he explains.

He is a fit-looking forty-seven, born and brought up just ten miles away in Chertsey. He went to agricultural college and trained as a ranger, spending seven years at Ashtead Common in Surrey – where he worked with Bob Warnock, now the boss of Hampstead Heath.

Over the years he has acquired seven different country-side or environment qualifications, starting with a City and Guilds and more recently doing an MSc in arboriculture and community forest management. He is married to Hollie, who used to work as an intelligence analyst, and their two sons are named after trees – Linden and Rowan.

Did he not think of changing his own first name to something like Ash or Oak and therefore have four trees in the family? 'No, I am quite happy being Adam, a good gardening name. But I have worked out that an anagram of my name, Adam Curtis, would be A Mad Rustic . . .'

He admits to being a countryside nut, nature obsessed, but of course looking after such a big park, he has had to learn other more humdrum skills as well, such as road surfacing and fund-raising. He lives in the park with his family, one of four staff with tied houses. Another eight lodges in the park, once used by staff, have been rented out to raise money.

'I could easily live here in the park for ever, and never go out. I would be quite happy never going into the so-called real world. But I have to go out for Royal Parks meetings and conventions.'

Of 150 full-time staff, most are contract workers, around fifty of whom work at Pembroke Lodge. The core staff, directly employed by the Royal Parks, comes to nine.

In the last ten years, Adam has seen a large rise in the number of visitors, almost doubling to its present six million a year.

'I wonder if it is a sea change in our lives and attitudes, and in our emotions and values.'

Traditionally, British people, in their leisure time, went to pubs, drinking and smoking, and to football matches. Football is still as popular but pub attendance has decreased. Pubs have been closing. But all parks report increased attendance.

'Is it because people like to look at a sunset, watch a

dragonfly, listen to birdsong? Then for a moment they stop and think about what it is to be a human being, living on this planet? They do appreciate finally what matters. It reminds me of that quote from Wordsworth: "Nature never did betray the heart that loved her." There is also a good quote from W.H. Auden I like, which I hope I have got right – "A culture is as good as its woods."'

(I looked it up later and the meaning was spot on and the wording was almost correct. It should read, 'A culture is no better than its woods'.)

Meanwhile, back to Adam, still musing away. 'Is it because of the increased pressure of modern life, people wanting to get away and forget their normal stresses?

'Cynics might say it is neither a spiritual release nor an escape. It's just all part of modern consumption. A lot of people do come into this park to consume – to eat in the cafes, play golf, meet friends. All parks today have to have modern attractions to bring in people, such as velodromes and gyms.'

At Richmond Park, however, they are firmly on the side of nature, not consumption. They see themselves as a nature reserve, protecting their woods and rare bushes, and providing a home for wildlife. No surprise to find out it's a Site of Special Scientific Interest, or SSSI.

Traditionally, the deer at Richmond Park provided venison for the Royal tables and tummies, and also for other notable national personages, such as the Archbishop of Canterbury and the prime minister, holders of the so-called Royal Warrant. This was suspended as recently as 1997, ending the centuries-old practice.

'It cost us a lot of time and money, dishing out the royal

venison,' said Adam. 'Now when we cull deer, which we have to do each year, we sell them to a licensed game dealer. Even so, it does not cover the cost of managing the deer and their welfare.'

Most years there is an incident with a deer. Usually a visitor with a camera goes too near a young deer and alarms the others. Or it happens when they are rutting and the male deer gets protective of his space. Deer also regularly come to grief on the park's roads, ending up injured or dead.

The only blemish on Richmond Park, detracting from its image as idyllic, wild countryside, is the presence of those two rather busy roads which cross it. It is easy to avoid them, when walking, and never realise they are there. So it is a bit of a shock when you suddenly come across a long line of traffic bustling through such natural countryside. There is a 20 mph speed limit, but as many as twenty deer a year are killed or injured by drivers who did not manage to avoid them in time. The deer of course think it is their park, their own private playground. An injured deer, usually with its ribs bashed in, has to be destroyed. It is normally a fallow deer, which can be nervous, liable to a make sudden mad dash. Red deer seem to have more traffic sense.

'Unfortunately, people use the park as a short cut, commuting to work in London. Most people take it easy, but of course we do get drivers belting along like mad.'

There are also thousands of people who drive in the park not for work but for pleasure, to enjoy themselves. There are seven car parks in all, which can cater for 1,700 cars. All the same, people do like to drive straight off the roads into the bushes and have a picnic or walk around. Hence along all their seven miles of park roads there are small, stout wooden posts, two feet below ground, one foot above, called Thomson's Teeth, after the 1950s superintendent, George Thomson, who installed them to deter naughty drivers. But some still do ignore the posts, such as Chelsea tractors with their high wheels. Or when the poles have started rotting they just charge through. Repairing the 10,000 little wooden poles is a constant problem – but not as much as looking after the roads themselves.

Their seven miles of roads are private, owned by the Royal Parks, thus the charity has to maintain and repair them. It is the biggest single expenditure each year. I can't think of another public park in London that has to carry the costs and repairs and problems of having a public highway running through it. It means Adam and his staff have to know about road surfacing: what to use, when and how to do it, which of course is a science in itself. If they put down salt, for example, it has to be spread so it will not ruin the trees, plants and grazing.

'Recently we had to do some expensive road repairs because of a badger sett. The badgers had made fourteen holes under the road, to get from one side to the other. We had to dig up and repair the road, then make underground tunnels for them so they could move across without the road caving in on top of them. Badgers are of course protected.

'We keep the roads safe for cyclists and motorists. We don't want anyone to hurt themselves. But occasionally we do have to deal with a motor insurance claim against the park. Motorists blame potholes in our roads for damaging their cars. Cyclists blame oil spillages from a car. Or they say they skidded on ice which we should have gritted.

'It can take up a lot of tine – just reading the claims, and then writing our reply. For the last ten years I have kept a daily climate record for the park. So when someone alleges we neglected to grit the icy surface, I can prove that the forecast that day was not for snow or ice, so I could not have put grit down in advance.'

The claims have increased because the number of people driving through the park has almost doubled in the last few years while the blame and compensation culture has also risen. This is all set against a fall in funds.

All the Royal Parks share from a communal pool of income and must find ways of contributing to it. Filming, catering and, most recently, car parking charges help. (Horse riders already make a donation.) What about all the wealthy people living nearby? Could they not have their arms twisted more? Adam says they do help, but the problems come when money is urgently needed for something like regular dog poo removal, or emptying litter bins. Generous people tend to want to be associated with something more glamorous, such as nature and preservation.

There are around 200 volunteers, while the Friends of Richmond Park are very supportive and helpful. There is a busy schedule of events in the park each year, which brings in a bit of money, though most are small, usually run by charities. The two big annual events are the London Duathlon and RideLondon, when all the roads are closed to allow competitors to run or cycle freely.

'We don't allow pop concerts. That would be inappropriate in a park which is a National Nature Reserve.'

On that day in Richmond Park there were three film

crews on location – two making TV programmes and one a feature film.

'I do worry what the park will be like in ten years if the visitor numbers grow even more and our incomes reduce. How will we be able to afford all our wildlife welfare and nature conservation work? That is the main purpose of our life and work in Richmond Park, why we are here.'

I asked Adam if it was true that Richmond Park had an excellent safety record.

'In my fourteen years here I have never heard of anyone being mugged or robbed or assaulted in the park. We don't get local youths hanging around, looking for mischief. There has never been any vandalism. We don't get rough sleepers, either. I think the worst crime we have had is fly tipping.

'I suppose the reason is that we are fairly remote. It is an effort to get here, not like the inner London Parks.'

After speaking to Adam, I had another wander, remembering I had meant to look for memorial seats, as I always do. In a little garden near Pembroke Lodge, I came across quite a collection of them. I wonder what the collective name for them is? A congregation of memorial seats? A gathering?

I noticed one in French. It said: 'C'est comme Trivy, Jean-Claude Seraisse.' I wrote it down and then on my mobile asked my son-in-law Richard, who is French, if knew what Trivy meant. By return, he told me that Trivy is a place in Bourgogne in France, and that the Loire flows through part of it. Perhaps Jean-Claude, sitting here overlooking the Thames, was reminded of his home land.

There were several other memorial seats inscribed to Brits with Christian names such as Violet and Herbert, which gave away their age even before I'd looked at their dates. You don't come across many babies with those names today. They will of course come back. Names always do.

There was also a more modern memorial seat, to a very modern sort of hero – a pop singer. I don't think I have ever seen a memorial seat in a park to a pop star before. The nearest, I suppose, is George Michael, whose grave is in Highgate Cemetery, next to Waterlow Park. But its exact location is private, to deter fans. The Richmond Park pop star is Ian Dury, who died in 2000, aged fifty-seven. I met him once, not to interview him, but at a house party in our street. The house belonged to a rather prim, very serious man, so I was surprised that he should be friends with a 1970s punk singer.

Dury got polio at the age of seven, which left him crippled. He went to a school for the disabled, but eventually got to the Royal College of Art, where he studied under Peter Blake. He was a talented lyricist and lead singer with Kilburn and the High Roads, then Ian Dury and the Blockheads. One of his best-known songs was 'Reasons to be Cheerful', the words of which are inscribed on the back of his memorial bench. I personally preferred his 'Hit Me with Your Rhythm Stick'.

The bench was put up in 2002 by his family, to commemorate him at a place he loved. It included a state-of-the-art piece of solar-powered audio magic, enabling you at the press of a button to hear some of his music, plus an interview with him. A fab idea, and what fun. I am amazed more memorial seats have not gone into the modern techy audio-visual age.

Alas, the chair was being repaired the day I was there, so I did not get to hear him. I have since gathered that when the chair is repaired, there will be instructions to download an app on your mobile phone. So, no need for solar power. But it means you can still sit on his memorial bench and listen to his music.

I wonder if I should update my bench on Hampstead Heath? Perhaps get a famous actor with a lovely voice to read out extracts from some of my lovely books.

My final port of call was with Adam, the superintendent, at his home. He had told me where he lived, but asked me not to reveal it here, otherwise he would get people knocking at his door all day long with their car-insurance claims. He had said that after he had finished work, I could pop in and meet his wife and family. And he would also let me see a non-public area.

Adam took me first down a little path, clearly marked PRIVATE. We came to a little wood and I wondered what he was going to show me. It turned out to be a charcoal burner. It's one of the oldest chemical processes known to mankind. Before the invention of coke, charcoal was used in the making of iron because it was hotter and cleaner than wood. It was used in the production of bronze and copper and later in medicine, art and weaponry. With 10 tons of wood needed to produce 2.5 tons of charcoal, charcoal makers were by tradition forest workers, working next to the raw materials they needed rather than hauling hard woods to a distant base.

Adam pointed out a large pile of logs waiting to be burned, and the kilns in which this would be done. This is one of the park's minor income-producing enterprises. The woodland area itself is let out to a charcoal burner who uses the spare wood, from coppicing or fallen trees, to make charcoal. Adam explained that the charcoal burner is now only working part time, to keep the skills alive. He doesn't make much money from it and works as a contractor as well. But Adam likes the fact that a charcoal burner is still there, in that little wood, in ancient and historic parkland.

Back at his house, I met his two boys, Linden and Rowan, who had not long come home from school. They go to a primary school in Richmond. It seemed idyllic, having their home in the heart of the park, with a charcoal burner on their doorstep. I wondered if his boys would grow up to be nature lovers, or nature workers, like their dad. It does not always work out that way. They probably want to work in the City and be hedge-fund managers.

'When I grow up,' said Linden, the elder, aged eight, 'I want to be a cephalopodist.'

You what?

He slowly explained that cephalopod is a name that covers a group of molluscs – notably squid, cuttlefish, nautilus and octopus. Octopus was his favourite.

Jolly interesting I said, though hardly any the wiser.

Having a tied cottage in such a sylvan situation does look at first like a wonderful perk of the job for Adam's wife and his family, and for him, not having to commute to work. But of course once you lose or move your job, you have nowhere to live. Places you might otherwise have bought twenty or thirty years ago will have zoomed up in price. Adam and Hollie have been canny. They kept the house where they used to live, and let it out.

'Working in a park is not a career you go into if you want to make money. You will never be well off. You have to have some other source of income.

'Working in a park, any park, is a way of life.'

He then got his two little boys ready to go out. He was taking them into Richmond to a local pool for a snorkelling club session. I wondered if they would come across any cephalopod. Or should it be cephalopods? Or even cephalopoda . . .?

Best Things About Richmond Park

1. Isabella Plantation – a man-made, but ever so natural 42-acre hidden-away woodland area, with ponds, streams and probably the country's best collection of azaleas: forty-five different varieties. Stunning in the spring when they burst into colour.

2. Pembroke Lodge, one of three lodges in the park, more like stately homes really, and the only one you can visit. Ever so tasteful restaurant and gardens.

3. Memorial bench in Pembroke Lodge gardens in memory of pop singer Ian Dury. From the bench, you can download some of his music. If, of course, it is working . . .

4. Telescope on King Henry's Mound, from which you can see straight to St Paul's Cathedral, ten miles away.

11

BATTERSEA PARK

During this year of walking London's parks, I have become introduced to one in south London which I'd never visited before, though of course I had heard about it, as it is so well known, so famous, so loved, not just in London but in British history. So many national events, public happenings and famous folks have been connected with it.

The reasons for suddenly, in my old age, getting to know this park are personal. Two years after the death of my wife in 2016, I acquired a girlfriend, someone I had vaguely come across many years ago. I did not want to go online, join a dating agency. I did not want to meet a stranger. I reckoned I must have met enough women in my long-legged life, some of whom must have ended up, like me, single and living alone, and looking for a companion.

In my mind, this fantasy woman would have been around seventy, so not too glaringly much younger than me. I wanted her to have had a career, still have interests and occupations, a family and her own teeth. That was a euphemism for, well, being fit, healthy and active. She must also have her own house.

Amazingly, all this came to pass. Claire has three grand-children, while I have four, and a busy life, doing good works in the neighbourhood with lots of friends. She is an active member of the Battersea Society. When I first met her, she was their membership secretary.

Her house is near Battersea Park. That means south of the river, a foreign country to me, but I was brave and became a regular on the Overground railway link from Gospel Oak to Clapham Junction. And through Claire, I got to know and love this park I had never visited before.

There are two bridges over the Thames which take you into Battersea from Chelsea – the Albert Bridge or Chelsea Bridge. The former was opened in 1873, when users paid a toll. However, it was less sturdy than its builders might have hoped and soon it became known as 'The Trembling Lady' for its vibrations. That's why there's a sign on Albert Bridge urging commanding officers from the nearby Chelsea Barracks to have their soldiers break step as they crossed, mindful of the 200 soldiers killed in France when the Angers Bridge collapsed as they crossed in 1850. Tolls disappeared when London's bridges were bought up in 1879 by the Metropolitan Board of Works, the precursor of the London County Council, although the vacant toll booths remain. Albert Bridge is painted predominantly pink and decorated with 4,000 LED bulbs, not for the purposes of Disneyfication but to stand out better to river users.

Today's Chelsea Bridge dates from 1934, a construction which replaced a suspension bridge built in the 1850s.

The land on the southerly bank between the bridges was possibly where Julius Caesar crossed the Thames on his way to subdue British tribes in Middlesex in 54 BC – though plenty of other places have been nominated for this prestigious link with Caesar. But many human bones and Roman weapons were found when the original Chelsea Bridge was excavated in the 1850s, giving this claim some historic legs, at least.

In the sixteenth century, a rough embankment was built next to the river, rendering the marshy land beyond it usable for farming, and for a while it became famous for lavender and asparagus. It became known as Battersea Fields. In 1829, the Duke of Wellington – who'd won victory over Napoleon at

Waterloo some fourteen years previously – met the 10th Earl of Winchilsea there to have a duel, which clearly was more symbolic than bloody. The duke deliberately fired his duelling pistol wide while Winchilsea fired his up into the air. At the time the duke was PM and had eased the Catholic Relief Act into law, which permitted Catholics to sit in Parliament at Westminster for the first time in a while, when sectarianism was still rampant. Winchilsea accused of him of trying to introduce popery all over the land, which the duke took as a heinous slur. However, after the shots were fired, the earl apologised for his churlish remarks.

Battersea Fields became a veritable pleasure ground for the city's poor. On Sundays there were fairs with horse and donkey races, roundabouts, theatre, dancing, conjurors and fortune-tellers. In the summer, gypsies camped there and competitive pigeon, starling and sparrow shooting took place nearby. The brick-built Red House Tavern, distinguished by green shutters and a boisterous clientele, also stood on the site. Gamblers, drinkers and hawkers from all over the capital headed there at weekends, causing some consternation at the time. In 1805, the recently established Society for the Suppression of Vice was told, 'a great many disorderly people frequent Battersea Fields'.

With parks being all the rage, an act was passed in 1846 to create a Royal Park on the site at a cost of no more than £200,000. More than 750,000 tons of gravel excavated from Surrey Commercial Docks – being enlarged at the time to accommodate more ships than ever on its 372-acre site at Rotherhithe – was brought along to level it and the notorious Red House Tavern was pulled down. The den of iniquity that was once Battersea Fields gave way to trimmed grass and flower beds.

When I first started visiting Claire, we constantly walked around Battersea Park, getting to know one another, and probably paying more attention to each other perhaps than the park itself. She took me to an art event there, in a massive hall, which just seemed to grow up overnight then disappear. We got free tickets, as she had a guest pass. That's why I remember it. At the end of the year, as we still seemed to be getting on well, and by this time had been on several holidays together, I decided to make Battersea Park my tenth London park. Lucky Battersea.

Battersea Park, being bordered on one side by the River Thames, historically has caused visitors some rather nasty health issues. In 1858, after Queen Victoria did the opening honours for the park, London was enveloped in what was termed 'the Great Stink' after unexpectedly hot weather combined with human faeces to make the city intolerably smelly. The source of the stink was the Thames itself, which was none too clean, with effluent pouring into it from sewers and cesspits. The city's population boomed at a time when the advent of the flushing toilet fast-tracked faeces into the network of rivers that crossed London, with the Thames being the biggest artery. Scientist Michael Faraday had described the river water as 'an opaque pale brown fluid' in 1855.

In a letter dated July 1858, Charles Dickens wrote that the Thames in London was most horrible. 'I have to cross at Waterloo or London Bridge to get to the railroad when I come down here and I can certify that the offensive smells even in that short whiff have been of a most head-and-stomach-distending nature.'

At the time, people feared it was this horrible smell that caused cholera, of which there were major outbreaks in London in 1831, 1848, 1853 and 1854, claiming about 32,000 lives in total. In fact, polluted water was to blame. Not all heroes wear capes, and on this occasion it was civil engineer Joseph Bazalgette, more of a top hat and tails man, who rode to the rescue, drawing up plans for 1,100 miles of street sewers for effluent and rainwater, which would feed into a further 82 miles of main sewers.

This effective new system brought with it some fresh street furniture to London, which filtered around the country, rejoicing in the name of stinkpipes. Have you ever noticed those hollow, metal poles, loftier than street lights, perhaps painted verdigris and sometimes topped with a crown or cowl that may or may not bear a manufacturer's name? You've probably never clocked them before, but they were installed to vent the sewers, releasing dangerous gases above street level for dispersal. You will certainly be on the lookout for them now. If you are in the vicinity of the park you will find one on Albert Bridge Road.

It was an altogether sweeter moment in 2012 when Battersea Park was packed by people watching the Thames-borne Diamond Jubilee celebrations for Queen Elizabeth in 2012. A rain-soaked but good-natured crowd watched as 1,000 boats passed by the park. It was, organisers insisted, the largest flotilla on the Thames since the reign of Charles II. The park then hosted the Diamond Jubilee Festival.

Battersea Park feels today more like a Royal Park, not a

municipal park. It has a handsome, broad carriageway which goes round most of the park, reminiscent of Rotten Row. You can imagine the aristocracy driving their carriages around the park to admire the gardens, and themselves. This broad walk is today always popular with parents and prams, dog walkers and cyclists, as it affords them so much car-free space. It also helps with the park's income. It is a perfect place for parking when there are big events requiring heavy gear.

There's a zoo with lemurs, otters, meerkats, Scottish wild-cats and wallabies, among other animals. Although pint-sized, it is well liked among younger visitors. There's also works by two of the twentieth century's best-known sculptors. Henry Moore's *Three Figures*, inspired by women in London shelters during the Blitz, made from Darley Dale sandstone is one. Then there's *Single Form* by Barbara Hepworth.

But perhaps the more surprising and compelling sculpture is of a brown dog, a rather small statue and easy to miss, which is now hidden away near the Old English Garden. It's hard to believe now all the ancient controversy and demonstrations that this little canine likeness represents – a century-old row which is somehow awfully modern.

In 1903, a pair of Swedish feminists reported on a London University medical lecture where a professor was cutting open a brown terrier dog. The women were ardent anti-vivisectionists and trumpeted that it was cruelty. The dog was conscious and in pain, although most of the medical students justified the experiment, saying the dog was anaesthetised and animal investigations were vital for medical research. It led to riots and demonstrations which split the country during the Edwardian era.

The anti-vivisectionists later commissioned a statue of the little dog and it was erected in the Latchmere Recreation Ground in Battersea, outside newly developed housing. It was made by sculptor Joseph Whitehead at a cost of £120, with his bronze dog sitting tall on top of a drinking fountain.

An inscription read:

In memory of the Brown Terrier Dog Done to Death in the Laboratories of University College in February 1903 after having endured Vivisections extending over more than two months and having been handed over from one Vivisector to another till death came to his Release. Also in memory of the 232 dogs vivisected in the same place during the years 1902–3.

Men and Women of England, How Long shall these things be?

The site was chosen as the statue's new home, not least because the Battersea General Hospital was known as 'the Antiviv', or 'Old Anti', for its stout opposition to vivisection. But medical students were upset and there was a series of attacks on the statue with various implements until police mounted a round-the-clock guard. In 1907, 1,000 students demonstrated through London, waving effigies of the brown dog on sticks, leading to clashes with suffragettes, trade unionists and assorted protestors. It was one of the best known in a series of Brown Dog Riots. In broad terms, the anti-vivisectionists tended to be suffragettes, fighting ever more fiercely for equality. Medical students, on the other hand, typified the establishment that was firmly blocking votes for women.

In 1910 Battersea Council, fed up with all the controversy and the costs, sent some workmen under darkness to remove the brown dog statue. It was then melted down, or so it was alleged. In 1985, modern-day anti-vivisectionists commissioned a small, discreet statue of the brown dog and it was placed in Battersea Park, but rather hidden away.

I eventually found the modern statue, near the Old English Garden, and examined it carefully. It seemed all in one piece, with no sign of the vandalism that had plagued its predecessor. Perhaps dog lovers are in the majority today, certainly in Battersea.

London parks do contain, often hidden away, references and mementoes to people and events once of national importance, now almost totally forgotten. I had certainly never heard of the Brown Dog Riots.

War memorials, of which there are some 50,000 scattered in our parks and towns throughout the country, don't tend to get forgotten or overlooked – or attract controversy. And their significance is still understood by everyone.

War artist Eric Kennington was responsible for an exceptionally elegant example in Battersea Park that's intended to recall the 10,000 men killed or missing from the 24th Infantry Division in the First World War. Unusually, the memorial, made from Portland stone, is three soldiers in full kit and in such close formation they are gripping hands. On the left is poet Robert Graves, who was seriously injured during the conflict, then nearly killed by Spanish flu at its end. The central figure is one Sergeant Woods, who acted as a bodyguard for Kennington when he worked as a war artist, while on the right stands strong-jawed Maurice Thomas, a machine gunner in the division.

Around their feet winds a serpent, probably representative of the insidious legacy of mental illness. The statue was unveiled in 1924, and fellow artist Augustus John observed that Kennington's figures looked as if they had no trousers on. Thereafter it was dubbed 'the Trouserless Tommies'. Despite its nickname, its realism was warmly admired by all the old soldiers who saw it. For his part, Kennington refused to accept payment for the work but was nonetheless presented with a gold cigarette case by way of reward. In 2005 the memorial became listed.

The creation and laying out of the park was partly instigated by Thomas Cubitt, the famous architect and builder, who several times urged the government of the day to buy land and earmark it for parks before it was all snapped up for development. He himself envisaged some choice mansion blocks going up around Battersea Park when it was completed, which indeed happened. But when he died in 1857, his obituary pointed to a philanthropist who recalled his own humble beginnings.

He established a workman's library; a school-room for workmen's children; and, by an arrangement to have supplied to his work-people wholesome refreshments at low rates, did much to establish habits of temperance among them, in place of those of drinking which formerly existed. To those under him, and holding responsible situations, he was generous and kind, blending his position as master with that of a friend. He was a liberal benefactor to churches, schools, and charities, in those places with which he was connected, and always valued, in a peculiar degree, the advantages resulting to the poor from the London hospitals.

Battersea Park features in the early history of football. In 1863, football first got itself a proper set of a rules and an organisation when the Football Association was created. One of the early FA teams, comprising former public schoolboys, was Wanderers FC – so called because for a long time it did not have a proper home. Battersea Park became one of several 'home' venues for matches. The Wanderers were winners of the first FA Cup in 1872, beating the Royal Engineers by a goal to nil at the Kennington Oval in front of a 2,000-strong crowd. Captain C. W. Alcock, who held the silver cup aloft that day, codified many of the game's rules.

Most early football clubs were mainly made up of public school and Oxbridge old boys, who ran football for the first few decades until 1887, when professional football was at last allowed and, oh horrors, it was never the same again. The park turf was disturbed again during the Second World War when it became the site of a bomb shelter and dig-for-victory allotments.

However, the biggest event in Battersea Park's more recent history was its involvement in the Festival of Britain, held between May and September 1951. This was a massive national celebration, encouraged by the post-war Labour government, to cheer up a nation still in the doldrums at a time when bomb sites remained commonplace and sugar, butter and meat rationing was still being imposed on households. It marked the centenary of the Great Exhibition of 1851, which had reflected the might of Empire. But this time the festival would be a purely British event, letting ourselves see how jolly good and clever and artistic and scientific and pioneering we all were – and fun as well.

There were lots of events spread throughout the UK, but the main focus was on the South Bank of the Thames, right in the middle of London, on the other side of the river from Parliament, centred round the brand new Festival Hall. That is still there today, though most of the other structures and creations have long gone, such as The Dome of Discovery, the largest dome in the world at the time, focusing on the wonders of exploration, and its neighbour the Skylon, a cigar-shaped modernist monument some 300 feet high. This was soon ridiculed by most newspaper columnists and questions were asked in Parliament about what would happen if it got struck by lightning. A few days before the king and queen visited the exhibition in May 1951, Skylon was climbed at midnight by a student, who attached a University of London Air Squadron scarf near the top. A workman was despatched to take it down.

I remember as a boy in Carlisle in 1951 reading loads of articles in my father's *Daily Express* about the wonders of the Festival of Britain, all the exciting events and exotic attractions, but not really quite understanding what it was all about. I knew I would never go there as it was so far away. At that stage in my life, I had never been south of Penrith.

I was particularly confused by Skylon when I saw photographs of it, trying to work out its purpose and symbolism. Most sensible northern folks scoffed at it, dismissing it as another example of southern artsy-fartsy modern art, eh.

Both Dome and Skylon were quickly ditched by a triumphant Conservative government, elected later in 1951 and led by Winston Churchill, keen to erase any lasting legacy of the Labour administration. They were then sold for scrap.

Further along the south bank of the river, just two miles

away in Battersea Park, was the fun part of the Festival. This was the Battersea Pleasure Gardens, which took over almost half of Battersea Park. The Pleasure Gardens harked back, in name and concept, to the eighteenth-century Vauxhall Pleasure Gardens, written about by Thackeray in *Vanity Fair* and in other novels and publications of the times.

Battersea Pleasure Gardens included a funfair, two theatres, a miniature railway, a station, beer gardens, shops, fountains, and entertainments of all sorts, going on all day and throughout the evening. During a five-month spell, over eight million people visited. Most of them were British, and mostly, in the case of Battersea Park, from London and the south.

The programme for the 1951 Pleasure Gardens is now a collector's item. I have my copy in front of me now, fifty-four pages long, full of information and fun (just like this very book you are reading, I hope). It includes contributions from the leading humorists, artists and cartoonists of the day, many of whom worked for *Punch* (as I did for ten years). These included A. P. Herbert, Rowland Emett, Bernard Miles and Osbert Lancaster.

The Riverside Theatre, which held 1,200 people, was distinctive for its Regency blue and white cladding.

The 1951 Battersea Fun Fair had everything for a family, including a carousel, a helter-skelter and a boating lake. It also became famous for its scary rides, and this heady combination drew thousands of people through its gates until the song 'Goodnight, Sweetheart' was broadcast, indicating to sideshow operators, ride pilots and the general public that it was time to shut. The most spectacular of the rides was the Big Dipper roller-coaster, until 1972, when five children were killed when one of the wooden carriages detached from its steel drive and rolled back, colliding with another behind. After queuing for a turn and paying 15 pence, it was those at the back – the most sought-after seat – who perished. It is still thought to be the worst-ever accident in the history of theme parks. Although the Big Dipper was torn down and replaced with the far more modern Cyclone ride, the funfair failed to shake off the grim associations forged by the accident and was eventually closed in 1974.

Still remaining, however, are the foaming fountains, a great hit with the 1950s crowd. The fountains are amazing – over-decorated, but so dramatic and grandiose, shooting so high up in the sky, out of synch with their surroundings. They struck me as a relic of some Eastern European People's Republic, the sort of 1950s architectural grandeur you still come across today in out-of-the-way corners of Croatia and Romania. As it was winter, they were not working, but I had seen them in the summer and they are still a big attraction for tourists.

Having decided I must include Battersea Park, I did what I had been doing all year, which was to contact the superintendent and make an appointment.

I had, during the last year, strolled round Battersea Park many times with Claire, often with a friend's dog, but I had not noticed where the park office was, or the depot, where the superintendent might be lurking. Claire did not know either, which she was a bit ashamed about, being a proper local who had lived here for eighteen years. I assured her that almost all superintendents in London parks have their office hidden away. They don't want to be doorstepped by people coming to moan.

Battersea Park's person in charge has his office in the far north-west corner of the park, at the Chelsea Bridge end, beside the herb garden, which itself is rather hidden. Once past the herb garden, thinking by now I was lost, or trespassing, I came to a row of sweet little cottages. This is where all the resident staff have their offices, including the park's police – so near the thundering traffic of Chelsea Bridge, yet so quiet and rural I could have stumbled into Trumpton.

Neil Blackley, the man in charge, is in fact head of parks for the whole of the Borough of Wandsworth, but Battersea Park is the jewel in the crown. There is no designated superintendent for Battersea Park itself. Everything that happens there comes under Neil's command. In the old days, there was an army of full-time staff, just for Battersea Park. Now, as everywhere else, a lot of the work is contracted out. Nonetheless, Neil reckoned that at the height of the summer, with lots of events going on, all the contract labour working full time, plus volunteers and visiting Wandsworth Borough specialists, there are probably about 100 people coming into the park each day to work. Now, in the middle of December, as many facilities were closed for the winter, his immediate staff looking after Battersea Park numbered about twenty.

You could tell it was December because of the strange shapes I passed in the semi-tropical garden. Each year, when winter comes, the palm trees and tropical bushes are wrapped in white plastic to protect them from snow and frost. It made them look like Christmas presents, about to be given out to the deserving poor of Battersea.

Neil had been in the job only six months, so it was a bit unfair to expect him be able to give detailed answers to all my

Battersea Park questions, especially about its history, which he was still learning. He is in his mid-forties, slender and trim, married with three young children, brought up in Essex. From the local comprehensive he went to Oxford Brooks University to study town planning. He then did a diploma in landscaping. His first job was working in an office for a media firm, till he decided he much preferred the outdoors, and to be among gardens.

He set up his own landscaping firm, which did well for a while, then ran out of money. He joined a bigger, established landscaping company, working his way up to managerial level over seven years. His firm had contracts with many local councils, which is how he heard one day that the job at Wandsworth was being advertised. His blend of commercial experience combined with his landscaping qualifications proved to be just what they wanted.

Technically, he does not work for Wandsworth Borough. He works for Enable. You what? I got a bit lost in his explanation, but apparently Wandsworth has set up a charity called Enable, which runs all their leisure and park services. Goodness, the lengths councils have to go to these days to save money and spread their resources around. He looks after thirty-two parks in the borough, plus allotments and cemeteries, and has a total staff of around 100 to do so. There are three major parks – Tooting Common (221 acres), Battersea Park (200 acres) and Wandsworth Common (177 acres), plus King George's Park (55 acres) and Wandsworth Park (20 acres). The rest are much smaller, some hardly more than greens. The grand total of public green in the borough comes to 1,500 acres.

Battersea Park is the glamour park, the most visited, but Neil has to tread carefully and not spend all his time or energies there. Wandsworth and Tooting might well get upset.

So far, his main regular problems are the same as in any other London park – people complaining about litter, dog walkers and cyclists. Raising money is not directly his concern – he just has to accept whatever budget is allocated for the year – but he knows he cannot do all the work he would like to do unless he can generate funds. These funds come from regular events held in the park, the biggest of which is the firework display every 5 November. Over 50,000 people turn up to watch the splendid displays – which of course leads to loads of health and safety concerns and the need for extra staff.

One of the main and most spectacular features in Battersea Park when it opened was the lake, which is man-made and covers some 50 acres. In Neil's office I studied an aerial photo of the park as it is today, and the lake looks enormous.

The lake is in fact only 3 feet deep, and in the early decades there were a lot of problems with silting and the water getting polluted, despite a large pump house, erected nearby in 1861. The pump was driven by a steam engine, which circulated the water and fed the cascades and fountains. Today there is an underground bore hole, which provides the water, and electricity now provides the power. The previous year, the biggest single expenditure was £250,000 on the pumps for the fountains, which I had earlier admired.

Battersea Park could raise more money as, each year, they get more requests than they accept from commercial bodies to stage events in the park. But the authorities don't want more than they can deal with.

Rough sleepers do not appear to be much of a problem. The park is closed each night at dusk and the parks police stop intruders getting in. However, Battersea Park is a popular spot to dump your stolen moped, after you have been up West and attempted a bit of ram-raiding or mugged a few pedestrians for their mobiles. A lot of rental bikes are likewise dumped, the scourge of all London parks at present.

Around the park are dotted six rather attractive staff cottages, lived in by parkies or retired parkies. Neil doesn't fancy one. His children are nicely settled in their home and schools in Beckenham.

There's one big central covered exhibition site, which was where the art show I attended was held. Officially it is called the British Genius Centre – for reasons he did not know. I suspect it must be to do with some previous exhibition. It is a temporary structure, though it does not look it. When erect, it dominates the centre of the park and can house massive exhibitions and corporate events. It gets taken down and packed up for two months every year. There is an agreement with the Friends of Battersea Park that it will operate for only ten months annually. It attracts thousands of visitors and involves loads of vehicles and equipment, and sensitive locals relish a short break for peace and quiet.

Back in the 1990s, Battersea Park hosted only around 100 public events a year. Now the number is nearer 600. That includes all the fun runs, as well as the regular fairs, concerts and exhibitions, most of which of course produce a decent income.

'I have to ration what funds I receive, but I can already see all the things I could improve, if I had more money,' said Neil.

'The sports provisions here are excellent, with so many facilities, but they get a lot of wear and tear. They do need to be repaired and improved. The football pitches will never be up to Premier League standard, but I think they are pretty good.

'My budget this year for maintenance is £4.5 million. I could easily spend four times that every year. There are sewage pipes I know will need repairing very soon. But people are not aware of these problems as they don't see them. They worry about things they can see, such as litter.

'We have two collections of litter every day of the year. But in a hot summer with tens of thousands coming into the park all day long, it is hard to keep on top of it.

'It is because we have so many different facilities. I am still amazed by what we offer the public. I don't think there is another park in London of this size which offers so many diverse attractions for all sorts of people, of all ages.'

I had to admit that on my walks round the park with Claire, I had not been aware of any excess litter, so he must be winning his battle. But there did seem to be lots of volunteers, in bright uniforms, working brightly away in little jolly gangs.

My main initial impression of Battersea Park, first coming to it as an outsider, was of the quality of the park. Compared to say, Burgess Park and Victoria Park, excellent though they both are at what they do, Battersea Parks feels like an affluent park. Not just because of the class of some of the locals, who like to think Battersea is nicer and more discreet than Chelsea, but because of the quality of the park itself.

Battersea has given its name to several nationally recognised institutions, the best known being Battersea Dogs and Cats Home. First established in Holloway, north London, in 1860, as a Home for Lost and Straying Dogs, it moved to Battersea in 1871, by which it time it also catered for cats. It now has other centres in Old Windsor and Brands Hatch. It is probably the nation's best-known dogs' home, where you'd go if you wanted to adopt Woody, the capable collie, obedient Oscar, a young husky, or ten-year-old Stitch, a brindle Staffie. One of my daughters got a dog from Battersea and it entailed lots of visits to her house before they were satisfied she was going to be a good owner.

Inside Battersea Dogs and Cats Home, there are usually about 260 dogs and 220 cats at any one time, waiting for caring people. It is estimated that, in all, over three million dogs and cats have found new homes, thanks to Battersea.

The other local monument with a national profile is the nearby Battersea Power Station. You can spot the four famous vast towers from most corners of Battersea Park. This coal-fired power station was built in the 1930s, covering 42 acres, and at one time supplied power to a great swathe of London. It ceased operation in 1983 and lay dormant for decades. During that time it changed hands several times as developers came up with grandiose plans, most of which came to nothing. The building was granted Grade II status, so no one was allowed to knock down the landmark towers, though in fact the present ones are phoney, rebuilt to look like the originals.

Now the whole site has been completely rebuilt, with an extensive riverside walk, new pier, shops and accommodation. I have walked there with Claire, and it is enormous. We got lost trying to pick our way around. In all, it will have cost around £10 billion. By the time it is all completed, it will be one of the biggest developments in London in recent years.

Battersea Power Station is considered an art-deco masterpiece and its towers have become an iconic image. It has
featured in many films, from Hitchcock to the Beatles' *Help*.
But its best-known appearance was on the cover of the 1977
Pink Floyd LP, *Animals*, one of the most recognisable album
covers. It's the one with a pink pig floating over one of the
chimney towers.

The inflatable pink pig was created by a German artist
and tethered to a tower for the photo shoot in 1976. It broke
loose and drifted off in the direction of Heathrow Airport,
causing police helicopters to be called out, who followed it,
tracking its progress. It eventually came down safely in a field
in Kent. Phew.

Battersea Park itself has featured in countless films, TV
programmes and commercials. It is so photogenic, awfully
handy for central London and, perhaps most attractive of all,
has that brilliant parking, ideal for luxury caravans for the
stars, electricians, lorries and mobile canteens where workers
can stuff themselves with bacon sandwiches.

Feature films have included *The Day the Earth Caught Fire*,
a Mr Bean film and a Muppets film. Among pop singers
who have used the park is Petula Clark. In 1954 she had a
hit with 'Meet Me in Battersea Park', co-authored with her
father. More recently, One Direction devoted a whole fifty
seconds of their video for their hit 'One Thing' to a scene in
Battersea Park.

There is one art gallery in the park. It is housed in the old
steam-powered Pump House beside the lake, the one which
provided the water for the lake and fountains. It is now a
listed building. I had passed it several times while walking

with Claire, but it never seemed to be open. For the purposes of research, I was desperate to get in and poke around. Eventually, on one of my walks, I did find the door open – hurrah – so I went in.

It seemed to be totally empty, perhaps abandoned. I couldn't work out if it really was an art gallery or just a place of rest and refuge. It was all very arty, but rather confusing. Then I noticed a young woman preoccupied in a corner of the entrance hall on a computer. I coughed and asked if I could look around. And, er, was there an admission fee? Entry was free, she said. And so was coffee. Goodness, I had landed lucky. I always love free things. I also went to the lavatory, which was beautifully clean – and also free. I was having a great day.

She eventually broke off from whatever she was doing on her computer to give me a leaflet. I could still not quite understand what it was all about, as the prose and the layout was so convoluted and arty. The title of the current exhibition was 'A Modest Proposal (In a Black Box)'. What could that mean? It talked of 'interface protocol, memory sticks, encrypted electronic data, black boxes, 3D printed metal lattice structures and Peripheral Electronic Devices' – still no wiser.

I then realised that, despite all the modern arty language, the current exhibition was in theory exactly what I was looking for – a history of Battersea Park itself. It had been created by two Belgian artists, who displayed blow-ups of ancient, original documents covering the history of the park. So that was interesting. I read about all the battles that went on to create the park. But there were also some art exhibits whose purpose I could not understand.

The exhibition was spread over the four storeys of the Pump House, with a display on each floor. I was warned when I got upstairs to the first room that 'one work in this room uses magnetic field and may interfere with your pace maker'. Hmm. Good job my triple heart bypass hadn't needed anything like that. I went over to look more closely at whatever it was in a glass case. Just seemed to be a little sort of dynamo, doing nothing in particular.

I wondered what connection it had with Battersea Park, and also how two artists from Belgium had got the commission and all the finance to spend two years creating this exhibition. Well done them, of course. I like people who can successfully work the system.

There were some video screens which looked easier to follow, but when I stood for a while listening, I couldn't understand their purpose, either. It was just folks talking.

But it was all lovely, really, such a nice building, all beautifully laid out, so clean and warm and well heated. It was a perfect place to loiter on a cold December day – and all just for me. How kind, how thoughtful.

While on the top floor, I heard footsteps coming up the stairs behind me. The Pump House has an open brick staircase going up the four floors and I could hear voices before I could see any people.

'Bollocks, it's all bollocks,' a man was saying. 'Let's go to Regent's Park. That's what I wanted to do anyway.'

They were a couple in their mid-sixties, both retired, and lived in Essex. Once a month they go up to London and visit one of the famous parks. It sounds a perfect and cheap hobby for anyone's retirement – or any age, really. This was their first time to Battersea Park. Like me, they had just wandered into the Pump House as it was open, and seemed to be the only place in the park that was open in December.

They both said they would not be coming to Battersea Park again. There was nothing to see. I reassured them there was loads to see, such as the fountains, when they were on, but also the statues were interesting; they would like the little dog statue, and they could walk round the lake and sit down in the nice caff. There was the history of Battersea Park, which was fascinating. I started to tell them about the Festival of Britain, which possibly they might remember from their childhood, but they had lost interest.

You can't actually visit history, or enter it. It's all gone. You have to be told about it, or read about it, then look out for relics and traces of it, then it will make sense. The London parks, all of them, have so much history. Each has its own particular story, plus reflections of the national history, of great events and personalities.

All year long I often had such trouble getting useful maps, leaflets, booklets, information, aimed at helping the first-time visitor. They mostly do exist, somewhere, but you can't find them, as so few parks have tourist stalls or visitor centres. They all have active Friends these days, and keen volunteers, so I am surprised that in the season, in the bigger, best-known parks, they don't all have information stalls or human guides available, local experts or enthusiasts you can go to for advice and suggestions.

Yes, I know you can find most stuff on the internet. I was told that all the time when I asked for a map or a brief history. And I know they have financial restrictions and printing costs are expensive. But there must be so many folks like me, not necessarily all oldies, who find going on the internet a pain and would prefer some printed information, which they can carry around with them and consult.

The whole world expects you always to log in to find out anything and everything, which makes those managing the attraction lazy at providing physical information such as leaflets. Leaflets can be kept, reread, reused, passed on, a souvenir from a memorable visit.

My Essex friends at least did not have their faces glued to their mobiles. They did not appear to be carrying anything. When I remarked on this, they said they prefer to walk around, just wandering, seeing where their steps take them. If anything strikes them as memorable, they can research it afterwards.

I like to idly mooch around as well, hoping for chance encounters and unexpected sights, but of course, in writing a book, I always research as much as I can beforehand, so as not to miss anything. And I always talk to everyone I meet – park officials or park walkers – in case I might still have missed something, and might learn something to my advantage.

Had they had the free coffee?

They look mystified. I said downstairs, in the entrance, did they not notice the girl on her computer? Talk to her and she will tell you where it is. It's rather good.

They rushed back downstairs at once. I do like to help.

In my list of things to see in the park, I forgot to tell them to go and look at the Peace Pagoda. This is the most surprising monument in Battersea Park. It is just beside the Thames, practically on the shore, as you come into the park from Albert Bridge. I was going to make it my last stop. Neil, the boss of the park, had told me something about it I had never known.

I had often admired the pagoda, walking along the riverside with Claire, but had never properly investigated it. Why is it there? Who put it up? Who looks after it? I suppose regular walkers in Battersea Park take it for granted, having become used to it. On Hampstead Heath, I am sure many people take Kenwood House for granted, having passed it so many times and perhaps never been in.

But I was rather stunned the first time I saw the pagoda. Claire had not mentioned it, and it is so unexpected, so unconnected with the river or the landscape, or the park itself and its history. It is magnificently and beautifully painted, the colours and decorations always gleaming.

It stands about 100 feet high, with a two-tier roof like an upturned hat, and a little spire on the top. There are steps leading up to a lower level, from which there is a good view along the Thames and over to Chelsea. You can then walk round a balcony, inspecting each of the four large and glistening Buddhas made of gilt bronze. Each Buddha is slightly different in hand gesture, which must have religious significance. Once again I am sure visitors could do with a good leaflet or, better still, someone knowledgeable to explain it all. It is always in sparkling condition, clean and gleaming, which is remarkable considering it is out in the open beside the tidal Thames, liable to be lashed by winds and spray. Claire had said it gets regularly painted, but did not know by whom.

This time, for my visit, I had of course looked up the basic facts about it. The pagoda is in fact fairly modern, erected in 1985 to honour the victims of Nagasaki and Hiroshima, killed at the end of the Second World War when two atomic bombs were dropped on Japan. Up to 226,000 civilians and soldiers lost their lives. In 1985, Battersea Park was still under the jurisdiction of the Greater London Council, as most London parks were, apart from the Royal Parks. Granting permission for a peace pagoda was one of the last acts of the GLC, before being dismantled in 1986. Today, a local borough would struggle to get political agreement for such a memorial.

It was the inspiration of Nichidatsu Fujii (1885–1985), a Japanese Buddhist teacher, and pupil and friend of Gandhi, who conceived a plan to have 100 peace pagodas erected around the world. Since then, 100 have been erected on all five continents. There are two in the UK, the other being in Milton Keynes.

Each year several events take place around the Battersea Peace Pagoda, notably in June, on the anniversary of its erection, and on 9 August, Nagasaki Day, when peace lanterns are floated nearby on the Thames. There are interfaith speakers and pro-peace events. I have never happened to be in the park when either of these two big celebrations are taking place, and neither has Claire. I made a note to attend at least one of them.

I later contacted Neil Blackley again, and said how pristine and sparkling the pagoda appeared, considering it is now well over thirty years old. Who kept it in such good condition – his parkies?

He said no. There is a monk who lives in the park who cleans it every day, alongside volunteers. A Buddhist monk living in Battersea Park? Who knew. I never did, and neither did Claire, a Battersea local and park lover – so she is always telling me.

Neil explained that it was a Japanese monk, Reverend Nagase, who has lived here and looked after the pagoda since it was put up. Can I contact him? Alas, said Neil, he has not got a phone. Where does he live? I eventually persuaded Neil to reveal where his cottage is located. He even agreed to take me past it. I would never have found it otherwise, as it is hidden behind some trees and appears little more than a converted shed.

Wandsworth Borough allows the monk to live there for a minimal rent while volunteers raise money for his living expenses. Every morning, before dawn, he goes to the pagoda and checks all is well. The monk is also a peace activist and attends peace demonstrations in London.

I walked over to his shed to get a better look and was about to knock, to doorstep him and ask to talk to him, but Neil dissuaded me.

'He will be praying. You don't really want to disturb him now.'

But Neil agreed to pass on a message to him, a request for me to talk to him. He does have occasional post, which is delivered to Neil's office. Every so often the monk turns up to collect it. Sometime, at a suitable a moment, Neil promised to put in a good word for me, and pass on my request.

When I told Claire all this, she too was amazed. She never knew the park had a resident monk who tended to the pagoda. Ha ha, I said, yet you are supposed to be a big cheese in the Battersea Society – membership secretary, no less.

I am now waiting to hear from Neil whether in the coming year the Battersea Park Buddhist monk will grant me an audience. I have promised to take Claire, if she is good.

And of course if we are still chums.

When we first got together, each of us said that we did not want to get married again. But you never know: if and when we eventually meet the Reverend Monk, and he grants me an audience, he might even give us a blessing as well.

In Battersea Park, of course. I won't expect him to come all the way to Hampstead Heath.

Best Things About Battersea Park

1. The Peace Pagoda, near Chelsea Bridge, by the Thames, just because it was so unexpected to find it there, so stunning, so gleaming.

2. The fountains – one of the leftover attractions from the Festival of Britain in 1951. Make sure you go at a time when they are turned on.

3. The Battersea Park Pleasure Gardens during the Festival of Britain. Do try to read or acquire a copy of the 1951 guidebook. It has an excellent map, list of excitements, and you can work out and wander round and ponder all the things that were once happening in this very park.

4. The 1924 war memorial with its immortalisation of Robert Graves.

5. The Genius Exhibition Hall, which only goes up for ten months of the year and hosts lots of great events. Its size and structure is a wonder in itself. Then they take it all down again and store it away.

6. The Pump House, built in 1861, which used to house an old steam engine that supplied the lake and fountains. It is now a museum, but an interesting building in its own right. If you're lucky, you might get a free coffee.

7. The lake and the cafe. Rather classy and attractive, which of course is only fitting in a rather classy, attractive park.

Appendix

Parks of London with Over Twenty Acres

Greater London stretches at its broadest point 34 miles across and encloses an area of 610 square miles. Inside this giant there are some 50,000 acres of parks and open spaces, ranging from massive parks like Richmond Park, 2,500 acres in size, to 1-acre open spaces that are little more than large gardens or playgrounds. Over half of London is green. This is based on 40 per cent being public parks and another 20 per cent being private gardens.

There are around 1,000 stretches of grass throughout London that are known officially or informally as parks, some quite small. The main problem about finding exact details is that they are run by so many different bodies. Also their names have often changed over the years.

In the meantime, the following is a list of all the parks and open spaces I can find of over 20 acres, and their respective owners. Total acreage of parks in each borough is what they tell us, and is often out of date, and definitions of what constitutes a park vary. Some count squares and gardens in their total and others don't. In many cases I have had to round up figures. So beware of making comparisons or showing off if you think you live in an ever-so-green borough.

Royal Parks, total acreage: 5,000

Bushy Park	1,100	Regent's Park	472
St James's Park	93	Richmond Park	2,500
Green Park	53	Hampton Court Home	
Greenwich Park	200	Park	1,000
Hyde Park	360	*(Royal but not run by*	
Kensington Gardens	275	*Royal Parks)*	

CITY OF LONDON, TOTAL ACREAGE: 11,000

Burnham Beeches, Bucks	504	Highgate Wood	70
Coulsdon Common,		Queen's Park, Kilburn	30
Surrey	430	Spring Park, West Wickham	
Epping Forest	6,000	Common, Kent	76
Hampstead Heath	800	West Ham	77

Within the City itself there are only 35 acres of open space, mainly gardens, squares, walks and churchyards. The largest are the Barbican (8 acres in all of open space), Finsbury Circus Garden (3 acres) and St Paul's Churchyard (1 acre).

LONDON BOROUGHS, TOTAL ACREAGE: APPROX. 30,000

Between them, the thirty-two London boroughs own or control most of London's parks and open spaces. These are their parks over 20 acres plus the total acreage of parks in each borough. Amazing, really, just how many decent-sized parks there are, well loved and well walked by locals, which you have probably never heard of.

Barking and Dagenham, total acreage: 708

Barking Park	76	Old Dagenham Park	70
Castle Green	42	Parsloes Park	148
Central Park	135	St Chad's Park	41
Goresbrook Park	37	Valence Park	24
Mayesbrook Park	116		

Barnet, total acreage: 1,226

Arrandene Open Space	55	Bethune Park	32
Barnet Playing Fields	82	Brook Farm	56

Brunswick Park	24	Montrose Park	26
Clitterhouse Park	47	Oak Hill Park	90
Copthall Sports Centre	140	Sunny Hill Park	54
Edgwarebury Park	39	Tudor Sports	24
Friary Park	23	Watling Park	21
Glebelands	46	West Hendon Playing	
Hendon Park	29	Fields	70
Lyttelton Park	35	Woodfield Park	39
Mill Hill Park	51		

Bexley, total acreage: 1,580

Bexley Woods	27	Lamorbey Park	130
Bursted Woods	30	Lesnes Abbey	215
Chalk Wood	69	Martens Grove	29
Danson Park	185	Mayplace Sports Field	36
East Wickham Open		North Cray Meadows	60
Space	60	Northumberland Heath	23
Foots Cray Meadows	48	Sidcup Place	37
Franks Park	41	Southmere Park	40
Hall Place	146		

Brent, total acreage: 1,036

Alperton Sports		Roe Green Park	38
Ground Rec.	22	Silver Jubilee Park	32
Barham Park	25	Northwick Park	65
Brent Reservoir (popularly		One Tree Hill	26
known as the		Roundwood Park	35
Welsh Harp)	340	St Raphael's Way	
Fryent Country Park	253	Open Space	20
Gladstone Park	93	Vale Farm	63
King Edward VII Park	26	Willesden Sports Centre	31
Neasden Recreation		Woodcock Park	28
Ground	37		

Bromley, total acreage: 2,000

Chislehurst		Marvels Wood	22
Recreation Ground	28	Mottingham Sports	
Coney Hall Rec.	24	Ground	30
Croydon Road		Norman Park	56
Recreation Ground	23	Parkfield	
Crystal Palace Park	106	Recreation Ground	44
Elmstead Wood	85	Priory Gardens 35	
Goddington Park	64	Ravensbourne Open	
Harvington Sports		Space	27
Ground	47	Riverside Gardens, St	
Hayes Common	225	Mary Cray	21
High Elms Country Park	350	St Pauls Cray Hill	
Hoblingwell Wood	210	Country Park	82
Jubilee Country Park	62	Scadbury Park	250
Kelsey Park	80	Sparrows Den	31
Keston Common	55	Well Wood	43
Martins Hill Open Space	23		

Note: Bromley is by far the largest London borough in area, covering 38,000 acres. The next biggest are Harrow and Hillingdon with 28,000 acres each. The rest average about 12,000 acres each.

Camden, total acreage: 101

Waterlow Park	27

Note: Camden Borough's total looks very small but inside the borough is also the City of London's Hampstead Heath and the Royal Parks' Regent's Park. The borough itself owns only two parks – Waterlow Park and the much smaller Kilburn Grange Park (8 acres). The rest of its open spaces are gardens or squares, including London's biggest square, Lincoln's Inn Fields, 7 acres.

Croydon, total acreage: 2,583

Addington Hills	130	Millstock	57
Addington Park	24	Norbury Park	28
Addington Vale	48	North Down	33
Ashburton Playing Fields	49	Norwood Grove	34
Betts Mead		Purley Way Playing Fields	108
Recreation Ground	30	Purley Way West	21
Birch Wood	37	Riddlesdown	37
Bramley Bank	23	Rowdown Fields	29
Croham Hurst	84	Rowdown Wood	34
Croydon Sports Arena	27	Sanderstead Plantation	21
Duppas Hill	34	Sanderstead	
Foxley Wood	26	Recreation Ground	20
Grangewood Park	28	Shirley Heath	68
Happy Valley Park	246	South Norwood	
Hawkhirst	35	Country Park	125
Jewel's Wood	38	Threehalfpenny Wood	25
King's Wood	147	Upper Norwood	
Littleheath Wood	64	Recreation Ground	20
Lloyd Park	114	Wandle Park	21

Ealing, total acreage: 1,957

Acton Park	28	Gunnersbury Park 188 *(jointly*	
Belvue Park	25	*owned with London Borough*	
Churchfields		*of Hounslow)*	
Recreation Ground	20	Hanger Hill Park	20
Ealing Central		Horsenden Hill	245
Sports Ground	37	Islip Manor Park	63
Ealing Common	50	King George's Playing	
Elthorne Park	37	Field	25
Glade Lane Canalside Park	26	Lammas Park	27
Greenford Park	33	Lime Tree Park	75

North Acton Playing Fields	23	Ravenor Park	32
		Rectory Park	63
Northala Fields	68	Southall Park	26
Perivale Park	110	Southall Sports	20
Pitshanger Park	50	Walpole Park	30

Enfield, total acreage: 1,658

Albany Park	45	Forty Hill Country Park	273
Arnos Park	44	Grovelands Park	91
Bramley Sports Ground	20	Hadley Wood	33
Broomfield Park	54	Hilly Fields Park	66
Bush Hill Park	27	Jubilee Park	37
Church Street Recreation Ground	24	Oakwood Park	64
		Pymmes Park	53
Durants Park	54	Town Park	23
Enfield Playing Fields	128	Trent Park	413
Firs Farm Recreation Ground	50	Whitewebbs Park	232

Greenwich, total acreage: 1,400

Avery Hill Park	86	Maryon Park	29
Birchmere Park	40	Maryon Wilson Park	32
Blackheath	272	Oxleas Wood	216
Bostall Heath	150	Plumstead Common	103
Charlton Park	43	Shrewsbury Park	32
Eltham Park	122	Sutcliffe Park	52
Horn Park	26		

Hackney, total acreage: 352

Abney Park Cemetery	32	London Fields	31
Clissold Park	54	Millfields Park	64
Hackney Downs	42	Springfield Park	38
Hackney Marshes	335	Well Street Common	21

Hammersmith and Fulham, total acreage: 580

Bishops Park	25	Wormwood Scrubs	192
Ravenscourt Park	35		

Haringey, total acreage: 713

Alexandra Park	200	Markfield	
Bruce Castle Park	20	Recreation Ground	25
Coldfall Wood	32	Muswell Hill Playing	
Finsbury Park	110	Fields	25
Lordship Recreation		New River Sport and	
Ground	123	Fitness	31

Harrow, total acreage: 1,239

Alexandra Park	21	Kenton Recreation	
Bentley Priory	163	Ground	52
Byron Recreation Ground	30	Montesole Playing Fields	20
Canons Park	48	Newton Park	25
Centenary Park	23	Pinner Park	250
Chandos		Roxbourne Park	54
Recreation Ground	27	Stanmore Common	120
Harrow Recreation		Stanmore Country Park	77
Ground	27	West Harrow	
Harrow Weald Common	47	Recreation Ground	26
Headstone Manor			
Recreation Ground	57		

Havering, total acreage: 2,800

Bedfords Park	214	Duck Wood	20
Bretons Outdoor Centre	184	Gaynes Parkway	59
Brittons Playing Field	26	Grenfell Park	27
Cranham Playing Fields	22	Harold Wood Park	45
Dagnam Park	146	Harrow Lodge Park	129

Havering Country Park	167	Little Hatter's Wood	94
Haynes Park	27	Oldchurch Park	50
Hornchurch Country Park,		Raphael Park	55
Ingrebourne Valley	644	Rise Park	23
King George's Playing Field		Upminster Hall	
(formerly Mawny Park)	24	Playing Fields	35

Hillingdon, total acreage: 3,314

Bayhurst Wood		Mad Bess Wood	186
Country Park	98	New Pond Playing Fields	20
Copse Wood	157	Northwood	
Cranford Park	148	Recreation Ground	24
Field End		Park Wood	238
Recreation Ground	27	Pole Hill Open Space	46
Grange Park	30	Poor's Field	40
Hayes End		Stonefield Park	98
Recreation Ground	23	Ruislip Lido	77
Hillington Court Park	56	The Closes	23
Kings College Fields	54	Yeading Brook Open	
Little Harlington		Space	113
Playing Fields	20		

Note: Hillingdon Borough owns more parkland and open space than any other London borough.

Hounslow, total acreage: 1,323

Avenue Park	20	Gunnersbury Park	188
Bedfont Lakes Country		Hanworth Park	145
Park	170	Lampton Park	43
Boston Manor Park	35		
Chiswick House Gardens	67		
Dukes Meadows	25		
Feltham Park	38		

Islington, total acreage, 174

Caledonian Park	20	Highbury Fields	29

Royal Borough of Kensington and Chelsea, total acreage: 150

Holland Park	54

Note: there are no other parks in Kensington and Chelsea over 20 acres: the next biggest are Royal Hospital South Grounds, 13 acres, where the Chelsea Flower Show is held, and Kensington Memorial Gardens, 7 acres. Kensington Gardens, a Royal Park, is also in the borough.

Royal Borough of Kingston upon Thames, total acreage: 236

Alexandra Recreation Ground	20	King George's Recreation Ground (also known as King George's Field)	33
Churchfields Recreation Ground	22	Manor Park	20

Lambeth, total acreage: 623

Brockwell Park	127	Ruskin Park	36
Clapham Common	206	Streatham Common and the Rookery	61
Kennington Park	37		
Norwood Park	38		

Lewisham, total acreage: 800

Beckenham Place Park	237	Ladywell Fields	52
Blythe Hill Fields	20	Mayow Park	20
Chinbrook Meadows	31	Mountsfield Park	28
Downham Fields	37	Summerhouse Fields	20
Forster Memorial Park	43	Sydenham Wells Park	20
Hilly Fields	46		
Horniman Gardens	25		

Merton, total acreage: 742

Cannizaro Park	34	Morden Recreation	
Cannon Hill Common	53	Ground	25
Commons Extension	79	Sir Joseph Hood Memorial	
Figges Marsh	25	Playing Fields	31
Joseph Hood		Wimbledon Park	66
Recreation Ground	21	Mitcham Common	442
King George's Playing		*(managed by Conservators of*	
Field	20	*Mitcham Common)*	
Morden Park	123		

Newham, total acreage: 358

Beckton District Park	47	Central Park	25
Canning Town		Plashet Park	20
Recreation Ground	22	Memorial Gardens	26

Redbridge, total acreage: 2,631

Ashton Playing Fields	52	Loxford Park	20
Clayhall Park	34	Ray Park	30
Fairlop Waters Country		Roding Lane Sports	
Park	300	Ground	26
Forest Road Playing		Roding Valley Linear	
Fields	40	Park	196
Goodmayes Park	69	Seven Kings Park	34
Hainault Forest	958	South Park	32
Hainault Recreation		Valentines Park	136
Ground	46		

Redbridge Borough also contains 1,250 acres of Epping Forest, run by the City of London.

Richmond upon Thames, total acreage: 1,116

Crane Park	72	Marble Hill Park	66
Fulwell Park	70	Old Deer Park	80
Ham Common	126	Palewell Common	39
Ham Riverside Lands	124	Sheen Common	53
Hatherop Park	20		

Richmond Borough also contains the Royal Parks of Richmond, Bushy and Hampton, plus Kew Gardens and the London Wetland Centre, 75 acres, which brings the total park space in the borough up to 5,500 acres, making it the London winner – counting all the various owners. Lucky Richmond.

Southwark, total acreage: 1,000

Belair Park	25	Peckham Rye	96
Burgess Park	135	Russia Dock Woodland	25
Dulwich Park	75	Southwark Park	63
Greendale Playing Fields	25	Sydenham Hill Wood	23

Sutton, total acreage: 1,500

Beddington Park	140	Poulter Park	51
Carshalton Park	23	Rosehill Park	79
Cheam Park	65	Seears Park and	
Cuddington		Perrett's Field	27
Recreation Ground	25	Stanmore Country Park	78
Mellows Park	20		

Parks of London with Over Twenty Acres

Tower Hamlets, total acreage: 432

Mile End Park	51	Queen Elizabeth	
Mudchute Park	32	Olympic Park	560
Victoria Park	218	*(in three boroughs: Tower*	
Tower Hamlets		*Hamlets, Hackney*	
Cemetery Park	28	*and Newham)*	

Waltham Forest, total acreage: 1,000

Highams Park	24	Mansfield Park	23
Larkswood Park	42	Marsh Lane Playing	
Lee Valley Playing Fields	21	Fields	39
Leyton Jubilee Park	30	Walthamstow Marshes	100
Lloyd Park	36	Walthamstow Wetlands	
Low Hall Sports Ground	46	Nature Reserve	520

Wandsworth, total acreage: 554

Battersea Park	200	Wandsworth Common	177
King George's Park	55	Wandsworth Park	20
Tooting Common	221		

City of Westminster, total acreage: 116

Paddington	
Recreation Ground	27

Finally, there are two other types of organisation which control London Parks:

CONSERVATORS, TOTAL ACREAGE: 1,500

Mitcham Common	440	Wimbledon Common	1,100

These 1,540 acres are open to the public but owned independently. Wimbledon Common is financed by a rate levied on local residents living in the nearby area and managed by an elected body called Conservators. The Conservators of Mitcham Common have appointed Merton Borough Council as their agents to maintain the Common.

NATIONAL TRUST, TOTAL ACREAGE: 892

East Sheen Common	53	Morden Hall Park,	
(managed by London Borough		Morden	124
of Richmond upon Thames)		Osterley Park	140
Ham House, Richmond	21	Petts Wood, Chislehurst	171
Hawkwood, near		Selsdon Wood, Croydon	198
Chislehurst	245	*(managed by London Borough*	
		of Croydon)	